Bushmen

M000188615

The hunter-gatherers of southern Africa known as 'Bushmen' or 'San' are not one single ethnic group, but several. They speak a diverse variety of languages, and have many different settlement patterns, kinship systems and economic practices. The fact that we think of them as a unity is not as strange as it may seem, for they share a common origin: they are an original hunter-gatherer population of southern Africa with a history of many thousands of years on the subcontinent.

Drawing on his four decades of field research in Botswana, Namibia and South Africa, Alan Barnard provides a detailed account of Bushmen or San, covering ethnography, archaeology, folklore, religious studies and rock-art studies as well as several other fields. Its wide coverage includes social development and politics, both historically and in the present day, helping us to reconstruct both human prehistory and a better understanding of ourselves.

ALAN BARNARD is Emeritus Professor of the Anthropology of Southern Africa at the University of Edinburgh. He has over 40 years' experience of field research with Bushmen or San in Botswana, Namibia and South Africa. His publications include *Language in Prehistory* (2016), *Genesis of Symbolic Thought* (2012) and *Social Anthropology and Human Origins* (2011), all published by Cambridge University Press.

Bushmen

Kalahari Hunter-Gatherers and Their Descendants

Alan Barnard

University of Edinburgh

CAMBRIDGE
UNIVERSITY PRESS

CAMBRIDGE
UNIVERSITY PRESS

University Printing House, Cambridge CB2 8BS, United Kingdom

One Liberty Plaza, 20th Floor, New York, NY 10006, USA

477 Williamstown Road, Port Melbourne, VIC 3207, Australia

314–321, 3rd Floor, Plot 3, Splendor Forum, Jasola District Centre,
New Delhi – 110025, India

79 Anson Road, #06–04/06, Singapore 079906

Cambridge University Press is part of the University of Cambridge.

It furthers the University's mission by disseminating knowledge in the pursuit of
education, learning, and research at the highest international levels of excellence.

www.cambridge.org
Information on this title: www.cambridge.org/9781108418263
DOI: 10.1017/9781108289603

First published 2019

Printed in the United Kingdom by TJ International Ltd, Padstow Cornwall

A catalogue record for this publication is available from the British Library.

Library of Congress Cataloging-in-Publication Data
Names: Barnard, Alan (Alan J.), author.
Title: Bushmen : Kalahari hunter-gatherers and their descendants / Alan Barnard,
University of Edinburgh.
Other titles: Kalahari hunter-gatherers and their descendants
Description: Cambridge ; New York, NY : Cambridge University Press, [2019] |
Includes bibliographical references and index.
Identifiers: LCCN 2019010800 | ISBN 9781108418263
Subjects: LCSH: San (African people) | Ethnology – Africa, Southern.
Classification: LCC DT1058.S36 B354 2019 | DDC 968.83/004961–dc23
LC record available at https://lccn.loc.gov/2019010800

ISBN 978-1-108-41826-3 Hardback
ISBN 9781-108-40687-1 Paperback

Contents

Figures

Tables

Preface

This book represents nearly a lifetime of research on Bushmen. The research has been enjoyable, and so has the teaching, both in the Department of Social Anthropology and in the Centre of African Studies at the University of Edinburgh. I thank the University for its many years of support in this endeavour.

But most of all, I thank the Bushmen, San, Basarwa, Kua or N/uakhoe themselves, *collectively*. That is probably the way at least most of them would want to be thanked. Many have suffered a great deal, as governments have repeatedly let them down. It is not easy to live as a hunter-gatherer, and pursuing that lifestyle means giving up the accumulation of wealth in favour of having more free time. That may sound great, but it does mean making considerable sacrifices and, above all, being grossly misunderstood by outsiders. Throughout history, Bushmen have had to put up with discrimination as well as vile insinuation and threats of imprisonment and death. Happily, things are better now than they once were, but we should always remember that our own ancestors were also once *pure* hunter-gatherers. And by 'our ancestors', I really do mean the ancestors of all human beings on the planet.

So what do 'we' call 'them'? In the past I have occasionally used *San*, which is common in South Africa and in Namibia. It is also especially common among archaeologists. I shall occasionally, where appropriate, use it in this book too. I have sometimes used *Kua* or *N/uakhoe*, which are preferred terms in some languages. Here though, I shall generally use *Bushmen*. This term is very well known and can always, as here, be used without prejudice. *San* is especially common in government circles. *Bushmen* is more common among Bushmen themselves and with NGOs. However, because of past discrimination, virtually every term has its drawbacks. *San*, for example, is recorded as meaning 'vagabond' or 'rascal' in the language from which it comes. It is also grammatically problematic, as it is spelled incorrectly. It is in theory common gender plural and is not *originally* meant as an ethnic group name at all. Originally, it probably did mean something like 'food-gatherer' and probably is best spelled (in the plural) *saan* or *sān*. The 'doubled vowel' or macron indicates a change in tone in the Khoekhoe language (Khoekhoegowab). The word is quite unknown in the only dialect of Khoekhoe that might be expected to have it:

Hai//om (or in conventional Khoekhoe orthography, Hai‖om, with a vertical double-stroke click symbol). That group is also sometimes known as ≠Akhoe or ≠Ākhoe. I shall not bother with the Khoekhoe preference for vertical click symbols though. For the sake of consistency, I shall use slanted symbols in all languages. And without meaning any harm, I use my own preferred word: *Bushmen*. This term is now gaining popularity again in some Bushman areas of the Kalahari. That is, some Bushmen now employ it to refer to themselves.

I finished my PhD in 1976, and I finished the book that is based on it in 1992. Both are very heavily referenced: the PhD thesis because that is the nature of the beast, and the book, I suppose, because I was still showing off. One reviewer commented that in the latter I had cited more than 600 books and articles, many in languages other than English. The present book will have fewer, if only because the Internet makes unnecessary reference citation a little less important. The population of Namibia at the time I started this book, in late 2016, was 2,522,325: I know because I looked it up on the Internet! That sort of reference is not necessarily worth citing by date and page.

I gratefully acknowledge the British Academy, the Economic and Social Research Council, the European Science Foundation, the James A. Swan Fund, the Japan Society for the Promotion of Science, the National Science Foundation, the Nuffield Foundation, the University of Edinburgh and my parents, all for their generous financial support. I am also grateful to the Office of the President of Botswana and to the governments of Namibia and South Africa for enabling my work.

Lastly here, let me acknowledge the kindness of the many *non-Bushmen* who have aided my Bushman or San research through the years. Probably there are too many to name, so I will simply list here some of them. A few are now deceased, and some helped so long ago that they will not remember. Yet I am grateful to them all: John Argyle, Joy Barnard, Megan Biesele, Gertrud Boden, Maitseo Bolaane, Peter Bradley, John Brearly, Peter Carstens, Liz Cashdan, Wallace Craill, Janette Deacon, Jim Denbow, Mary Douglas, Tom Dowson, Anne-Maria Fehn, Maurice Freedman, Jack Goody, Rob Gordon, Julie Grant, Tom Güldemann, Mathias Guenther, Willi Haacke, Doc Heinz, Roger Hewitt, Bob Hitchcock, Kazunobu Ikeya, Ray Inskeep, Hiroaki Izumi, Pieter Jolly, Aglaja Kempinski, Sue Kent, Klaus Keuthmann, Chris Knight, Adam Kuper, Jessica Kuper, Blesswell Kure, Jenny Lawy, Bob Layton, Richard Lee, David Lewis-Williams, Bill McGregor, Kennedy McIntyre, John Marshall, Lorna Marshall, Junko Maruyama, Bob Murry, Ellen Murry, Hirosi Nakagawa, Emmanuelle Olivier, John Parkington, Motsamae Phiri, Camilla Power, Rick Rohde, Karim Sadr, Beatrice Sandelowsky, Sidsel Saugestad, Isaac Schapera, George Silberbauer, Pippa Skotnes, Jan Snyman, Anne Solomon, Jackie Solway, Hendrik Steyn, Kazuyoshi Sugawara, Sian Sullivan, James Suzman, Akira Takada, Jiro Tanaka, Mike Taylor, Phillip Tobias, Tony Traill, Carlos

Valiente-Noailles, Helga Vierich, Ben Visser, Coby Visser, Hessel Visser, Rainer Vossen, Ian Watts, Martin West, Ernst Westphal, Thomas Widlok, Polly Wiessner, Ed Wilmsen and James Woodburn. I also must thank Andrew Winnard and Stephanie Taylor of Cambridge University Press for their help during the production process. I am also particularly grateful to Gertrud Boden, Bob Hitchcock, Emmanuelle Olivier and James Suzman for the offer to donate photographs to be included here, and to one San, Job Morris, for the same priviledge. My own photos are mainly from the 1970s and not digital, and therefore not perhaps ideal for the book. Yet I have decided to use them anyway in the hope of capturing something of my own research through them.

I dedicated my last book to the Naro and their language. This book therefore probably needs no such dedication. But let us hope that the Naro language does survive another 100 years. As I hope to show in this book, language is highly significant for identity, and not least for Bushmen, whose languages contain not only a sense of identity but also so much wisdom from the past.

Pronunciation and Orthography

For many people, the correct pronunciation of Bushman words seems to be difficult. Yet, in fact, things are not necessarily as difficult as one might imagine. There are at most five basic clicks, and these are always at the beginning of words or at least at the beginning of morphemes, never in the middle or at the end. Sometimes orthographic rules kick in, though, so that a word may begin with a 'g' or an 'n', for example. This just indicates that given click is respectively voiced or nasalized. Sometimes the 'g' or 'n' is placed after the click symbol, sometimes before, but in general this really does not matter. There is rarely any difference in pronunciation. An apostrophe means a glottal stop, as might a question mark with the dot below missing.

Let me go through the basics, bearing in mind that the rules of the most difficult languages, such as !Xoõ (the tilde on the 'o' meaning nasalized) and Ju/'hoan, may make things a little more complicated. The final 'n' on the latter is just another way of indicating nasalization. It was the preference of the linguist who standardized the orthography, the late Patrick Dickens. The 'j' in the word is meant to be pronounced [ž], as in 'treasure'.

Finally, there are a few complications in the Khoekhoe language, which among Bushmen is spoken only by one group, the Hai//om. I shall leave discussion of that language until the end. Further details are given in my *Hunters and Herders of Southern Africa* (Barnard 1992a: xviii–xxv) and similarly in *Anthropology and the Bushman* (Barnard 2007a: 8–10), but those details are not so important now. They include various click releases, such as 'h', 'x' and 'q', placed after the click.

Here are the five clicks and where, geographically, they occur. They are presented in the customary order, which is, in terms of the point of articulation, from front to back of the mouth.

⊙   This is the so-called kiss click. It is a kissing sound, produced on the lips. More technically, it is the bilabial click. Found only in Southern Bushman languages.

/   This is the 'tisk' click. Use it twice to express annoyance or disappointment: 'tisk tisk'. It is alveolar-dental, produced on the teeth or just behind them. This is the 'c' in Zulu, Xhosa and other Nguni languages. Sometimes this and other slanted-line clicks are written with vertical strokes: |. This is always the case in Khoekhoe, although in this book I will standardize the usage by showing only slanted strokes. The only exception is in the list below where I discuss 'official' usage in Khoekhoe.

≠ The alveolar click. Produced in the same place, though with the blade or your tongue rather than the tip.

// The 'giddy-up' click. Use it twice to make your horse go! Sometimes called the lateral click, since it is always produced on the side of the mouth (mine is always on the right side, but yours may be on the left). This is the 'x' in Zulu, Xhosa and other Nguni languages, as in the word 'Xhosa'.

! The 'pop' click. More technically, the palatal, cerebral or retroflex click. Simply make a loud 'pop' by drawing the tip of your tongue quickly from the roof of your mouth. This is the 'q' in Zulu, Xhosa and other Nguni languages.

Other anomalies sometimes occur in Bushman orthography. Normally these revolve around the use of the intrusive 'k', which may be there phonetically but which is not necessary orthographically. Therefore it is not (in general) used in this book except in quotations. The official motto of the Republic of South Africa, for example, is *!Ke e: /xarra //ke* (officially translated as 'Diverse people unite'). Other phonetic symbols are all standard ones, as now employed by the International Phonetic Association (IPA). For example, an 'x' is a voiceless velar fricative, not to be confused with the 'x' of Nguni languages: the latter being the click //. Some authors use idiosyncratic spellings, but I simply use the most common. Where there exists an 'official' orthography, such as in Ju/'hoan, I stick to it. The *-si* added to the word Ju/'hoan simply makes the word plural. In theory, plurals may be added to other words, but by convention only Ju/'hoan does this. Occasionally, one will see Bantu prefixes. The most common are in the Tswana language, where *Bo-* refers to the country, *Se-* to the language, and *Mo-* (singular) and *Ba-* (plural) to people.

One further complication regarding 'official' usage. In Hai//om (Hai‖om), which is a dialect of Khoekhoe or Nama-Damara, orthography follows the rules of Khoekhoe. Since this language makes no distinction between voiced and voiceless consonants, normal 'voiced' and 'voiceless' rules are not followed. Rather, the rules are as follows:

| In the *standard* Khoisan orthography, this would be given as /'. In other words, the Hai//om glottal stop is *not written* but is there *only in speech*. Hai//om is pronounced (with the morpheme division added) phonetically [hai-//'om] or in the plural [hai-//'om-n]. In the dialect itself, the // would be written with the click vertically, as is standard in Khoekhoe

orthography. However, I do not bother with writing clicks vertically in reference to the Hai//om dialect, since this would be inconsistent with usage in this book generally.

|g   In standard Khoisan orthography, this would simply be /. The 'g', which would otherwise mean voicing, is in Hai//om (likewise, other dialects of Khoekhoe) there simply to indicate *the lack of* a glottal stop. The 'g' here, by convention, is placed *after* rather than *before* the click symbol. Likewise, with the 'n' in a nasal click: |n.

All Khoekhoe dialects use the macron to indicate a 'doubled vowel', in other words, one with two tones, either rising-falling or falling-rising. An example is the word 'San', or more correctly, 'Sān' or 'sān', meaning 'Bushman'. This word, incidentally, is unknown in Khoekhoe dialects today. It occurred, though, in the now extinct ones formerly spoken in the Cape: usually in the masculine plural form and written as 'Soaqua' or 'Sonqua'.

Finally, in this book I have done my best to avoid unnecessary diacritics: for example, in a word like ≠Hoã or ≠Hoan I prefer to keep the tilde to indicate nasalization, but I avoid accents otherwise. However, with the word Ju/'hoansi, which has the same nasal sound, I keep to the official and now well-known orthography. All the ethnographers of the Ju/'hoansi do prefer to use the word in full, so it would be strange for me not to do so. Likewise, the northern Ju/'hoan group who call themselves !Xun are called that here, because this is in the official orthography. These (northern) !Xun are not to be confused with the !Xoõ, an entirely different (southern) group. Phonetically, the former is [!xũ], and the latter is [!xoõ].

I apologize for any confusion, but it is best to get the pronunciation straight first. It is no wonder that one expert (Traill 1974: 9) recorded the name for !Xoõ variously (and probably jokingly) as !ku, !kõ, !kũ, Koon, Lala, /ŋu//en, '//ŋaʰmsa, tuu'⊙ŋaʰnsa, !xong, //no, Tshasi and more than a dozen other possibilities. I just use !Xoõ. Traill's suggestion of 'Koon' is not as odd as it may seem, for it is fairly common to skip an initial click and use a 'K' instead. Much easier to pronounce!

1 Bushmen
Unity and Diversity

The most important thing to note about 'Bushmen' or 'San' is that they are not a single ethnic group. They are several such groups. They speak a diversity of languages, which are more different from each other than Hindi or Sanskrit is from English. Genetically, Bushmen are in fact the most diverse 'people' on the planet (see Hublin *et al.* 2017). Also, they have many different patterns of settlement, some of which are *opposites* in terms of seasonal aggregations and dispersals. They have a wide range of kinship systems too, and these are as complex as anywhere on earth outside Australia. They even possess a variety of economic practices, not just in terms of hunting and gathering but also through gift exchange. And their social values are often the *reverse* of expectations about what we in the West assume is 'normal' and 'natural'. Given that they have lived in southern Africa for at least 25,000 or maybe 50,000 years, why should we expect otherwise?

The subcontinent is difficult to define exactly, but the distance from the Cape to the Cunene, for instance, is nearly 3,000 kilometres. It is bounded by rivers, and in between is the Kalahari – a plateau consisting of a vast sand system. This includes the landlocked Republic of Botswana, which became independent from the United Kingdom in 1966. To the west is another desert, the Namib, from which the Republic of Namibia takes its name. Namibia was German from 1884 to 1915, then a UN Mandated Territory under the control of South Africa until the eve of independence in 1990. The Republic of South Africa gained its own freedom from apartheid in 1994. To the east lies a tropical ocean and a former Portuguese colony, the Republic of Mozambique, and a former British colony, the Republic of Zimbabwe. Two further countries in the region are the Kingdom of Lesotho and the Kingdom of Eswatini (Swaziland). The latter reflects a recent name change, but both names are still in use. It is also landlocked, and Lesotho lies completely within the boundaries of South Africa. To the north are the Republic of Angola, a Portuguese colony for 400 years (1575–1975), and the Republic of Zambia, formerly British. The latter has had a chequered history and was the site of various kingdoms. These followed Khoisan habitation to about AD 300 and the arrival of Bantu-speaking groups in the twelfth century. Most of southern Africa is Bantu-speaking. Bantu is a large language family, and Bantu languages are spread across most of Africa through recent centuries. Their point of origin was around modern Cameroon. The remaining languages spoken by Bushmen are very tiny in terms of numbers of speakers, though vast in their diversity.

Bushmen as a Unity

We often tend to think of Bushmen as a unity. This is not as strange as it may seem, for all such groups share a common origin as an original hunting-and-gathering population (or populations) of southern Africa. Their diversity includes biological difference (there are 'black' as well as 'yellow' or 'red' people among them), linguistic affiliation (some speak Khoe or so-called Hottentot languages rather than 'San' ones) and so on. Even what we call them reflects a kind of diversity. Many experts, especially in archaeology, call them 'San', a term derived from the word *saan* or *sān* (common gender plural) in Khoekhoe dialects. It occurs in no Bushman or San language. Other experts prefer to use Bushmen or Basarwa, and a few have used Kua or even N/uakhoe (literally, 'red people'). Kua is the preferred generic term in a few languages. Red People is a fairly common self-description in my own fieldwork language, Naro (formerly known as Nharo or Naron). Etymologically though, each of these terms is quite problematic. This introductory chapter will explore all these issues and some related ones.

Like Bushmen, we are all hunter-gatherers in our essence. That is, modern humans have existed for about 200,000 years (the traditional date) or perhaps for much longer. For at least half of this time we modern humans lived as a symbolic species, with language, animistic beliefs and symbolism at the core of our self-awareness. There is recent evidence that humans have existed more than 100,000 years longer than that, thanks to a study from Jebel Irhoud, in Morocco. Through thermoluminescence dating, it appears that modern humans have lived there since around 315,000 BP (Hublin *et al.* 2017). The implication is that humans were spread across Africa, rather than just in eastern or southern parts of the continent. The data suggest further that early modern humans, and the symbolic culture they possessed, had an origin in the Middle Stone Age. This was a long and Africa-specific period of human prehistory. We shall learn more about it in Chapter 3.

Early Humans and Bushmen

It may be tempting to imagine that early humans and Bushmen are much the same. They are not! If Bushmen possess attributes of early humans, so do the rest of us. There is little that is 'early' about Bushmen: they are fully modern people. What does set them apart is a dependence for subsistence on hunting and gathering, or *mainly* on hunting and gathering. Yet this comes with a large number of attributes of Middle Stone Age life that are retained by Bushmen, even today.

'Middle Stone Age' and 'Mesolithic' may literally mean the same thing, but they are not identical. The Middle Stone Age was the period when humans *became* modern. It marks the beginning of symbolism, personal decoration, art, language and so on, in eastern and southern Africa. It took place perhaps around 280,000 BP and lasted until 50,000 or 25,000 BP (see McBrearty and Brooks 2000). The Mesolithic is largely technological and marks the beginnings of the use of smaller stone tools and changes in hunting techniques. It took place much later, more like 15,000 to 5,000 BP in Europe and similar dates elsewhere in the world (Bailey and Spikins 2008).

Another version of human evolution comes from work on the Dali skull, discovered in 1978 in northern China but only fully analysed much more recently (Arthreya and Wu 2017). This suggests a high degree of hybridization and gene flow among Chinese hominins. There is also some hybridization among Denisovans (descendants of *Homo heidelbergensis*), Neanderthals and *Homo sapiens*, indicating further genetic complexity (see Barnard 2012: 118–20). However, the crucial thing is what effect any of this might have had on symbolic thought and behaviour, including the development of any kind of language. Here, at least, it is African data that is at the forefront. Africans exhibit greater phonological diversity than any other part of the world. Within Africa, Bushmen show this to a greater extent than anywhere else. This suggests that their languages are of greater time depth than those of anywhere else (Atkinson 2011). The presence of language is, of course, closely related to the origins of symbolism, and it would appear that both of these, language and symbolic thinking, did indeed originate in eastern or southern Africa (see also Stringer 2011: 105–37; Barnard 2016b: 73–8). There is more work to be done on issues such as these, but there is no doubt that science is gradually coming to firmer conclusions.

Food production only came into being with the Neolithic, roughly 12,000 years ago (depending on how it is defined). The technology that first produced it is hardly natural. The archaeologist-filmmaker team of Peter Nilssen and Craig Foster (2017: 2) put it this way:

[H]umans lived in and connected with nature for at least 95 per cent of our time on earth. It is only the last five per cent or so that we have been manipulating nature for our own short-term benefit, to the long-term detriment of life in general. It is hardly surprising then that most of us find comfort, peace and joy in nature as opposed to the discontent associated with the sights, sounds and smells of industry and modern life. Our deep-seated relationship with nature, and 95 per cent of our genetic coding and heritage, is part of the original human design – gatherer-hunters are at the core of who and what we are.

Gatherer-hunters is simply another way of saying hunter-gatherers, less sexist perhaps because most such populations subsist mainly by gathering. That is done mainly by females. Nilssen and Foster (2017: 4) go on to suggest that early humans had two 'ingredients in their recipe for success'. These were: (1) cognition through intelligence and (2) symbolic behaviour, evidenced through their belief systems and their spirituality. We can still see these in the animistic elements of Bushman religions today, including trance dancing. This is depicted in rock paintings, the earliest form of art in southern Africa.

Bushmen, therefore, are at the apex of human culture. In genetic terms, Bushmen are the most diverse population, or sets of populations, anywhere. This means that they are the groups that the rest of modern humanity is descended from. More specifically, the Israeli geneticist Doron Behar and his team (Behar *et al.* 2008; cf. Pickrell *et al.* 2012) argue that Khoisan populations diverged from other populations through the paternal line sometime between 150,000 and 90,000 years ago. The maternal line remained separate until around 40,000 years ago. Yet, as all this implies, Bushmen are not a single ethnic group but several. We must forget about the idea that 'the Bushmen' are a uniform bunch of people. Except in religious belief and practice, they are in fact quite *diverse*. Religion is excepted because it is similar throughout Bushman culture.

Bushmen are not particularly small in stature. They do tend to be fairly light-skinned, although many are dark-skinned. Above all, descriptions like 'Bush crania' as 'sub-doliochcephalic, metriocephalic, orthognatic, mesomeme, platyrhine, leptostaphylinic, cryptozygous, and microcephalic' (Shrubsall 1898: 280) should, of course, be consigned to history. There is no 'typical' Bushman. Indeed, as the study by Behar's team shows, Bushmen are genetically diverse. The reason why the rest of us are so similar is due to what biological anthropologist Marta Mirazón Lahr has labelled the 'Holocene filter'. This similarity is due, in other words, to the adoption of farming for subsistence (see also Scerri 2018). And finally here, and importantly, we should forget about a lot of what we imagine Bushmen to be. Their struggle for freedom from all encumbrances is pretty obvious. But it also entails a choice they make, *for doing less work*: they work far less than we in the West do, only about two to three hours a day. As one expert has said, they eat more meat than Texans. That said, their nutrition is very good. If there is a true struggle for existence, it is among their agricultural neighbours. Peoples with cultivation, rather than hunter-gatherers, are the ones who tend to be most affected by drought.

How Many Bushmen Are There? What Should We Call Them?

This is a more complicated question than we might imagine. We do tend to think of Bushmen as a unity. In a way, this is not as strange as it may seem, for all Bushman or San groups do share a common origin as the original hunting-and-gathering populations of southern Africa. For a variety of reasons though, it is extremely difficult to estimate their numbers. There are about 90,000 in total, with significant populations including some 55,000 in Botswana, 27,000 in Namibia, 10,000 in South Africa (many of them being migrants from Angola and Namibia), fewer than 5,000 in Angola and about 1,200 in Zimbabwe. There are also small numbers in Zambia and Lesotho, and in South Africa near the Swazi border. Megan Biesele and Robert Hitchcock (2011: 4) give a total Bushman population of 96,800 in 2010, with numbers by country of 48,000 in Botswana, 34,000 in Namibia, 7,500 in South Africa, 3,500 in Angola, 2,500 in Zimbabwe and 1,300 in Zambia. These figures come from survey work done by the Working Group for Indigenous Minorities in Southern Africa. For the sake of comparison, remember that Botswana is about the same size as France and has a total population of just over 2,000,000 (including the 48,000 Bushmen). France has a population of around 67,000,000.

The present estimates for population groups are shown in Table 1.1, and the locations of the most prominent groups are illustrated in Figure 1.1. These details are the ones proposed by the linguist Matthias Brenzinger (2007: 188–90; see also Güldemann 2014: 40–1; Lee, Hitchcock and Biesele 2002b: 10). However, there do seem to some anomalies. Brenzinger says that about 10,000 people have Ju/'hoan (which he refers to as !Xũ) as their first language, whereas other authorities claim a rather higher figure. (The people are referred to as Ju/'hoansi, whereas their language is simply Ju/'hoan.) Interestingly too, Brenzinger (Brenzinger 2007: 186) gives a figure for Naro (including Ts'ao or Ts'aokhoe) of 9,000 and notes that about the same number have Naro as a second language. He suggests that the Deti have a population of 'few' and notes that the status of their language is 'critically endangered' or 'extinct'. I certainly encountered people claiming this language in the 1970s, and Traill did too, earlier in that decade. Brenzinger does not record the *ethnic group* known as Hai//om or ≠Ākhoe, since he includes them under the heading 'Khoekhoe-gowab', the term that designates the *language* they speak. *Gowab* simply means 'language'. There are about 200,000 Khoekhoe (formerly known by the derogatory term 'Hottentots'), and of these perhaps as many as 16,000 are Hai//om hunter-gatherers or former hunter-gatherers (see also Widlok 1999: 15–41).

The click-using Hadza and Sandawe of eastern Africa, respectively of Kenya and Tanzania, are often said to be related to the Khoisan peoples of southern Africa. The Hadza language seems to be an isolate and is spoken by fewer than 1,000. Sandawe appears to be very distantly related to the Khoe languages of Central Bushman groups, as well as to Khoekhoe cattle, sheep and goat herders of southern Africa (see Sands 1998). The Sandawe

Table 1.1 *Approximate populations of Bushman groups today*

	Speakers	Total population	Time period
Southern Bushmen			
/Xam	0	0	1920s
N//u	0	600	1930s
//Kx'au	0	0	1930s
//Ku //'e	0	0	1930s
!Gã !ne	0	0	1930s
//Xegwi	0	0	1988
ŋ/u	10–20	500	
! Xoõ	6,000	6,000	
Central Bushmen			
Naro, Ts'ao	9,000	9,000	
G/wi	2,300	2,300	
G//ana	1,500	1,500	
Khwe	6,000	7,000	
//Ani	1,100	1,300	
/Xaise	600	800	
G!oro	1,200	1,200	
Deti	Few	Few	
Shua	1,700	1,700	
Ts'ixa	400	400	
Danisa or Tshara	670	670	
Kua	2,500	3,000	
Tshoa	380	380	
Northern Bushmen			
!Xũ or !Xun and Ju/'hoan	10,000	10,000	
Unclassified isolates			
≠Hoã	200	?	
Kwadi	0	0	1960s
Hadza	800	800	

Source: Adapted from Brenzinger (2007: 188–90)

today have an agricultural subsistence base, but in the past were 'pure' hunter-gatherers. Estimates of their numbers vary between 20,000 and 70,000 (Brenzinger 2007: 189). I have not included the Sandawe in the table as they are not in any sense thought of today as 'Bushmen'.

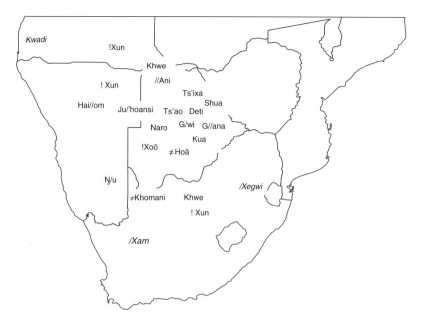

Figure 1.1 Locations of prominent Bushman groups
Source: Barnard (1992a)

Until the dawn of the Neolithic, all the world's peoples were hunter-gatherers. Tiny groups of hunter-gatherers remained in central and eastern Africa until fairly recently: that is, Bushmen or San are the last remnants of this once-widespread way of life. One often sees references in earlier literature to people such as the 'Dorobo'. This term today is a derogatory one for people without cattle, and much the same is often true for 'Bushmen' as well. Other eastern African languages were spoken until the last century or two by a great number of groups who have since then lived at least mainly by hunting and gathering: these means of subsistence were in the past more widespread than we find today. Brenzinger (2007: 192–5) includes here Aasáx, Yaaku, Elmolo, K'wadza, Dahalo, Akie, Okiek, Omotik and Nyang'i. Often linguistic change is accompanied by cultural change at the same time, and we see this in southern as well as eastern Africa. The way of life of earlier hunter-gatherers must have been quite different from that of recent ones. For this reason, some experts, such as Thomas Widlok (2016), have argued that we should be talking about hunter-gatherer 'situations' rather than hunter-gatherer 'societies'. There is no doubt that such 'situations' are on the decline, which is another reason to be careful about any such labels.

If Bushmen are not a single ethnic group, nor are they homogeneous. Studies of both male and female lines (for example, A. Knight *et al.* 2003; Pickrell *et al.* 2012) have suggested that southern African traditional hunter-gatherers are probably the most unlike and disparate peoples on earth. This includes biological difference (there are 'black' as well as 'yellow' or 'red' Bushmen), linguistic affiliation (some Bushmen speak Khoe or so-called Hottentot languages rather than San ones) and so on. Even what we call them reflects a kind of diversity. Many experts, especially in archaeology, call them San, a term that occurs in no Bushman or San language, whereas others prefer Bushmen or Basarwa, and a few have used Kua (for example, Valiente-Noailles 1988, 1993). Kua, Kúa or Kūa is the preferred generic term in a few languages, although Valiente-Noailles and a few others employ it specifically for the people of the Central Kalahari Game Reserve, especially the G//ana. Helga Vierich (1982) used Kūa in her PhD dissertation, and Valienate-Noailles (1994) used Kúa in his. Basarwa is very common throughout Botswana. Although they are used more in eastern Africa, the general terms Twa or Batwa and Baroa are also heard in some parts of southern Africa. Etymologically though, each of these terms is problematic. That is why it is so difficult to find an appropriate label for them.

My own choice of the traditional word 'Bushmen' is used in this book mainly because it is so very well known. One academic who is himself a 'Bushman' has expressed a preference for 'Kua' (Kiema 2010: 67–77). Yet even his preference is still not without ambiguity. Kuela Kiema (2010: 67) is a native speaker of G/wi. He explains further:

If I meet a Tswana or other Bantu I say I am a Kua or a Mosarwa, but if I meet a Naro or any other people of my people I refer to myself as a Dcuikhoe. When speaking Setswana, I call myself a Mosarwa, but when speaking English I use the term Bushman or San … . I do not care whether the terms San, Bushman and Basarwa are popular in academic fields or not. My aim is to fight against such stereotypes in the struggle to regain my identity. I am a Kua not a San.

Still, *kua* can simply mean serf, and in the Okavango this meaning occurs (see Kiema 2010: 68). It has been used to refer to some specific ethnic group, and Brenzinger seems to use it in that sense.

Basarwa implies a people who have nothing: 'no tribal territory, no livestock, no culture, no property, no rights, no language, no ethnic identity, no human dignity, even no chief' (Kiema 2010: 69). Of course Kiema exaggerates here, but his understanding is not beyond the feelings of many in Botswana in the 1970s or even now. In the 1970s, during Botswana's Remote Area Development Programme (RADP), it was common to call Bushmen 'RADs' or Remote Area Dwellers. The Tswana phrase was actually *matengnyanateng*, literally 'deep inside deep', presumably meaning *beyond* civilization. The RADP was to imply a social welfare initiative, but among Bushmen it did (accidentally) imply a sort of new form of ethnicity. Calling Bushmen 'San' does not really help, and the latter term has conferred an academic and a social development legitimacy born more of ignorance than of understanding (Kiema 2010: 69–70). As Kiema (2010: 70) says later on, the term San, or in its masculine singular form, Sāāb (his spelling), 'refers to a man who picks up food from dustbins or the ground'. Roie Thomas (2016: 33–5), among others, comments on this dilemma: there exists no neutral term at all. That is why I do not often use the word San. It is very common, but using it simply does not help.

Establishing how many Bushmen there are has always been difficult. As Widlok (1999: 19) points out, 'counting Bushmen' is more problematic with some groups than with others, even with a census designed to exclude from consideration either ethnic identity or language. Even indicating 'language spoken' on a post-apartheid census form in modern Namibia is problematic. In his words, 'there are, for instance, Hai//om (by self identi-fication) who tend to speak Owambo. Implicitly it buys into the apartheid claim that ethnic identity is a "given" category that requires no further deconstruction.' There does not seem to be any way to win in this game, and a Hai//om who is clearly not Ovambo (or Owambo, Ambo) but Bushman in appearance either *has* rights to the use of communal land designated for Bushmen or *does not have* this right. Nor has that problem been alleviated by the removal of apartheid legislation. Hai//om Bushmen do not live in 'Bushmanland' and are, in effect, off the map even in modern Namibia. Ju/'hoansi (!Kung) have it a little better, since their traditional territories are mapped according to collective ownership, and their land area does more or less coincide with the boundaries of apartheid 'Bushmanland'. All that can be said in a positive way is that when we talk of Bushmen we tend to know whom we mean.

Once More, What about 'San'?

In the Preface I commented on the problematic nature of the word 'San'. Let me now make it clearer what that word might really mean. Here I quote extensively from Theophilus Hahn (1881: 3). He was the son of a missionary among the Nama, and he grew up with Khoekhoegowab (Nama) as virtually his native tongue.

In the Nama language, one of the Khoikhoi idioms, the Bushmen are called Sā-n (com. plur) [*sic*]. The meaning of this term is not quite intelligible, and I frankly confess that, after nine years, of which I have spent nearly seven among the Khoikhoi, I did not succeed in arriving at a quite satisfactory etymology, and I must still adhere to the interpretation which I gave in the *Globus*, 1870, where I traced the word Sā-(b) to the root SĀ, to inhabit, to be located, to dwell, to be settled, to be quiet. Sā(n) consequently would mean Aborigines or Settlers proper. These Sa-n or Sa-gu-a, Sonqua or Saunqua, &c. (obj. plur. msc.) as they are styled in the Cape Records, are often called Bushmen – the Bossiesman, Bosjesman, Bosmanneken of the Colonial Annals, a name given to them to indicate their abode and mode of living.

The word Sā(b) has also acquired a low meaning, and is not considered to be very complimentary. The Khoikhoi often speak of *!Uri-Sān* (white Bushmen) and mean the low white vagabonds and runaway sailors who visit their country as traders. One also hears, '*Khoikhoi tamab, Sab ke*', he is no Khoikhoi, he is a Sā, which means to say, '*he is no gentleman, he is of low extraction, or he is a rascal*'.

Of course, Hahn was writing in the late nineteenth century. It is true that the use of San and its variants (Soaqua, etc.) is slightly older than the use of Bushman (Bosjesmans, etc.) in either colonial Dutch or in English, though this does not matter that much. Archaeologist and historian M. L. Wilson (1986) notes that variants of *San* (Soaqua, Saoqua, Sanqua or Sonquas) first occurred in Jan van Riebeeck's journal on 9 January 1653. This was at the same time that the label *Quena* (Khoekhoe) first occurred. *Que* (meaning 'person') is the root, and *-na* or *-qua* is a plural indicator. Neither *Que* nor *San* caught on, however, at least not at that time, although variants of *San* were more common in the second half of the seventeenth century. It seems it was most commonly as a synonym for *Visman*, meaning fisherman or, more literally, fishman. The label 'Hottentots' (now always a derogatory term) was generally employed for both hunters and herders in the earliest days, and on 31 October 1685 we have the first occurrence of the word *Bosjesmans*. These were said to be a group of 'Hottentots' living along the Berg River, and they were also known as 'Somquaas' [*sic*]. In these times though, many writers did not see a difference between Bushmen and Khoekhoe, at least in part because the European category 'hunter-gatherer' simply did not exist.

The details of *why* it was the case that 'hunter-gatherers' did not exist as a category are explained more fully in my history of anthropological studies among Bushmen (Barnard 2007a: 11–21) and in other writings. Indeed, the idea of the 'hunter-gatherer' could not logically exist until European thought gave up the domination of *politics*, in favour of a turn to *economics* as the main driving force of social organization (Barnard 2004). Throughout southern African history, the terms 'Bushmen', 'Khoekhoe', 'Khoi' and 'San' have never been entirely stable in meaning (see Smith 1985). According to Wilson (1986), the term *Bosjesmans* seems to have become common by around 1770. In the early 1970s, as much as in 1881, 'Bushman' was in very common use and had long overtaken the undifferentiated 'hunter *or* herder' phrase or the use of the word 'Hottentot'.

'San' became a preferred term by the late 1970s, with the publication of Richard Lee and Irven DeVore's (1976) edited volume *Kalahari hunter-gatherers: studies of the !Kung San and their neighbors.* Lee's (1979) great monograph *The !Kung San* came a little later. His preference for Ju/'hoansi over !Kung came still later. In modern usage, 'San' seems to date from *The Oxford history of South Africa* (Wilson and Thompson 1969) and, in particular, from Monica Wilson's (1969) chapter, 'The hunters and herders'. Yet, at least in my view, the claim that the term 'Bushman' is somehow more derogatory, or indeed more sexist, cannot be sustained. One of my colleagues in Bushman or San studies alternated between 'Bushman' and 'San' half a dozen times throughout his career, and I have done much the same through mine. Those who claim that 'Bushman' is sexist seem to ignore the fact that the feminine version is correctly, if awkwardly, rendered as 'Bushman woman'. It is never correctly given as 'Bushwoman', although that version is sometimes heard. Obviously, there is no truly correct version of any of these terms. They have changed frequently over the years, although I believe we are currently in a period of lexical stability.

The Long Duration of Bushman Settlement

I first learned about 'theory' in Bushman linguistics from the late Ernst Westphal. That was in around 1973. When, in the following year, I first encountered Bushman languages for real, rather than in a language class, it truly hit me. The language in question was *Naro*, then generally written as Nharo or Naron. It had some twenty-eight click sounds (if we include clicks and all the click releases), loads of grammatical complexity, three tones (some linguists say just two) and, I later learned, 86 person-gender-number suffixes. It also had about thirty-three words for 'talk', 'talking', 'tell' and so on (see Guenther 2006: 242, 256–7). Most Naro spoke not only this language, but several other ones too.

Clearly, these were not, as they are sometimes called, 'stupid Bushmen'. Naro though is only one Bushman language, and not even the most complicated of Khoisan languages. I did learn a lot in my early field research in the 1970s. However, I was still learning, gradually, about the great diversity that existed among Bushman peoples. This should have been pretty obvious from the very considerable time span, between the suppositions then talked about by anthropologists and the first definitive encounters of Bushmen with the outside world. That means between 25,000 and 50,000 years ago, as paleonologist Phillip Tobias (1978: 19) once tentatively suggested, and the earliest record of Vasco da Gama, which is 1497 (Da Gama 1947 [1497]: 5). As we shall see later, a recent effort gives around 44,000 years ago (d'Errico *et al.* 2012: 13214) for the duration of Bushman-like material culture, and this indeed vindicates Tobias's earlier suggestion.

Given at least 44,000 years of continued existence on the subcontinent, it should not be surprising that many languages are spoken. Indeed, in my experience most Bushmen can speak several, and the languages have such great antiquity that they are not even traceably related. Language families enjoy a timespan of only about 7,000 years. That is, the Indo-European Language Family, for example, which includes English, French, Latin, Greek, Russian and Sanskrit (among many other languages) is around that old. All these languages may seem very different, but they are all *genetically* (in a linguistic sense) related. We know this because of a magnificent eighteenth-century discovery: the fact that Indo-European Language Family *is* a 'language family'. This fact we owe to an Anglo-Welsh judge, working in colonial India.

In 1786, Sir William Jones (1824: 28) wrote these now-famous words:

[N]o philologer could examine all three [Sanskrit, Greek and Latin], without believing them to have sprung from some common source, which, perhaps, no longer exists; there is a similar reason, though not quite so forcible, for supposing that both the *Gothic* and the *Celtic*, though blended with a very different idiom, had the same origin with the *Sanscrit* [*sic*]; and the old *Persian* might be added to the same family.

Jones was an extraordinary polyglot. The phrase 'sprung from some common source, which, perhaps, no longer exists', is the telling one. Bushman languages are very different from one another, and I have known many individuals who could speak a great many such languages. With a timescale of many thousands of years, at least many hundreds of Bushman tongues have been spoken. Think about it: we know today that the distance in time between any two Indo-European languages could not be more than 7,000 years. Assuming d'Errico (d'Errico *et al.* 2012: 13214) and his colleagues are correct, Bushmen have been around and speaking some language or other for around 44,000 years. I must admit to being surprised, therefore, when a Tswana or an English-speaker asks me if Bushmen all speak the same language. Of course not! And it must have been much the same for Jones. He lived for only forty-eight years (from 1746 to 1794), and by the end of his short life he spoke at least eight languages, and some authorities credit him with a knowledge of twice that number or even as many as twenty-eight languages.

However, there is no one Bushman (or Khoisan) language family. There are a great many, and the individual languages are often of extreme complexity: phonologically they are of greater intricacy than any others on earth, and grammatically too they rich in their ability to express almost anything. At best then, Khoisan is not a language family at all, but rather, a *Sprachbund*, or a group of languages that share a geographical area. In other words, they are 'related' through convergence, rather than through divergence from a common source (as in a language family). That idea can be dated to a 1904 paper and later work by, among others, linguist Nikolai Trubetzkoy. It appears that he used the word 'language union' in a Russian paper (Trubetzkoy 1923), and later used it in German in other work too. His colleague Roman Jakobson also employed the idea of a *Sprachbund*, albeit with a slightly different meaning.

In parallel with this concept, it may be useful to think now also in terms of what might be labelled a *Kulturbund*. What similarities there are can be accounted for through this assumption, and similarities include things like religious belief, mythology and folklore. The same such ideas are widespread among Bushmen, and were it not for which language they are speaking, sometimes it is difficult to tell where in southern Africa one is. Obviously it is pretty much impossible to date the origin of a people or a 'culture' in quite this way, but this is an idea worth thinking about. This is especially true since individual Bushmen often speak a great number of languages, and children will sometimes speak different ones from their parents and spouses different ones from each other. The notion of diversity (as well as a unity) among Bushmen was fairly prevalent from the nineteenth century onwards, although it is to this day not really appreciated among the general public. Because of environmental differences there is great variation in patterns of settlement too, for example with Ju/'hoansi (commonly known as !Kung) aggregating at waterholes in the winter dry season and dispersing in the summer wet season. Central Kalahari groups (G/wi and G//ana), because they have no surface water at all in the dry season, cannot easily aggregate then. They are dispersed as family-sized units at that time of year (see Barnard 1979a, 1986; Cashdan 1983). In other words, the settlement patterns are *reversed*. These four groups can be ranked from least water to most water: !Xoõ, Central Kalahari groups, Ju/'hoansi, Naro. This correlates exactly with degree of nucleation: the !Xoõ are the most dispersed, the Central Kalahari groups next, then the Ju/'hoansi and finally the Naro. Relatively speaking, Naro tend to be the most nucleated. We shall look into this in more depth in later chapters.

All Bushman groups are heavily dependent on environmental conditions, but these affect groups in different ways. It is sometimes said that Bushmen know their environment well. Probably 'environment' should be understood in the plural though, because Bushmen actually inhabit different environments, from the very dry and unsustaining southern Kalahari to the very wet reaches of the Okavango delta. The Okavango has the peculiarity of a *dry* wet season and a *wet* dry season, since water levels depend not on seasonality there but what happens much further north in Angola. Be that as it may, it is a fact that they utilize these environments to the best advantage. They have lived in them for long enough to know where each species of plant and animal resides, and how best to make use of them.

How to Pronounce (and Spell) Bushman Group Names

By now it should be clear that there are many Bushman groups. There are also any number of ways to write their ethnic group names. Wilhelm Bleek (1858: 6), who along with the Prussian Egyptologist Karl Richard Lepsius was responsible for the orthography we now use, counted twenty-eight ways to write clicks. Or indeed, thirty-one ways, according to a manuscript version I have seen. Four of these were invented in the seventeenth century, the earliest being that of Sir Thomas Herbert in 1638. Finally here, in addition to the idiosyncrasies of the Khoekhoe dialects mentioned in the guide to pronunciation and orthography, I should mention the system employed originally by Oswin Köhler (1962). He marked voiced click consonants with a squiggly line underneath, and nasalization with tilde above the click symbol. A few German linguists have since followed this practice, but it is not very common. We shall not bother with it further.

That still leaves the question of how to write things in click languages, given the proliferation of spellings. Some Bushman specialists prefer to use diacritics, as, for example, for Nàró. This is especially true for linguists, who might actually use tones in the word when speaking English. Others omit diacritics, with the possible exception of a tilde for the nasalization of a vowel, for example, !Xoõ. To avoid clicks altogether or to substitute an unconventional system would surely cause confusion. Alternatively, one can use the Nguni system, as in Xhosa (isiXhosa), Zulu (isiZulu) or Swati (siSwati, the Swazi language). Nguni is the subset of Bantu languages that use clicks. They are found mainly along the east coast of South Africa. The other main subset is the Sotho branch, including Tswana, found mainly in the interior. Hessel Visser (2001) has given both Nguni and Khoisan representations in his standardization of Naro orthography, which uses the Nguni system. This system is based on the one chosen by the Rhenish Mission Conference of 1856, with some later minor changes.

My solution for this book is very simple. As I have suggested above, keep the clicks, use conventional Khoisan spellings, with slanted click symbols, and use the most common spellings in all cases. For example, use G/wi (rather than G|wi), and rather than G/ui, /Gwi, /Gui, /gwi, /gui or, for that matter, G/wikhoe or G/wikhoena. G/wi was the preferred spelling of their main ethnographer, George Silbebauer (who, incidentally, pre-ferred the form G/wikwena as the full form for 'G/wi people'). Occasionally too, I omit the '-khoe' in the names of the River Bushman groups. *Khoe* simply means 'person', and suffixes are added to indicate number and gender.

I have frequently been asked how often clicks occur. For the record, the answer sort of lies in Joseph Greenberg's (1955: 82–3) count. His *Studies in African linguistic classification* includes details for several languages of the ratio of clicks to the number of words in connected discourse. At the risk of thinking too much about what constitutes a 'word', I shall simply report Greenberg's figures in the five Khoisan languages he lists:

- Hiechware (Shua), 16 per cent
- !Kung (Ju/'hoan), 18 per cent
- Nama, 26 per cent
- /Kam (/Xam), 30 per cent
- Korana (!Ora), 44 per cent

Nama and Korana (or !Ora) are actually two dialects of the same language, so the figures may indeed be very questionable. In any case, the time depth between any of these is so considerable that we have to ask if this indeed is the right question. Greenberg's effort was admirable at the time, but we now know so much more about click languages. The only thing that counting clicks can tell us is the rate at which these are lost. Among the languages of the Okavango, for example, they are lost fairly rapidly, and in some other Central languages they are too: in G/wi one says *n!abe* for 'giraffe', and in (closely related) G//ana one says *nabe*.

The existence of clicks is pretty much irrelevant. What Greenberg did not realize is that Bushman languages have been around for tens of thousands of years, so the relation between one and the next one is certainly not one of having a common source. This is why the study of these languages is so fascinating, and why it is, and remains, a major area of research in Khoisan studies among both linguists and others who use linguistic data.

What Have We Learned So Far?

So, in summary, what have we learned? Let me list just a few things touched on thus far and hint at a few whose details are to come later.

- Bushmen are at the apex of human culture: they are early, but they are not primitive.
- They live in small groups in environments that they know well and have learned to utilize very effectively.
- They are not a single people, but a large number of peoples who have inhabited southern Africa for a very long time.
- In a sense though, they are related peoples who have long shared ideas, as they have shared evolutionary history, languages and material culture.
- As they have shared this simple material culture, they have also shared a simple way of life; this has been difficult at times, but it has also been resilient

(hunter-gatherers are still here, as they have been for nearly all of human-kind's time on earth).

- Bushmen and other hunter-gatherers shun accumulation of property, though not the accumulation of time: they spend less time than people in the West in daily activities and at no loss except materially; this is famously described in an essay by Marshall Sahlins (1974).
- Hunting and gathering life can be troublesome, but it also involves good things: the ethos is one of *sharing* rather than *hoarding* (see Barnard 2017), and learning this can only be of benefit to the rest of us.

These last two points are highly significant, and they will be discussed shortly. What they show is that the ethos of Bushman society is quite different from that of Western society. We accumulate, and they do not. We hoard, and they share. They do not share because they are better people than we are; they share because sharing is the essence of cultural life for them.

The remainder of this book is structured as follows. Because of its importance to Bushmen today and for their future, the next chapter is on the politics of indigeneity. Then we take a step back and examine the prehistory of Bushmen. After that, roughly from south to north, we look at the major ethnic groups in turn. Here also we follow the history of Bushman studies, since 'south to north' coincides to a great extent with this history. Then we look at the dealings between Bushmen and non-Bushmen. And finally, there are some theoretical conclusions.

Further Reading

Usually, 'further reading' consists of lists of books and articles. However, in this book further reading will be presented less in list form and more often in prose. Also, readers will note that this work has no footnotes. The reason in both cases is that I find the use of such devices as lists and footnotes distracting, whereas prose (without footnotes) can usually better express the nuances required.

The great classic has always been Isaac Schapera's (1930) *The Khoisan peoples of South Africa*. Although Schapera did not invent the word 'Khoisan', he certainly popularized it. The forms KhoiSan, KhoeSan, Khoesan and Khoe-San also occur, though today most scholars have reverted to Schapera's preferred term. Khoe (Khoekhoe for 'person') is simply an updated form for Khoi, in use since the 1970s and especially since the 1980s for the Khoekhoe ('person of persons', that is, 'the best people'). *The Khoisan peoples of South Africa* is now very out of date. My own *Hunters and herders of southern Africa* (Barnard 1992a) was, at least in part, designed to update it.

Another excellent, though also very dated, work is Phillip Tobias's (1978) edited collection *The Bushmen*. Unfortunately too, it is out of print. For those who would wish more bibliography, I suggest my short monograph *The Kalahari debate* (Barnard 1992b). This was essentially an essay made up of material left over from my much longer *Hunters and herders of southern Africa*. *Hunters and herders* was later supplemented by an additional essay (Barnard 1996) summarizing some of its main points.

2   The Politics of Indigeneity

The right to land is among the most significant interests for San today. Very often, these interests are couched in terms of 'indigeneity' or being indigenous to some particular territory, and therefore having rights that others will not enjoy. Several International Labour Organization (ILO) Conventions, especially ILO Convention 169 (1989), as well as pronouncements by the World Bank and the UN Working Group on Indigenous Populations, have altered definitions of who is to be considered indigenous. Some writers prefer to call indigenous status 'indigenousness' rather than 'indigeneity', but it comes to the same thing.

However, several anthropologists, especially Adam Kuper (2003), have made clear that neither the definition nor the rights are obvious. It is much more complicated than that. What about someone who is exactly half Bushman and half something else? Or one quarter Bushman? What special rights might such a person enjoy? Is a claim to such privileges not the same as those made by the whites in the 'old' South Africa? Much ink has been spilled on these questions, and the decisions of Botswana courts on Bushman claims to land and other resources, especially in the Central Kalahari Game Reserve (CKGR), have been ambiguous. Even the designation 'game reserve' hides the fact that its original intention was that it was to be a reserve *for Bushmen*, as much as for game. This chapter will review the literature on these often highly politicized issues.

Bushmen or San, whatever 'we' choose to call 'them', have certainly lived in southern Africa longer than anyone else. Yet the outside world encountered them little more than a few centuries ago. Like it or not, they are afforded positive discrimination, against the wishes of the vast majority of the citizens of Botswana. The situation is similar in neighbouring countries. As critics, most prominently Kuper, have suggested, this is the very problem with the concept of indigeneity. Kuper was, in fact, born in South Africa, and he points out that an overwhelming majority of people on earth have no claim to the exclusionist concept of indigeneity. So it is a little like the 'old' South Africa, whose policies he always opposed. Yet, on the other hand, it is not like this at all. Very simply, the 'old' South Africa gave rights to the highest of the high, whereas the 'indigenous' claim is a claim by or for the lowest of the low. Indigenous people are those who are 'non-dominant' over other peoples.

This latter, alternative view is that of Sidsel Saugestad (2001a: 43–4), one of Kuper's leading opponents. The two claims are opposites. Which view is correct is a politically charged issue. Both Kuper and Saugestad lay claim to such a right for their side in the debate through their anti-apartheid credentials. The context is complicated by the fact that the occupation of land implies a relational aspect. This is not always clearly defined in terms of genealogy. In other words, is ownership implied because one's *grandmother* was born there, or rather because one lives and works there now?

Saugestad emphasizes four things: being considered indigenous implies that (1) a group of people got their first (2) they are culturally distinct from other people (3) they identify themselves as 'indigenous' and (4) they are not dominant. To me the one of these that does *not* seem problematic is *self-identification*, though that turned out to be the one that was tricky for Kuper (2003: 389). What happened was that, a few years ago, a group of Afrikaners arrived at an 'indigenous peoples' conference. They were there in order to lay claim to such an 'indigenous' status. They felt that they were being discriminated against by the new, post-apartheid, South African government. Boer or Afrikaner farmers have lived in South Africa since their settlement there in 1652, in other words for longer than, say, some peoples who claim to be indigenous in some other parts of southern Africa. The Himba of northern Namibia are an obvious example. Are the Himba to be regarded as indigenous just because they have unusual customs?

Let us look at Kuper's position first, then at the views of some of his opponents and later at the reality of the dismal place of most Bushmen in southern Africa today (Figure 2.1).

Kuper and His Allies

Neither the definition of indigeneity nor the rights claimed are obvious. People are just 'pure Bushman' or *not* 'pure Bushman'. How far back in time would we have to go to determine this? And how? Genetically? And how far *forward* in time? What about someone who is genetically 'pure' (if that can ever be defined), but who has never *personally* lived a hunter-gatherer lifestyle? If Bushmen or San are defined by their lifestyle rather than by their 'race', this is what we might expect *being one* should involve. What about someone whose ancestors once lived as hunters and gatherers? What special rights might such a person enjoy? A great many people who claim San ancestry are a half or a quarter San, and hardly any live today as pure hunter-gatherers. The charity Survival International recently launched a campaign in support of 'uncontacted tribes', mainly in the Amazon Basin. Are these 'uncontacted' people not

Figure 2.1 At Ghanzi airfield, Botswana

perhaps more 'indigenous' (even if they practise horticulture) than any Bushmen?

As Kuper (2003: 389) notes, 'culture' is often a euphemism for 'race', and the words 'natives' and 'indigenous peoples' in the indigenous peoples movement are little more than what used to be called 'primitive peoples'. ILO Conventions, pronouncements by the World Bank (see Griffiths 2005), the UN Working Group on Indigenous Populations, the International Working Group for Indigenous Affairs (IWGIA) (see, for example, Vinding and Mikkelsen 2016: 431–59) and other organizations have all altered definitions of indigeneity. By implication, the rest of us are not to be considered indigenous. ILO 169 (International Labour Organization C. 169, 1989) has in fact been ratified by virtually every country in Latin America but by very few countries outside Latin America. The only non–Latin American countries to ratify to date are the Central African Republic, Denmark (including Greenland), Dominica, Fiji, Nepal, the Netherlands and Norway. To some extent this is to be expected, since few countries outside Latin America have any dealings with 'indigenous' peoples. However, several African countries, for example, *do* include such populations. Obviously, the reason African countries are not interested is political.

According to Kuper (2003: 390),

The rhetoric of the indigenous-peoples movement rests on widely accepted premises that are nevertheless open to serious challenge, not least from anthropologists. The initial assumption is that descendants of the original inhabitants of a country should have privileged rights, perhaps even exclusive rights, to its resources. Conversely, immigrants are simply guests and should behave accordingly. These propositions are popular with extreme right-wing parties in Europe, although the argument is seldom pushed to its logical conclusion given that the history of all European countries is a history of successive migrations. Even in the most extreme nationalist circles it is not generally argued that, for instance, descendants of the Celts and perhaps the Saxons should be given special privileges in Britain as against descendants of Romans, Vikings, Normans, and, of course, all later immigrants.

But what does all this mean in terms of who is *really* to be counted as indigenous? IWGIA (Vinding and Mikkelsen 2016: 432) includes pastoralist groups like Himba and Nama, for example. Certainly, the Himba have only been in southern Africa since the seventeenth or eighteenth century when they and other Herero-speakers settled there. The Nama are more recent migrants to Namibia, but had previously lived in South Africa. Does this count? Indigenous to where? A few Himba groups, namely the Twa (Ovatwa) may have been traditional hunter-gatherers, but does this make *all* Himba indigenous people? Himba are Herero-speakers, but they dress differently from other Herero: Himba are virtually naked, while most Herero groups, especially the women, typically wear modest clothing. Does this matter in terms of indigeneity? I am not going to pronounce on this question, but it does raise many serious issues. Not least is the effect that resettlement would have on the Ju/'hoansi, who would be outnumbered if all the 20,000 Herero-speaking refugees were to take up the Namibian government's offer to resettle them on Ju/'hoan land (see /Useb 2002). These are the refugees from the dreadful War of 1904–1908, between Germany and the Herero (see Olusoga and Erichsen 2010). When cattle as well as people are added to the mix, the effect would be devastating, especially as the land is already short of water.

A notion of being 'primitive' is almost always in the equation. André Bétaille (1998: 187) begins his commentary on 'The idea of indigenous people' with the words: 'Anthropology has from the beginning had a special interest in the customs, practices, and institutions of simple, primitive, or preliterate societies or cultures.' A little later he explains: 'The phrase "indigenous people" is a little like the term "native" in colonial usage, with the moral signification reversed to some extent' (1998: 190). So indigenous people are primitive, but this is regarded (in anthropology) as a good thing. Bétaille does

not disagree with Kuper, and both Bétaille and Kuper see the issues as involving a complexity that is fairly peculiar, as well as embedded in the discipline
which the three of us (myself included) practise. We in anthropology are a long
way ahead of some in other disciplines who see, for example, Bushman
languages as lying somewhere between chimpanzee and Indo-European in
their complexity. This was argued by the linguist Roman Stopa (1972),
whose fanciful notions were the subject of lectures in African languages at
the University of Cracow some years ago. My view, along with that of several
other recent scholars, is rather the opposite. Bushman languages are languages
of great complexity and diversity, and there is nothing in any of them to support
the idea that they are at all primitive. The fact that many people, and even
apparently the courts in Botswana, think of Bushmen as 'primitive' is no
argument that they really are in any way truly primitive.

The decisions of Botswana courts on Bushman claims to land and other
resources have been ambiguous. This is especially true for the CKGR.
Some decisions, such as the *right to occupy* their traditional lands, have
gone in their favour, and others, such as *access to water*, have not (see
High Court of Botswana 2005). This may be because of an idea that San
retain a degree of 'primitiveness'. It also may simply reflect the notion
that they are different and that *difference* may allow for certain special
rights to be granted to them. Indeed, complexity is the order of the day, as
Roie Thomas (2006: 27–8), following Ning Wang (1999), has argued.
There are several forms of 'authenticity'. Thomas and Wang identify
three: objective, constructive and existential. *Objective authenticity* is
that which is either truly original or some imitation of this, perhaps as
understood in the tourist experience. *Constructive* is more nuanced, a kind
of hyper-reality with an embedded symbolic appreciation of it. *Existential*
is yet more profound: an actual belief in what lies behind the Bushman
trance dance comes to mind (see Thomas 2006: 116–71).

It is worth noting that this applies specifically to Botswana. The situation in
South Africa and in Namibia may be yet more complicated, if a little more
mundane. Let me now turn to the details in each of these three countries (South
Africa, Botswana and Namibia) and examine the status of San, Basarwa or
Bushmen in each. And for each, I shall use the most common term to refer to
them: San, Basarwa or Bushmen.

San in South Africa

South Africa is unique in southern Africa, as it has not one or two but eleven
official languages. None of these, however, is a San language, and the total
number of native speakers of any San language alive today is very tiny,
certainly no more than a few hundred. In any case, there is no such thing as a

distinctly San language: San is a cultural concept, and San across southern Africa speak many languages. They are unified only in the sense that all San are traditional hunter-gatherers and in that their many languages all possess click consonants. Nearly all San within South Africa today are relatively recent immigrants from Angola and the north of Namibia. They and their dependents arrived in South Africa only after serving in the South African Defence Force during the Namibian War of Liberation. This ended in 1989, a year before Namibia's independence.

Other South African San, such as the /Xam, have all died out, although the descendants of the /Xam still proudly claim the status of being the First People of South Africa (see De Jongh 2012). These latter people are the *Karretjiemense* (Donkey Cart People): the capitalization is deliberate and reflects their self-classification as an ethnic group. Modern technology has been of great advantage to them, as they now communicate through cell or mobile phones! Their traditional occupation is sheering sheep, and to do this they travel from farm to farm across the Great Karoo. None of them can speak the /Xam language, however. Their language is now Afrikaans.

In 1995 the South African cultural studies journal *Critical Arts* (1995) devoted an issue, 'Recuperating the San', to the plight of San in southern Africa. As the blurb on the back cover puts it, the journal 'aims to challenge and engage academic practices which reinforce undemocratic relations in society'. Much concern seems to be given over to the representation of San, especially in Keyan Tomaselli's (1995) introduction to the issue. For example, the film *The gods must be crazy* (Uys 1980) received great critical acclaim and box-office success, but it has not been highly regarded by anthropologists. Likewise, the documentary *People of the Great Sand Face* (Myburgh 1985) explores the everyday lives of the G/wi of Botswana's CKGR. It is factually accurate, but depicts a now past lifestyle without apology for its depiction. One of the most interesting things that the filmmaker, Paul John Myburgh (2013: 224), says is: 'We were all once "first people".' The subtle, and sometimes not so subtle, evolutionism that permeates his work is not to everyone's taste, but it does remind us of one of the reasons that San remain figures of fascination for many in the West.

South Africa became an independent country in 1910, after two civil wars between Afrikaners and British forces. The apartheid government ruled from 1948 to 1994, although the apartheid system became more relaxed in the period immediately preceding the introduction of democracy. South Africa has been a democracy since 1994, although the political stability that has existed since then has been marred by political scandal and continuing rural poverty. San have always faced discrimination, although for technical reasons they were not considered 'black' under apartheid. This, in fact, at least gave them some, if strangely dubious, privileges. They were considered a kind of 'Coloured' (supposedly, mixed race), and therefore they were not subject to the pass laws that constrained the majority population. This may have resulted simply from their rather low population.

The language statistics are:
- Zulu, 22.7 per cent
- Xhosa, 16 per cent
- Afrikaans, 13.5 per cent
- English, 9.6 per cent
- Pedi, 9.1 per cent
- Tswana, 8 per cent
- Sotho, 7.6 per cent
- Tsonga, 4.5 per cent
- Swazi (siSwati), 2.5 per cent
- Venda, 2.4 per cent
- Ndebeli, 2.1 per cent
- Sign language, 0.5 per cent

South African San today speak mainly Afrikaans, though the 4,000 migrants from Angola and northern Namibia and their descendants originally spoke !Xun (!Xũ) and Khwe (Kxoe). I would guess about 3,000 spoke !Xun and 1,000 Khwe in the 1990s. I visited the army camp of Schmidtsdrift in 1997. This was just after the inhabitants had been allowed to move their tents. Before this, they had to keep them in straight lines. Yet when I got there it was still obvious which group was which. Each group placed their tents in traditional fashion: !Xun in open, circular configurations and Kxoe with metre-and-a-half high windbreaks surrounding the huts. The windbreaks were there probably less for privacy and more for deterring any potential encroachment by snakes. The point is that the style of these was reminiscent of the Kxoe camps in the Okavango. Schmidtsdrift is near Kimberley, and the growing population has since then been moved to a nearby farm known as Platfontein. A wealth of ethnographers, both Afrikaans-speaking such as L. P. Vorster and H. P. Steyn, and English-speaking, including Linda Waldman, John Sharp and Stuart Douglas, have now descended on these locations (see Barnard 2007a: 120–2, where references to their numerous works are given).

In terms of ethnicity, South Africans are:
- Black, 80.2 per cent
- Coloured, 8.8 per cent
- white, 8.4 per cent
- Asian, 2.5 per cent

These figures, however, exclude the languages of all 'indigenous' South Africans, which is, if you think about it, quite strange in a country that has eleven official languages. And of course, some in South Africa, particularly

Khoekhoe, as well as the descendants of San, resent this linguistic policy. Their languages are simply not recognized.

In the year 2000, the then President Thabo Mbeki inaugurated South Africa's new Coat of Arms. It features a rock art figure, in order to represent the idea of 'coming together', and the country's new motto, *!Ke e: /xarra //ke*. It is worth thinking about Mbeki's (2000: 1) words:

The motto of our new Coat of Arms, written in the Khoisan language of the /Xam people, means: diverse people unite or people who are different join together. We have chosen an ancient language of our people. This language is now extinct as no one lives who speaks it as his or her mother-tongue. This emphasises the tragedy of the millions of human beings who, through the ages, have perished and even ceased to exist as peoples, because of peoples inhumanity to others. It also says that we, ourselves, can never be fully human if any people is wiped off the face of the earth, because each one of us is a particle of the complete whole.

Mbeki adds, by the way of further explanation, an invocation of human evolution, respect for diverse languages, opposition to racism, sexism and so on, and a nod to the 'ancientness' of the /Xam:

By inscribing these words on our Coat of Arms – !ke e: /xarra //ke – we make a commitment to value life, to respect all languages and cultures and to oppose racism, sexism, chauvinism and genocide. Thus do we pledge to respect the obligation which human evolution has imposed on us – to honour the fact that in this country that we have inherited together is to be found one of the birthplaces of humanity itself. Here in the language of our ancient past, we speak to present generations and those who are still to come about the importance of human solidarity and unity.

So, everything is there: San culture, common humanity and, at least by implication, indigeneity. My own translation of the motto is: 'People of different origins are joining together; people who differ in opinion are talking with one another' (Barnard 2003: 249). This captures yet another meaning in these /Xam words, and it is entirely literal. In short, the complexity of the idea of indigeneity is brought in at every turn, and South Africa is safe from that notion being stolen. There are hardly any indigenous South Africans left, which is perhaps the point. Of course, Mbeki did not come up with all this by himself. The Coat of Arms was designed by a professional draftsman on the basis of an object that was in the government's hands already (it was in a museum). The motto itself was drafted by David Lewis-Williams. He happens to be the foremost expert on rock art in the country and knowledgeable of the /Xam language.

Basarwa in Botswana

Botswana has two official languages, Tswana (Setswana) and English. The overwhelming majority of the population, about 79 per cent, speak Tswana as their first language. The country became independent of British rule in 1966. The Kalahari sand system covers about 70 per cent of the country as well as parts of neighbouring countries. It is indeed the largest continuous stretch of sand in the world (see Figure 2.2).

In Botswana, Bushmen are known as 'Basarwa'. The term is traditional, though the *Ba-* prefix was added to replace the older *Ma-* form in the late 1960s. This was at the instigation of a schoolchild. He noted that as 'Masarwa' are indeed *people*, they should be honoured linguistically, as in the word *Batswana* (the people of Botswana), with the prefix appropriate to people. *Ma-* would be grammatically appropriate for trees and the like. By ethnicity the population is:

- Tswana, 79 per cent
- Kalanga, 11 per cent
- Bushmen (Basarwa), 3 per cent
- Kgalagadi, 3 per cent
- whites, 3 per cent
- others, 1 per cent

The Kalanga are a Bantu-speaking (western Shona) group related to the majority population of Zimbabwe. The Kgalagadi are a Bantu-speaking group closely related to the Tswana. The Kgalagadi arrived in Botswana first, around the eleventh century. The Tswana came into existence within current South Africa by the thirteenth century and moved into modern Botswana in the eighteenth. Kgalagadi used to be regarded as a dialect of Tswana, but is now recognized as distinct.

Three per cent of the total population may not sound like very many, but the Basarwa have long occupied the heart of the country. The traditional land of the G/wi and G//ana is the vast CKGR or simply 'the Reserve'. It is about 52,000 square kilometres: larger than Switzerland, one and a half times the size of Belgium or twice the size of Massachusetts. The population at the time of George Silberbauer's fieldwork in the 1960s was only about 3,000 (see Silberbauer 1965: 14). In the following decade, the population was smaller. Silberbauer put down the first borehole in 1962, and he used to take the pump with him whenever he left the Reserve. This was for fear of spreading disease through a concentration of population at the site of the borehole, a place officially called Xade or, with the click, ≠Xade. Silberbauer was Bushman Survey Officer and District Commissioner of Ghanzi District at the time: this was before he became an anthropologist.

The trajectory of events is interesting. It is also depressing (see Kiema 2002: 159–62). The Reserve was declared in 1961. It had the dual purpose of protecting wildlife and providing sanctuary for the human inhabitants, as long as they lived according to their traditional means. Independence came to Botswana in 1966, and over the years the second purpose of the Reserve was gradually forgotten. Silberbauer's (1965: 134–6) recommendation that fifteen

Figure 2.2 Building a hut at Hanahai, Botswana

boreholes be drilled was never followed. Through the 1970s and 1980s, people moved to the one borehole, whose pump had been restored. Through those times the government provided facilities, including sporadic medical care. Diamonds were discovered at Gope in 1984, and after a fact-finding mission a year later government declared the Reserve ecologically unviable and set about relocating the population. Meanwhile, Bushmen had begun herding goats in the Reserve and hunting on horseback. Both, of course, were illegal. Botswana was relatively poor in those early days, and has only (thanks to the discovery of diamonds) become Africa's richest country quite recently.

The Botswana Society (consisting mainly of academics) organized a small conference in Gaborone in 1992, and the small number of Basarwa present raised objections to the dispossession of land by the government. The NGO First People of the Kalahari was registered a year later. The Christian missionary and advocate of Basarwa rights Braam Le Roux was declared a prohibited immigrant. That decision, though, was later reversed, and he lived in Botswana until his death in 2009. Back at Xade, things were not going well. Opinions differed on whether to accept relocation or not. Then wildlife officers tortured an activist, and he later died. Other activists campaigned against relocation, and in 1996 the Minister of Local Government, Lands and Housing (Patrick Balopi) visited Xade. He explained that the government had not intended the relocation of people, but simply the relocation of cattle posts to areas outside the CKGR. Struggles continued through the late 1990s, and the Working Group of Indigenous Minorities in Southern Africa (WIMSA) was established in late 1996. Leading activist John Hardbattle died of cancer in November that year. He was half Naro and half English. He could speak a great many languages (including English) eloquently, and his loss was considerable.

Despite the government's reassurances, some CKGR residents were selected to accompany representatives of the Land Board to locate a resettlement site. A CKGR negotiating team was formed, and delegates and supporting NGOs eventually examined the chosen site. This was at a place called Kg'oesakeni (meaning 'in search of life'), and in 1997 the relocation began. This settlement soon took on the name *New Xade*. Others were moved to a village south of Khutse known as Kaudwane. The NGO Survival International argued that relocation was linked to the mine at Gope, and many CKGR inhabitants refused to be relocated. Among others, the controversial Australian political scientist Kenneth Good (see, for example, Good 2003, 2008) famously took up their case, and he was ejected from the country in 2005. Good's arguments, rightly or wrongly, tended to focus on minutiae, but the gist was that everything tends to stack up against Basarwa: the power of the mining interests, the dominance of the Botswana Democratic Party and so on. I would only add that on the other side, the lack of political power, and as well a culture of compliance and compromise on the part of the Basarwa, has not made their plight any easier. Nor is outside intervention always a good thing: a point made by Sethunya Tshepho Mphinyane (2002), herself a Tswana commentator on the issue.

In late 2001, the Botswana government announced it was about to cut off basic services to those who remained in the Reserve. This was effected in the following year, and Reserve residents filed a case in the High Court at Lobatse. Botswana has always prided itself by its democracy and its independent judiciary. At first the case was dismissed on technical grounds, but by July 2004 a new case began, and with George Silberbauer himself appearing as an expert witness. This case was heard at New Xade. The CKGR NGO called Coalition, together with Survival International and First People of the Kalahari, took the case forward. Other relevant NGOs (such as WIMSA) held back. In September 2005, a disease that affects sheep and goats was discovered in the Reserve, and the gates of the Reserve were closed. The activist Roy Sesana of First People of the Kalahari was arrested for trying to enter it, and soon thereafter he was awarded the Right Livelihood Award (sometimes called the Alternative Nobel Prize). The court ruled on 13th December, 2006. The decision was ambiguous, as it allowed residence in the Reserve but without the guarantee of the provision of essential services. In other words, both sides could claim victory. The judges were divided, and the exact details of the decision were lengthy, to say the least (see High Court of Botswana 2005). Of the 243 original applicants, some died during the 130 days of the case, which was spread over two years. Hearings were held in several locations, and the typed record of the proceedings numbered 18,900 pages.

In January 2007, some former residents returned to the Reserve. Meanwhile WIMSA Botswana and First People of the Kalahari fell apart! Roy Sesana, Kuela Kiema and others met with the president, and the goats were returned to the Reserve and compensation awarded. In a way, the saga continues: some Basarwa of the CKGR are in effect dispossessed and deprived of water resources and other amenities, while others have been able to make a new home at New Xade (see also Ikeya 2016). I referred earlier to the situation as being depressing. What is probably most depressing is that no one can see an outcome that will please all parties. Alice Mogwe (1992: 1) employs the phrase *tengnyanateng* (deep inside deep) in an epigraph to her pamphlet *Who was (t)here first*. Her point is that Basarwa do not see themselves as 'remote'. 'Remote Area Dwellers' is, of course, a misnomer. As one put it, it is not that *they* are far from Gaborone, but that Gaborone is far from *them*. In other words, it is Gaborone that is *tengnyanateng*.

The legal issues involved have been quite complex and have been documented in a recent monograph by Maria Sapignoli (2018; see also Sapignoli 2015; Saugestad 2011). The purpose of giving San, Basarwa or Bushmen land rights, the nature of those rights, Tswana traditions that might conflict with them, mining in the Kalahari, interference by the United Nations, similar interference from local and international NGOs, and indeed other factors have all taken their toll. Indeed, Sapignoli's list of abbreviations cites literally dozens of NGOs. Nor is it all over: the Basarwa's struggle for indigenous rights continues. Saugestad (2001a: 232) writes: 'The development of indigenous representative organisations is probably among the most significant innovations in the relationship between indigenous peoples and the state.' She notes that this has taken a long time, not just in Botswana but also in many other countries: in Canada, in the United States, in Australia, in New Zealand and in Scandinavia.

San in Namibia

Namibian independence was officially granted in 1990, following a year under United Nations control. Before that, there had been direct rule from South Africa after South Africa's capture of the country from Germany in 1915. The history here is rather complicated. Following the Allied victory in the First World War, the Union of South Africa, and later the Republic of South Africa, had been granted control over South West Africa as a Mandated Territory. In effect, the South Africans ran South West Africa or Namibia from 1915 to 1989. The country was finally freed only after a number of skirmishes and a long War of Liberation. South Africa never recognized anyone else's right of control, since in their view the Mandate had been granted by the League of Nations (1920–1946), and the United Nations (1945–present) had no right to assume it. These dates are misleading in any case, since in effect the League had long since ceased to exercise any authority (see, for example, Wallace 2011: 205–308).

Namibia today has just one official language, English. In spite of a preference for other languages among many inhabitants and various political parties, immediately prior to independence English was chosen. Before that, hardly anyone had spoken English as a first language. However, the diplomatic corps, made up mainly from former exiles who had served in the Liberation Movement, *did* speak English. Nearly half the population speak a dialect of OshiWambo (like Kwanyama or Ndonga), though to have *this* language as the only one would have been rather difficult politically. So English then did seem an obvious choice.

Population statistics by ethnicity are:
- Ovambo, 49.5 per cent
- Kavango, 9.2 per cent
- Coloured (including Basters), 8 per cent
- Herero, 7 per cent
- Damara, 7 per cent
- Namibian whites, 7 per cent
- Nama, 4.7 per cent
- Lozi (Caprivian), 3.5 per cent
- San, 3 per cent
- Tswana, 0.6 per cent
- others, 0.5 per cent

Namibia has the largest population of San in any of the three countries: South Africa, Botswana and Namibia. However, Namibia remains very sparsely populated. Of the population groups, the Damara and the Nama speak *Khoekhoegowab* (the Khoekhoe language), as do the Hai//om, a San group of northern Namibia. The Hai//om traditionally occupied the area around Etosha Pan (see Dieckmann 2007). 'Bushmen' is a common term, though the government encourages the use of 'San'. The San population remains significantly disadvantaged, thanks to shortages of food and water, an absence of paid work and the presence of drug-resistant tuberculosis, malaria and HIV/AIDS.

A key factor for social development in recent years has been the influence of the Ju/wa Farmers Union from around 1986, and later its successors the Nyae Nyae Farmers Cooperative and the Nyae Nyae Conservancy (see Biesele and Hitchcock 2011: vii–xiii). Also important has been the involvement of the Nyae Nyae Development Foundation of Namibia (NNDFN), set up originally by John Marshall and Claire Ritchie. Marshall (filmmaker and son of ethnographer Lorna Marshall), along with Ritchie, long advocated that Ju/'hoansi make the transition from hunting and gathering to livestock production (see Marshall and Ritchie 1984). The debate over the possibility of this still haunts Bushman studies: it was not so much that anyone thought this impossible, but that, in the words of an agricultural adviser speaking in the late 1980s, Ju/'hoan families were welcome to apply for fenced-in farms as long as they had 'a hundred cattle and the means to operate a commercial farm' (Biesele and Hitchcock 2011: 87). Of course, virtually none of them did.

The NNDFN was a major effort designed to assist in social development for Bushmen. Activities included, for example, the Village Schools Project, which included education in the Ju/'hoan language, largely through the efforts of the linguist Patrick Dickens. Dickens had worked on the !Xoõ language some years before in Botswana, and the independence of Namibia brought him the opportunity he needed. Yet very sadly, Dickens died in 1992. Fortunately for the rest of us though, shortly before his death he was able both to complete a highly usable dictionary of the language (Dickens 1994) and to begin work on the school. Megan Biesele (2016) cites a vast (and now growing) literature related to this project, and the spinoff projects that this enabled still continue. They have benefitted a number of people, many later employed through them. Others have been able to learn to read and write Ju/'hoan because of this, and the orthography of the language has been standardized on Dickens's system. The only drawback (for me at least) has been the rather absurd usage of *Ju/'hoan* as an adjective and for an individual, but *Ju/'hoansi* as the plural. All ethnographers adhere to this, and in this book I do as well. Ju/'hoan may be an 'endangered language', but Dickens's efforts do indicate that there is hope for the future. Biesele estimates there are 17,000 first-language users. Of course, Biesele's own work benefits too, as she is trained as a folklorist as well as now practising as a development co-ordinator.

The main geographical area of concern here is the former 'Bushmanland'. This was the western half of the desert plain that had been the traditional location of these San. It was centred on the land known to the Marshall family as N//hoan!ai or Nyae Nyae. The latter term has caught on, and in English it tends to refer to a slightly larger area along the Botswana border. Above all, the location has a focal point today at the village of Tjom!kwe or Tsumkwe, which has a population of around 6,000 (Biesele and Hitchcock 2011: 5). As is customary in Anglophone literature, I shall refer to these by their Anglicized names Nyae Nyae and Tsumkwe. A problem in recent years has been that this area, which was once inhabited by Herero, has since independence seen an influx of significant numbers of Herero people and their cattle. Herero had lived in exile in Botswana ever since the War of 1904–1908, when the German occupiers of Namibia attempted to exterminate the entire Herero nation. It is estimated that they nearly did so, with (according to some) as much as four fifths of the entire Herero population being killed (see Olusoga and Erichsen 2010; Sarkin 2010: 5). It is estimated that between 34,000 and 110,000 Herero died in the conflict or in their escape, while many of the survivors were able to settle in what is now Botswana. It is no wonder that those who remained alive fled to British territory, present-day Botswana, in the years immediately after.

The presence of surface water is, of course, crucial to life in the Kalahari. This is true for both humans and animals, especially if livestock have been introduced. The Herero are cattle people, and as I have mentioned John Marshall also tried to bring cattle to the Ju/'hoansi in the 1980s. Even before that, there were also early attempts at livestock breeding. The first borehole at Tsumkwe was put down in 1961, the same year as the establishment of the CKGR in Botswana. Four gardens were started by 1964, and goats were introduced in 1965. The South West Africa Administration tried to introduce cattle as early as 1972, and the attempt was not unrelated to the growing militarization of the area around that time (see Biesele and Hitchcock 2011: 9–12; Hitchcock 2016). The proclamation of much of the land near Tsumkwe as another game reserve in the 1980s did not help matters, and by this time Herero had begun to return to their own ancestral Namibian homeland. They shared this territory with San, as indeed they do in north-western Botswana. Except for their different political histories, the trajectories of sometimes gradual and sometimes rapid developments in San affairs seem to have run parallel in the two countries.

Indigeneity and Self-Image

Ultimately, being an 'indigenous person' is about self-perception. In other words, indigenous people are those who truly perceive themselves as such (see also Saugestad 2001b). The rest of us cannot understand, and nor should we try to understand. In my view, Kuper is right that 'indigenous' is not a proper concept for anthropology, but he is wrong that it must be rejected in all circumstances (see Barnard 2006). It is a legitimate concept of self-definition, and it is useful in practice for those who claim it. The fact is: we are stuck with it! In a sense, it is like the concept of a 'refugee', defined in legal terms as a person who does not belong, or who is of the wrong culture to fit in. Other analogies may be relevant here too. The notion of *Urkultur* among the Vienna-based diffusionists of 100 years ago, and both the revisionist and the anti-revisionist positions in the famous Kalahari Debate (see Chapter 8) come to mind. Basically, revisionists reject the idea that Bushman culture is real and long-standing; anti-revisionists or traditionalists reject this assertion.

Urkultur was the idea that there existed a primitive 'culture circle', a kind of stratum with other culture circles built on top of it. That idea was prominent especially in the work of Father Wilhelm Schmidt (for example, Schmidt 1929,

1939), a Catholic priest whose diffusionist ideas were prominent in the early twentieth century. His notion of *Urkultur* was, among other things, of a kind of primitive monotheism. In his view, this existed long before shamanistic and polytheistic notions. He equated hunter-gatherer monotheism with his own. Later religious ideas were corrupt, he argued, while hunter-gatherers had retained the divinely revealed religion of very ancient times. Kalahari revisionists, most notably Edwin Wilmsen (1989), are those who reject ethnicity-based concepts in favour of class-based ones. Their opponents are often called traditionalists, and this position is exemplified in the work of Richard Lee (for example, Lee 1972, 2013). Both sides, in their different ways, are looking to find an *Urkultur*. The revisionists fail to find it among Bushmen, since it has been stripped away through centuries of contact with Iron Age Bantu-speaking populations. The traditionalists do find it, because they recognize its fundamental truth in what remains of Bushman culture. Of course, both this debate and the history of the Vienna School show rather more complexity than can be expressed here, but this is the gist of both positions (Barnard 2006). The big question really is: how primitive, or how modern, are Bushmen?

Let me summarize the comments on Kuper's original article and then look at the comments on my own 2006 piece. In his comments on Kuper (2003), Keiichi Omura says that Euro-American essentialist ideology is not applicable anyway. Indigeneity is in practice constantly redefined. He says we should focus on that. Evie Plaice says that Kuper's position may be 'the only tenable one', but that it does not address the issue of inequalities. Alcida Rita Ramos says that Kuper argues badly, and with casual generalizations. Steven Robbins says Kuper is right about essentialism, but his image of the indigenous rights movement is a caricature. Kuper should concentrate on the reconstruction of indigenous identities instead. James Suzman agrees with Kuper, but unlike Kuper comes at this from a practical point of view rather than a theoretical position. In other words, several subtly different positions are expressed, and most find fault with Kuper.

The views of the commentators on my 2006 article are not all that different from each other, but they do bring out further the complexity of the issues. Kuper's stance is, in essence, that the concept of indigeneity is *essentialist*: it should be abandoned in favour of universal human rights. It is like apartheid ideology. It is also like the earlier, now discredited, anthropological notions of 'the primitive' – attacked by Kuper (2005) in *The reinvention of primitive society*. This was part of traditional anthropological thinking at least through the nineteenth century. This position, say the commentators, does so-called indigenous groups no good. Mathias Guenther (see also Guenther *et al.* 2006) is largely in agreement with me. Justin Kenrick says that my position is interesting, but nevertheless that Kuper is wrong. Indigenous peoples are not looking for 'special rights', but are starting from a position of political weakness. Adam

Kuper, in his reply to me, argues that my position simply will not do. If he, Kuper, is right then in theory, it must follow that his own *full* position must hold. Evie Plaice says that she is not quite convinced about my separation of anthropological baggage and legal issues. Anyway, social justice, she says, is what is important. Trond Thuen agrees that indigenousness is indeed a political construct, but argues that anthropology should concentrate on changing relations between governments and minorities. Patrick Wolfe says that in my own effort to be fair to everyone, I have suggested two separate conversations, and that this simply will not do. In other words, Wolfe's position on my argument is similar to Kuper's, but Wolfe also strongly opposes Kuper. I am wrong, Wolfe says, on two accounts: one cannot separate being wrong for anthropology and being right for politics. Finally, Werner Zips seems to agree with me, but suggests that the legal questions have been neglected. I said in reply to these others that this is ironic, considering that the basis of social anthropology itself *is* legal theory: Maine, Bachofen, McLennan, Morgan and Radcliffe-Brown were at heart, if not professionally, legal theorists. As Kuper (2005: 3), who is critical of the 'myth of primitive society', puts it: 'Primitive society was initially regarded as a subject for lawyers' (see also Barnard 2000: 15–26).

In further discussion in *Current Anthropology* a year after Kuper, Michael Asch and Colin Samson (Asch and Sampson 2004) say simply that Kuper is wrong with regard to indigenous rights in Canada. Dieter Heinen says that Kuper is broadly right about a number of issues, and clarifies them, but that more emphasis should be placed on social justice. Justin Kenrick and Jerome Lewis argue that indigenous peoples want not *extra* rights, but *equal* rights. Sidsel Saugestad points out that Kuper makes factual errors. Terence Turner adds that Kuper's argument is based on false premises, and his image of indigenous peoples is a caricature. Kuper replies that none of the attempted definitions of indigeneity would exclude 'the English' as an 'indigenous people'. And all of them retain romantic imagery and false ethnographic visions. Furthermore, he says, these have dangerous political implications.

There have also been further discussions and related pieces, for example in the journals *Anthropology Today*, the *New Humanist* and *Before Farming* (now renamed *Hunter Gatherer Research*). The debate rumbles on. Neither side, in the sense that there are just two sides, can really claim victory. Yet, in a clear sense, Bushmen are at the forefront of the debate, for it is their claim to indigeneity and the consequences of having it that is really at stake. Bushmen may not know the English word 'indigenous', nor for that matter its near-synonym 'autochthonous', but they certainly do have a self-perception of having been in southern Africa a long time. But what do we really mean by 'Bushman groups'? I say that Bushmen speak many languages, but to what extent is this always true? Of course Naro speak the Naro language, which is very different from, say, the Ju/'hoan language. However, Naro and Ju/'hoansi were once essentially the same people. We know this from genetic evidence (Pickrell *et al.* 2012; Pakendorf 2014). The G/wi and the G//ana are separate peoples: we know this because they consider themselves to be separate peoples, even if they share the same lands. Jiro Tanaka's (1978) dictionary has separate listings for G/wi and G//ana, although the vocabularies listed are nearly identical (like British and American English). G//ana people sometimes say that they have a different ancestry because (supposedly) G//ana have some 'black' ancestry and G/wi do not. In what sense then, except through their own self-perceptions, are these really different peoples? It is the same with several other groups: Naro and Ts'ao or Ts'aokhoe, for example. They differentiate themselves, but from an outsider's point of view they are culturally and linguistically identical. The Ts'ao are simply northern or north-eastern Naro, although the Naro of the west, who *sometimes* call themselves //Aikhoe, are still Naro. //Aikhoe is simply a (western area) synonym for Naro. Other labels are known too, such as Qabekhoe and N/haints'e, but these may simply be other names for Ts'aokhoe or ≠Haba.

It is, of course, much the same with 'nations'. The United States considers itself a separate nation from the United Kingdom, and Scotland from England. Yet the boundaries between these, in both cases, were once fluid. The town of Berwick-upon-Tweed shifted between England and Scotland several times during the Middle Ages as armies conquered it and then relinquished it. Nor do boundaries always work in the same way. For example, I have two nationalities but am often thought to be one or the other. And even nation states can play this game too. In 1991, I travelled across the Namib Desert, from Swakopmund to Walvis Bay and back again. But in what country had I been? South Africa reckoned Walvis Bay was in its own territory and duly stamped me into South Africa. Going in the other direction, there was no border crossing: Namibia reckoned I had never left Namibia, so there was no need to stamp me in. Happily, there is no question about this now, since South Africa gave up its claim to the Walvis Bay area in 1994.

A Final Note: !Khwa ttu and Cultural Heritage

Bushman culture is to a great extent in the eye of the beholder. Nowhere is this more true than in the organization called !Khwa ttu, which is located near Yzerfontein, South Africa. This organization has a museum and engages in various educational activities, including what is known as the //Kabbo Academy. There is also a guest house, a bush house, a bush camp, some luxury tents and a publishing venture (see Von Wielligh 2017). The motto, in *Khwedam* (People-language) is 'San Spirit Shared'. The //Kabbo Academy at the moment trains some 150 young people from Botswana, Namibia and South

Africa. As its website declares: 'The entry level course focuses on improving students' cultural, heritage, nature and environmental education, builds life skills and provides work exposure. The course prepares San youth to make decisions about their future and walk the path of their choice – be it further study, entering the workplace or starting their own business.' More detail is available from the website !*Khwa ttu – San sprit shared*: https://www.khwattu.org.

A great deal more could be written, and has been written, about what it means to be indigenous in southern Africa. Yet this is not the place for that. I have tried here simply to set the scene and show the complexity of the issues. They have profound theoretical implications, but also illustrate real, and very practical issues for the peoples concerned. There are also disagreements involved, for example in the verbal confrontations encountered at the 'International Conference on Khoisan Identities and Cultural Heritage', held in Cape Town in 1997 (Bank 1998). Indeed, many of these involved disputes between Khoekhoe and San – disputes about who is, or is not, 'indigenous' in southern Africa. Both groups laid claim. The dust seems to have settled for the time being, but the battles will probably continue for some time to come.

But on a more positive note, in the words of Nelson Mandela (1997: vi) in reference to this conference, 'By challenging current perceptions and enriching our understanding of Khoisan cultural heritage, this conference will contribute to the renewal of our nation, our region and our continent.'

Further Reading

Developments in Botswana, including the court case in the Central Kalahari Game Reserve, are well covered in Kiema's (2010) book *Tears for my land*. Another treatment of legal issues is Sapignoli's (2018) recent book *Hunting justice*.

The best work on the topic of indigenous voices is Biesele and Hitchcock's (2011) *The Ju/'hoan San of Nyae Nyae and Namibian independence*. This is supplemented by an interesting update in the form of a film review by the same two authors (Hitchcock and Biesele 2014). The best opposing view of the idea of indigenous voices is represented by Kuper's (2003) article 'The return of the native'. At about the same time, there is the debate in *Before Farming* between James Suzman (2002) and Stephen Corry (2003). Suzman is in agreement with Kuper, and Corry (of Survival International) holds the opposite view.

A list of NGOs involved in San development is given in *Cultural Survival Quarterly* (Anon. [b] 2002: 59). There is also an extensive chronology of developments in Namibia from first encounters in the 1850s to the UN

Permanent Forum on Indigenous Issues in 2010, in *The Ju/'hoan San of Nyae Nyae and Namibian independence* (Biesele and Hitchcock 2011: xvi–xviii). See also Chennells (2014), who reflects on sharing the 'cultural riches' of the works of Bleek and Lloyd. The most up-to-date source is the volume edited by Fleming Puckett and Kazunobu Ikeya (2018).

3   How Far Back Can We Go?

When does prehistory begin? Tobias (1978: 19) once dated the earliest Bushmen to approximately 25,000 or 50,000 years ago. He gave both these figures simply because he was unsure. Recent findings at several sites trace the origin of symbolic culture in southern Africa to more than twice the latter figure. What this means in terms of either the origins of language or the relation between the earliest symbolism and living populations is, of course, open to debate. As I have said, a recent figure suggests 44,000 years ago (d'Errico *et al.* 2012: 13214). A clear solution to such a debate would also dissolve any difference between what in southern Africa are known as the Middle Stone Age and the Later Stone Age. Archaeological findings, such as those of early rock art, perhaps give a better clue to Bushman prehistory. Engravings and paintings can be dated to at least some 27,500 BP, in the case of Apollo 11 Cave in southern Namibia (Mason 2006). The newest evidence suggests a date of around 80,000 BP (Vogelsang *et al.* 2010). Namibian rock art boasts some 1,000 sites and nearly 50,000 paintings, in the case of the Dâureb or Brandberg Mountains. However, the connection with Bushmen today is far from certain. The same goes, and even more so, for much earlier sites like Blombos Cave on South Africa's Indian Ocean coast, with its etched red ochre and shell beads presumably long ago strung on now-decayed twine (see Henshilwood *et al.* 2009). That said, there is very little doubt that Bushmen are at least among the earliest painters, engravers and symbolic thinkers on the planet.

This chapter will explore these and other issues. Rock art studies will be covered in the next chapter, and the entry of Iron Age, Bantu-speaking populations into southern Africa will be dealt with in later chapters, especially Chapter 11.

Beginnings of the Bushmen

Ever since the 1920s, it has been recognized that the periodization of archaeological sites in southern Africa is rather different from that of the rest of the world. This is shown in Table 3.1. Symbolic thought began during the Middle Stone Age (MSA), a uniquely African period. It is, though, very roughly

Table 3.1 *'Stone Age' archaeological periods*

Worldwide archaeological periods	Southern African archaeological periods
Neolithic 12,700–5,300 BP	**Recent**
Farming, urbanization	contact with Iron Age agro-pastoralists
	development of herding lifestyle
Mesolithic 22,000–5,900 BP	modern hunter-gatherer lifestyle
Microliths, ceramics	extensive rock art: painting and engraving
Upper Palaeolithic 45,000–10,000 BP	**Later Stone Age 50,000 to recent**
Domestication of animals	ceramics, pottery c. 2 ka
Figurines, rock art	Wilton 4–8 ka
Diversity of artefacts, bow and arrow	Oakhurst 7–12 ka
	Robberg 12–18 ka (microliths)
Middle Palaeolithic 300,000–30,000 BP	**Middle Stone Age 300,000–50,000** BP
Mousterian	Sibudu 45–58 ka
Stone-tipped spears	Howieson's Poort 58–66 ka
Neanderthals, *Homo sapiens*	Still Bay 70–77 ka
Homo sapiens and Out of Africa migration	pre-Still Bay 72–96 ka
	Mossel Bay 77–105 ka
	Klasies River 105–130 ka
	development of symbolism and language
Lower Palaeolithic 2,600,000–100,000 BP	**Early (Earlier) Stone Age 2,600,000–300,000** BP
Acheulean	Acheulean 300 ka–1.5 Ma
Oldowan	Oldowan 1.5–2 Ma
Homo erectus and Out of Africa migration	*Homo erectus*
Australopithecus	*Australopithecus*

Source: Adapted from Barnard 2012: 26, with additional material from Lombard *et al.* 2012: 125

equivalent to the worldwide Middle Palaeolithic. There are perhaps hints of this in Schapera's (1930) *Khoisan people*. However, the definitive text was actually an archaeological one that was published a year earlier. In this text, A. J. H. Goodwin and C. Van Riet Lowe (1929), urged on through visits by the Cambridge anthropologist A. C. Haddon and others, recognized that European classification simply did not fit the South African scheme. So, they devised their own one, and this one has remained in place ever since. The key archaeological sites in southern Africa, many discovered prior to 1929, are illustrated in Figure 3.1. I have concentrated here mainly on those of the Middle Stone Age (300,000–50,000 BP) and Later Stone Age (50,000 BP to recent).

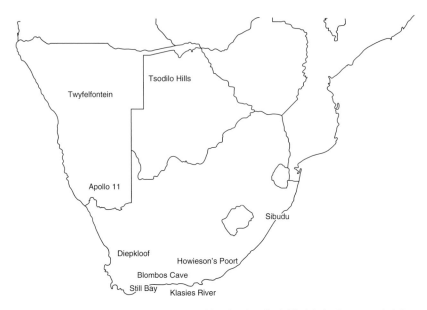

Other sites along South Africa's Indian Ocean coast include
among others Wilton, Oakhurst, Robberg and Mossel Bay

Figure 3.1 Southern African archaeological sites
Source: Details given mainly for MSA and LSA sites

So when did Bushman society begin? And how long is a piece of string? These two questions are actually quite similar and depend on what is meant by 'Bushman society' or 'a piece of string'. We cannot go by anything in the prehistory of language because language families all post-date Bushman origins (Barnard 2016a). That is, the farthest back we can trace any language family is about 7,000 years, or maybe just very slightly longer. Symbolic thought is much older than this. Just as in astronomy (where things have to be inferred through an understanding of gravitational pull), a great deal in prehistory does depend on inference, and in this case on reasoned speculation. The etchings at Blombos Cave, for example, are reputed to have been made about 77,000 years ago, and the shell beads assumed to be from an ancient necklace are even older. Likewise, tools at Border Cave and other MSA sites are said to resemble those of modern Bushmen (Grün and Beaumont 2001; Grün, Beaumont and Stringer 1990). Yet resemblance, one might well argue, is different from identity. Steven Mithen (1996) suggests that a cognitive shift occurred in humanity between the Middle and the Upper Palaeolithic. This was not because of a change in brain size, but simply because of changes in mental attributes. These are evidenced by material culture, burial practices, the emergence of cave art and so on – all between 100,000 and 40,000 years ago. Accompanying this was a change in religious thought, as humans became 'modern' (Winkelman 2010: 76–9). Shamanic ritual, healing practices, mysticism and a new consciousness all followed.

Nor will anything in genetics provide a clear answer. However, there are indications that today's Bushmen are at least one of the ancestral populations of the world. For example, according to Henn and her team (Henn *et al.* 2011: 5154): 'The observed patterns are consistent with an origin of modern humans in southern Africa rather than eastern Africa, as is generally assumed.' The team do point to significant interaction with herders and farmers over the last 5,000 years, as well as population bottlenecks and at least some hunter-gatherer migrations. Yet they do state that African hunter-gatherers maintain the greatest degree of genetic diversity in the world. This is part of their insistence that it is southern Africa, rather than eastern Africa, that is where modern humanity began. In this regard it is worth remembering that the *total* population of the world after the Toba volcanic explosion of around 74,000 BP was possibly as low as 2,000 (Wells 2007: 140). Toba, now a lake in Indonesia, was once the site of a huge eruption whose ash covered much of the globe. The Toba eruption led to a volcanic winter that lasted perhaps ten years or so. In spite of later interbreeding on many continents, we the people of the earth are all descendants of this tiny population. The rest mainly died out (see Ambrose 1998), although a handful entered the genepool through interbreeding with Neanderthals and Denisovans.

Bushmen, of course, are, or were until fairly recently, full-time hunter-gatherers. Even this, however, is a little problematic. All hunter-gatherers today live on the fringes of herding or cultivating societies. They may do some scavenging or live to some extent on handouts, or by theft from neighbouring groups. Some of them, like the River Bushmen of the Okavango delta, also do some fishing. The Okavango is a vast inland delta whose water flows down from the Angolan highlands in the north during the Kalahari's dry season, roughly March to July, and then simply soaks into the plant system, into the ground or simply evaporates (see, for example, Botswana Society 1976). This phenomenon is unique in the world, and these River Bushmen will be described in Chapter 10. Fishing was no doubt also practised by the ancestors of the early humans who migrated along the coasts, to Asia and Australia, but except among River Bushmen it is rare today.

Definitions of 'hunter-gatherer society' have changed through time, but generally fishing is allowed under nearly all definitions of 'hunter-gatherer'. A substantial portion of early humans apparently lived by eating shellfish as they travelled along the coasts (see, for example, López *et al.* 2015). There is some debate about when 'hunter-gatherer society' came into being. I once argued that 'hunter-gatherer society' is essentially an eighteenth-century Scottish invention. What is problematic is the idea that early humans lived in *societies*. This dates from late eighteenth-century Scotland. Hunting and gathering are *economic* concepts, and the existence of such a society implies a theory of economic relations (Barnard 2004). Before the eighteenth century, the idea was that societies were purely political and not economically constituted, and therefore that hunter-gatherers did not live in societies but in a pre-societal existence (for example, Hobbes 1991 [1651]: 86–90).

Another commentator, the archaeologist Sibel Barut Kusimba (2003: 112–36), goes further. She talks of the *emergence* of the hunter-gatherer and argues that this concept is meaningful only in the context of anatomically modern, and in a way *socially* modern, humans. These are humans who have developed dynamic technological systems, with innovation and creativity, ways to pass on ideas down through the generations and the means to exploit environments to best advantage. This may have included a sociality based on monogamy and principles of kinship, exchange systems, the development of trade and the notion of specific environmental awareness, and of course, language. These are all characteristics of a Middle Stone Age existence (see also Brooks 1984). Certainly, hunter-gatherers have great variation, not simply because they live in a wide variety of natural environments but because they have chosen to exploit them quite differently. Commentators have repeatedly remarked on this (for example, Kelly 2013; Finlayson and Warren 2017b), and it is the reason why humans have been able to make a living through millennia in a variety of habitats.

It really is impossible to say when Bushmen came into being. Although Henn and her colleagues are quite emphatic that southern Africa is the source of humanity, not everyone agrees. The geneticist Sarah Tishkoff, for example, argues for an eastern African origin, with a subsequent migration southwards between 10,000 and 50,000 years ago. This does seem that unlikely to me, and she argues her case on the basis of linguistic evidence (see Jobling *et al.* 2014: 303). She does not, however, specify that linguistic evidence. As I say, it does depend on what we mean by original populations. Certainly, hunter-gatherers have lived on the planet since the earliest times of the human species. Modern humanity came into being in some part of Africa, and from there humans colonized the world (see Barnard 2011: 39–45). It is a myth that hunter-gatherers are 'nomadic'. Of course, they migrated from Africa to Asia and Australia, to Europe and the Americas. Bushmen though are not truly nomadic, a point made by Ikeya (2017), among others. Basically, southern Africans are simply those who stayed put in Africa, while the rest of humanity went else-where. Occasionally, Asia (once assumed to be the continent of human origins) sees a resurgence of interest, for example in a recent article in *New Scientist* (Douglas 2018). This has to do with our species being assumed to be hybrids.

We should not imagine that Bushmen should be any less creative than we are, and indeed there is a bit of Denisovan and Neanderthal in all of us.

Bushmen are quite creative. For example, when I visited a Naro settlement in 1982 I heard someone say (in Naro), 'That's really "digging stick"!' I have never spoken Naro all that well, and I had to ask myself if I had heard this correctly. I was later able to confirm with a bilingual Naro-English-speaker that I really *had heard* this. This was a novel linguistic usage, and it caught on: normally 'digging stick' is simply a noun phrase, but here it was being used as an adjective to mean something like 'wonderfully crazy'. I do not know whether the phrase is still as trendy with this meaning, nor how widely it spread among the Naro. If in English I were to say, 'Hey man, that's like "crazy"', people might find this a strange thing to say, but they would understand me. Could the same not be true among the Naro in 1982? Or at Border Cave 40,000 years ago? The earliest evidence of modern Bushman-like artefacts dates from 44,000 years back, at Border Cave (d'Errico *et al.* 2012: 13214). This is more than twice the previous estimate, and 44,000 years ago would indeed seem to be an accurate date for early San culture. Yet this does not mean they are stuck in the 'Stone Age', for they have evolved to take best advantage of one of the most difficult environments on earth, technologically, socially and linguistically. It is well to remember this.

Instances of Bushman creativity include the Women's Drum Dance of the Ju/'hoansi, apparently introduced about 1960 (Lee 2013: 148–50; Katz, Biesele and St Denis 1997: 114–29). In this the roles of women and men are reversed: women dance and go into trance, while men watch. The dance is accompanied by drumming. The male equivalent is the Giraffe Dance, although at times (in the 1980s and 1990s) the Drum Dance has eclipsed it. In fact, the Drum Dance and the actual drum that represents it dates originally from 1915. At that time the woman who introduced the drum acquired it from the Mbukushu, a farming group from the Okavango swamps. Throughout the Kalahari, there are also many examples of people making fun of others, either individuals or whole ethnic groups, by imitating their stylistic actions. Naro not infrequently do this with regard to Herero: they pretend to be Herero in order to mock them. Nicknames are also common: Naro and Ju/'hoansi, and some of the groups that live nearby like Ts'ao or Ts'aokhoe (north-eastern Naro), need nicknames because so many people share the same 'real' name. That is, if my real name is //'Are, people may invent a nickname for me. Or distinguish me from someone else also bearing the name //'Are by adding a suffix: //'Are-*kiba* (old //'Are), //'Are-*g//oba* (prime-of-life //'Are), //'Are-/*uaba* (little //'Are) and so on. Sometimes individuals are referred to by specific characteristics: I once knew a man the Naro referred to as 'Ostrich' because his gait resembled that of an ostrich.

We can also look, in a sense, to natural humanity. By this I mean natural humanity in the way that this concept is conceived in modern science, *not* as understood by political philosophers of past centuries. One key paper that explores this is by Tobias Kordsmeyer, Pádraig MacCarron and R. I. M. Dunbar (2017). Kordsmeyer, MacCarron and Dunbar examine the size of permanent campsites among hunter-gatherers. They argue that these are of sizes that are constrained by natural conditions, including the sizes of personal social networks. The sizes of both these networks and of residential communities are typically 50, 150, 500 and possibly 1,500 individuals. These represent 'natural social attractors' or 'sweet spots' to which communities gravitate. Bushman groups do indeed fit the bill here, just as they adhere to Dunbar's (2003) earlier suggestion of a natural community size of around 150. This is the largest group that can be sustained without recourse to police, government institutions and so on: the *natural* size of a true anarchistic society. Even Western groups that attempt anarchy instead of government, such as Moravians, tend towards this figure. So too do military units.

Comparative Anthropology

It should go without saying that Bushmen have lived in the environments they have for a very long time. Contrary to what is often said, they are not constantly migrating. They are transhumant, but they do not generally leave their territories to move to other ones. As Hugh Brody (2001: 7, 86–90) once put it, it is *farmers* who throughout prehistory and history have been the migrants. They move about every five generations in search of new pastures and planting grounds, whereas hunter-gatherers tend to retain an attachment *to land*. This is for its local resources, but it is also for its symbolic value. The case is most strongly represented in Aboriginal Australia (see Maddock 1973: 21–44), a continent inhabited for far longer even than Europe. The date of first habitation is in dispute, but Australia has had a human presence for at least 42,000 or 48,000 years. Some experts assume an even greater time depth, possibly as great as 60,000 years (Cameron and Groves 2004: 268–9). Language, mythology, religion, practices such as burial and cremation, fishing and some sort of sailing (or rafting) had already begun. These customs must have been brought by the first inhabitants, and Australia was virtually separated from the rest of the world for the next several thousand years.

Southern Africa has had a similar length of habitation, possibly by Bushmen or by those who eventually became the Bushmen we know today. I am thinking here of archaeological discoveries such as those at the Klasies River Mouth (for example, Wurtz 2002), Blombos Cave (for example, Henshilwood and d'Errico 2011) and Pinnacle Point (for example, Marean 2010). These Middle Stone Age sites are very near the Indian

Ocean coast and indicate the use of ochre for body painting and the use of marine resources. The latter were for food, and also for body decoration (sea shells, originally strung on twine). The sites date from 125,000 years ago, with several from more than 70,000 years back. They indicate that ochre was transported and stored, that abstract drawing existed and that sea creatures were eaten. The use of seashells in jewellery may not seem that relevant to Bushmen in recent millennia, but their presence, in large number, points to early symbolic thought. Indeed, we could ascribe Bushmen to being present at the very dawn of modern humanity. From southern Africa, their descendant conquered the globe. There may have been people in Siberia or the Middle East before that, but it was 'the Bushman' who created humanity as we know it. I say 'the Bushman' here, but remember that this is not any single ethnic group but rather a great diversity of actual groups (see Henn *et al.* 2011).

Comparison is a key concept in social anthropology. It also provides a measure with which to think about prehistory in general. If we are concerned with the basis of hunter-gatherer social life, a good place to start might be with humankind's nearest biological relatives, such as bonobos and common chimpanzees. Another is with other hunter-gatherers, such as Australian Aborigines. They are a collection of modern hunter-gatherer societies that have maintained independence from African hunter-gatherers for, according to David Cameron and Colin Groves (2004: 268–9), some 60,000 years. Others do opt for a somewhat lower figure by a few thousand years. Whatever the exact time depth, the degree of distance in African and Australian contact is very considerable indeed, and in spite of similarities in way of life there are big differences. Aborigines hunt but have no bow and arrow, only hafted spears. Bushmen hunt with bow and poisoned arrow as well as spears and traps, though as Schapera (1927) noted long ago, their arrows, in general, have no flights. Aborigines and Bushmen have different ideas of the afterlife, very different religious ideas and so on, though Ian Watts (2017) has noted that there may be similarities and even a common origin dating back to before the great human dispersal tens of thousands of years ago. Watts and colleagues (for example, Watts, Chazan and Wilkins 2016; Knight 2010) have made similar point in other papers too, and it is high time for a rethink of the issues and the dates.

Another point of comparison is with our nearest human or nearly human relatives, the Neanderthals. They interbred with modern humans in Europe and the Near East some tens of thousands of years ago, but they have always been quite separate from African hunter-gatherers such as Bushmen. In their monograph *How to think like a Neanderthal*, Palaeolithic archaeologist Thomas Wynn and cognitive psychologist Frederick Coolidge (Wynn and Coolidge 2012: 35–6) suggest seven ways in which Neanderthals were similar to modern human hunter-gatherers and, perhaps more importantly, six ways in which they were different. The similarities include:

- cooperative hunting (i.e., hunting in groups);
- using terrain features to navigate;
- carrying meat back to home bases;
- dividing carcasses further, for sharing;
- cooking as a means to prepare meat;
- maintaining different tactics for different game; and
- having hunting trips lasting more than a single day.

The differences include, for Neanderthals:

- using a narrower range of meat and vegetable resources;
- having a more dangerous animal-killing technique;
- lacking a schedule within seasons but nevertheless varying prey according to season;
- employing, almost exclusively, an 'out and back' pattern for hunting and gathering trips;
- travelling shorter distances for both hunting and gathering; and
- possessing no clear gender difference in foraging activities.

What the various similarities and the differences tell us is that Neanderthals had evolved cognitively to a point that they were nearly like us. Yet nevertheless they were clearly different, and they possessed elements of culture that might be considered human universals. I would add at least one additional difference: human hunter-gatherers *do have* clear gender differences in hunting and gathering activities. Men are normally the hunters, and women do at least most of the gathering of vegetable foods. But of course, Neanderthals were Europeans; Bushmen are Africans. On these grounds alone, it should be obvious that Bushmen are certainly not either primitive or related to humankind's primitive ancestors any more than anyone else is. Exactly the same is true of Australian Aborigines. Kuper (2005) is right: a primitivist illusion surrounds these peoples, and this is our fault, not theirs.

In all probability, Neanderthals and other early humans had a form of language (see Wynn and Coolidge 2012: 27). Occasionally, people today assume that language evolved from simple to complex forms and that Bushmen and other hunter-gatherers possess just a simple form. In fact, nothing could be further from the truth! Hunter-gatherers speak languages just as complex as anyone else on the planet. If they are 'primitive' in any sense, they are not linguistically primitive. Naro, for example, is much *more* complicated than English, not less complicated. As I pointed out in Chapter 1, Naro has some thirty-three words for 'talk' and similar concepts (see Guenther 2006: 242, 256–7; Visser 2001: 209–11). Naro is also very rich in verbs and adjectives. Some other hunter-gatherer groups, notably Inuit and Athapaskans, have very complex grammars, with up to 450 or more affixes in any given dialect. Phonological complexity is also far greater among Bushmen than in any other group on earth (see Atkinson 2011). Namibian !Xun (!Xũ) has about 141 phonemes, compared to the Brazilian language Pirahã, which has only eleven. Other Khoisan languages, notably !Xoõ (which is not traceably related to !Xun), have *nearly* 141 phonemes. All other languages lie somewhere in between !Xun and Pirahã, with Oceanic and South American ones tending to have only a dozen or so, and Southeast Asian and European ones rather more. English (depending on dialect), by comparison, has around forty-six phonemes. Atkinson's study is based on comparisons of 504 languages and their distance from an African point of origin, and strongly supports an African beginning for language in general. It really is not unlikely that the ancestral languages of all humanity were ultimately derived from Khoisan ones. I say *derived from* them here because the time depth is so many times the duration of any language or even any language family.

Also, we must not think of language only as spoken. Language can also use signs: sign language is just as much *language* as is spoken language. Anne-Maria Fehn (pers. comm.), working in the Okavango, found a large vocabulary of signed words in two quite different Khoisan languages. Her colleague Susanne Mohr has had results in related 'River Bushman' languages (for example, Mohr and Fehn 2013). The two languages employed different means as well: mainly one-handed in Ts'ixa and mainly two-handed in //Ani. Among Ts'ixa, this sign language is still in use in hunting, whereas among //Ani its use is predominantly restricted to narrative. Among Ts'ixa, the overwhelming majority of words express only one morpheme, whereas among //Ani their use is mainly in compounds. In short, there is great divergence here even in sign language.

Village sign languages have been reported on several continents, often in villages or communities in which there is a large deaf community. The most famous example is Nicaraguan Sign Language. Its invention was actually observed by linguists around 1977, when a school for the deaf was established in Managua (Kegl 2002). Linguists were able to witness the creation and (rapid) development of a language for the first time. This may be slightly different from the River Bushman case, however, as the latter is specifically sign language employed for use in hunting, where it is important to keep silent in order to prevent animals from hearing anything said.

Prehistory for Social Anthropologists

Prehistory is, of course, part of the subject matter of archaeology. However, the sharp division between social anthropology and archaeology is, for me at least, rather difficult to accept. It is better to think of prehistory as a field that has a place in both of these disciplines or sub-disciplines. The problem arises when anthropologists seek to explain things like society and culture across the boundaries anthropology has drawn for itself. This is especially true in studies that seek to explain evolution, or indeed most anything involving temporal comparison. An overarching idea of anthropology is essential in order to look for answers to great questions that the discipline was, in the nineteenth century, formed in order to explain.

According to conventional wisdom, the genus *Homo* is about 2,300,000 years old. The human species, modern *Homo sapiens*, is only about 200,000 years old. This figure, however, is now contested, and social anthropologists would do well to follow developments in archaeology and in human genetics to keep up to date. The science writer Colin Barras (2017) has a good deal to say about this in his assessment of shifts in thinking in the early 2000s. Much of this depends on some startling new discoveries, like stone tools dated to 3,300,000 years ago, the small-brained Dmanisi fossil of 1,750,000 years ago, genetic evidence of the mysterious Denisovans 400,000 years ago and of their descendants since then, *Homo floresiensis* alive only 50,000 years ago and new discoveries about Neanderthals. Then in the year 2017, new fossils from Morocco seem to indicate that *Homo sapiens* can be dated to at least 300,000 years ago. This is only part of the story, and the saga continues. Table 3.2 is an attempt to capture some of this in tabular form. The table is, of course, derived from many sources, and the dates given are obviously difficult to verify.

Symbolic thought and language, it is said, first occurred in eastern or southern Africa some 130,000–120,000 years ago (see Barnard 2012: 12–14). However, we simply do not know for sure whether this date is correct or not, but evidence for a southern Africa origin is strong. This is based on excavations at Blombos Cave (for example, d'Errico *et al.* 2005). Neanderthals and other early human species seem to have had symbolic thought and human creativity too. Penny Spikens and her colleagues (Spikens *et al.* 2017) argue the case for this, and with comparisons to Ju/'hoansi regarding childhood and sociality. Modern humans first migrated from Africa either shortly before or not long after the volcanic explosion of Toba about 74,000 years ago. Because of the ensuing volcanic winter, that explosion led to a severe bottleneck in population size across the globe (see, for example, Oppenheimer 2004, 2009). Although the exact dates have long been disputed, such sources tend to date the first migrations across the then-existing Bering Land Bridge to the Americas about 25,000 to 22,000 years ago. Agriculture then evolved, independently, in the Americas and in the Near East. This began roughly 12,000 years ago. There is no doubt that biological and cultural evolution

Table 3.2 *Timetable of human evolution and Bushman society*

Earliest *Homo sapiens*	320,000 or 200,000 years ago
Early language	130,000 or 120,000 years ago
Symbolic culture: beads and etchings (RSA)	110,000 and 70,000 years ago
Homo sapiens outside Africa	85,000 years ago or earlier
Ostrich egg shell fragments	83,000 years ago
Earliest rock art in Africa	80,000 years ago
Toba volcanic explosion	74,000 years ago
Humans arrive in Australia	65,000 years ago (perhaps)
First Bushmen	44,000 years ago (perhaps)
Earliest rock art in Spain	40,000 or 35,500 years ago
Humans arrive in the Americas	25,000 or 22,000 years ago
Domestication of the dog	16,000 years ago (perhaps)
Very early agriculture: dawn of the Neolithic	12,700 years ago

influenced each other, and that biological evolution did not cease when culture took over as a dominant evolutionary force.

Adam Kuper and Jonathan Marks (2011) argue for a wider anthropological science that accommodates both biological interests and social ones. This is, in fact, a view that I now share. However, this is not the same thing as favouring the complete assimilation of one field into the other: a view that I was once accused of fostering. Biology and social or cultural aspects of the discipline do represent quite different areas, with legitimately quite separate research interests and research programmes. In reality, I have never argued otherwise, but my suggestion of a branch of modern social anthropology encompassing evolutionary ideas (Barnard 2011: 149–51) seems to suggest this to some people. What is important is to recognize that biology and culture both contribute to the making of humanity, and in that sense, that anthropology ought to be a single science, albeit necessarily a fragmented one. This is true on both sides of the Atlantic, but particularly true in Europe.

Things are particularly complicated when we are talking about Bushmen. The linguist Rainer Vossen (1991: 370), for example, talks of the *extra-linguistic factors* that affect linguistic factors: the social influence of one language on another, the way children acquire a language, 'the seemingly unmotivated variability within a single speaker', as he puts it, as well as the interview situation. There is also the geographical context of a region in which people speak a great many languages, many of which are related. All this has a profound impact on understanding the prehistory of life in the Kalahari.

Social Anthropology Enters the Middle Stone Age

Archaeology is perhaps the most obvious sub-discipline to expect, with regard to engagement with a wider anthropology. It is also a particularly strong field in Mexico, right from the beginnings of anthropology there. However, the most relevant sort of archaeology happens to be that rooted in African Palaeolithic and African Middle Stone Age (MSA) studies. African archaeology exhibits its own periodization, and the MSA lasted roughly from 300,000 until 50,000 BP. Or some refer the dates 280,000 to 25,000 BP. (Even Wikipedia does not seem to agree on this.) The MSA was preceded by the Early Stone Age (in some writings, Earlier Stone Age) and followed by the Later Stone Age. The latter label, which dates from the 1920s, was chosen precisely because it was a little vague (see Goodwin and Van Riet Lowe 1929). This was, of course, two decades before the invention of radiocarbon dating, in 1949, at a time when what we now refer to as 'relative' dating was indeed truly relative.

Today the main concern in the archaeology of the MSA is with the earliest stages of *symbolic thought*, and with the dawn of language – which may or may not coincide with it. At least on the former (symbolic thought), we have some good evidence. The clearest comes from South Africa. There is a major site called Blombos Cave, 100 metres from the Indian Ocean coast (sea level has changed very little in the intervening millennia). This site has yielded bead-work made from shells and several pieces of etched red ochre as old as 100,000 BP (for example, d'Errico *et al.* 2005; Henshilwood 2009a). We know that the ochre was brought to the site from several kilometres away, then carved and stored. Elsewhere, the earliest ostrich egg shell fragments in Namibia are dated at 83,000 BP (Miller *et al.* 1999). Early dates have become quite commonplace in recent years, and all of them reflect the use of symbols, and even the expression of ideas through language. All of this, of course, predates the migration of humans to the Americas. It also predates the invention of agriculture by tens of thousands of years.

The common culture that humanity once shared was a hunter-gatherer one. Hunter-gatherers do not accumulate, but find ways to redistribute their property through sharing as well as exchange. Although the details have been questioned, the idea of an 'original affluent society', popularized by Marshall Sahlins (1974), was a prehistoric reality. Typically, the hunter-gatherer or foraging mode of thought involved quite different sets of values from those of Western or other recent societies. The accumulation of wealth is considered antisocial, while giving it away is idealized. This is not the same as performing charitable acts, but it involves formalized giving within the family or the community. Likewise, followership is favoured over leadership. Following other people shows deference to the whole community, while seeking to lead shows self-interest. In kinship, the entire society is classified as belonging to kin categories, and there is no such thing as *not* being 'kin': everyone stands in some kind of classificatory 'kin' relation to everyone else. The very notion of 'society' entails this. People are seen as free individuals, and the land they occupy as sacrosanct. It is associated with inalienable rights of primordial possession. As has been shown in numerous ethnographic studies, such a notion of sociality persists among hunter-gathers to this day (see Barnard 2017).

Beyond hunter-gatherer ideology lies the Neolithic. For me, this was *and is* (since non-hunter-gatherers inherit this post-hunter-gatherer ideology too) a step backwards in social evolution. I am not saying that we as a species have not advanced a great deal since the Neolithic, but rather, that we have also lost a great deal! Language emerged in hunter-gatherer times, and with it came mythology and totemic thought. Most practitioners of social or cultural anthropology, and indeed of the whole of the anthropological sciences, are ethnographers. But what is the point of ethnography, apart from contributing to our understanding of human diversity and the details of how humans behave? The functionalist tradition of A. R. Radcliffe-Brown (1952) and others always emphasized society as consisting of four systems: economics, politics, religion, and kinship. Although other theoretical perspectives have seen things a little differently, this functional paradigm still makes clear the systematic relations within and between these elements. As the late Sir Edmund Leach (pers. comm.) used to say, fieldwork has only one tradition: the functionalist tradition. For example, *marriage* is in essence an institution within the kinship system. Yet it also has impacts within the others: in the economic sphere it affects the transfer of property through dowry and bridewealth, in the political sphere it reflects the power base, particularly in the case of relations between kin groups and in arranged marriages, and it also very frequently has religious dimensions. Were it not for ethnography, the full extent of human diversity would be unknown. The recognition of descent is an obvious example. Basically here there are four kinds of descent: matrilineal, patrilineal, double (through both mother and father, with children belonging to one matrilineal group and one patrilineal one), and cognatic or bilateral (with no recognized descent groups). There are also much rarer types, where gender is important: parallel (where women trace descent through women, and men through men) and cross or alternating (where women take membership in the group of their father, and men take membership in the group of their mother). Such differences are not trivial, but reflect both the organization of societies and the cultural understanding of individuals who live in these societies.

Political relations are generally bound to property relations. They are also embedded in symbolic relations: everything humans do has a symbolic dimension. For this reason, we as a species cannot live through biology alone. The most common forms of kinship structures on earth are not ones like ours, based on genealogical proximity and distance, but ones based on things like alternating generation equivalences and rules that assume that to be related through a same-sex sibling link implies a closeness that being related through an opposite-sex sibling link does not. In the *majority* of human societies, on virtually every continent (apart from Europe and in societies closely related to European ones), the incest taboo is usually defined to allow marriage between cross-cousins (children of a brother and a sister), but not between parallel ones (children of two brothers or two sisters) (Barnard 2012: 41–3).

These findings are largely social anthropological ones, but the data gathered reflect input from many areas, including human biology (in studies of nutrition), linguistics (in the form of data on knowledge and classification of plants) and even (in consideration of time depth of these practices) archaeology. This suggests that there are grounds for optimism: anthropologists working together, with a diversity of perspectives and interests. Nor indeed are related disciplines excluded: the impact of human genetics in evolutionary studies is obvious. Among the great contributor to such analyses, for example, has been Stephen Oppenheimer (2004) whose training and expertise lies in that field. It is difficult to see exactly how genetics and social anthropology could be united under a single theoretical perspective, but it is by no means beyond the realms of plausibility that they should agree to the same larger framework. By this I mean agree that the genetic domain is genetics and the symbolic domain lies clearly within a social and cultural domain beyond that. This latter domain is, of course, social anthropology, and a mutual recognition of this is necessary for both disciplines.

Obviously, an ethnographic focus on hunter-gatherers is desirable, but taking into account other perspectives, such as broadly evolutionary ones within psychology, may reveal insight as well. It is also worth some reflection that little over twenty years ago evolutionary linguistics did not exist. Today it is thriving: there may be a lesson here for social anthropology. After all, social anthropology's subject matter is essentially symbolic thought, especially as revealed through language. If this does not lend itself to evolutionary treatment, then what does? Symbolic thought is a significant force within virtually every branch and theoretical perspective within archaeology, as well as within social anthropology. Virtually every theoretical perspective in the history of social anthropology has considered it too, although because of postmodern approaches since the 1970s it has fallen into relative obscurity. In my view, all is not lost: social anthropology has everything to gain by recalling this interest. There is no reason for social anthropology not to be a core part of the subject, and to re-establish itself, possibly at the very centre of a newly invigorated but broad-based discipline. And this should not be seen as a threat to any other field, for all are needed in what I would like to see (if I can risk the phrase) as a *new anthropology.*

The only sense in which hunter-gatherers can possibly be primitive is in the sense of technology, although even here they possess a relatively high degree of sophistication when compared to ancient hominin species. This is perhaps particularly true of Bushmen. The classic story of archaeological classification in southern Africa dates from excavations by George Stow (1905). In 1877 he excavated a cave near Smithfield and found tools from what later became known as the Later Stone Age. He describes these in *The native races of South Africa* (1905). The classification became standard through the work of A. J. H. Goodwin and C. Van Riet Lowe, whose scheme dominated archaeological thinking in southern Africa for many years. Goodwin and Van Riet Lowe's (1929) classification was ultimately quite simple, though the rethinking of the classification proved a bit more complicated. The Early or Earlier Stone Age was characterized by hand axes. The Middle Stone Age by prepared cores, and the Later Stone Age by microliths. Wilton was essentially a coastal tradition, and Smithfield was found mainly in the interior. The former was a tradition of segments, and the latter essentially of large scrapers. Wilton was quite widespread, and Smithfield less so.

Later refinements proved relatively minor, and other complexes were added: Oakhurst (or Albany), with Robberg predating this, and coastal Strandloper (literally, 'beach walker'). And in the late 1940s, new dating methods made possible greater periodization, rather than simply a geographical description. Wilton and Smithfield had originally been thought to be contemporaneous, but later developments showed that what had been known as 'Smithfield A', later called Lochshoek, dated from 12,000 to 8,000 BP and was part of the Oakhurst complex. This non-microlithic industry, in turn, was contemporary with the Albany industry of the Cape Province. The classification does not meet everyone's expectations, and archaeologists debate the details. For example, the term Smithfield is generally used now for the Later Stone Age tradition dating roughly from 1300 to 1700 CE (see, for example, Mitchell 2002: 137–91; Barham and Mitchell 2008: 309–55). What used to be called 'Wilton' is now, according to the latest revision (Lombard *et al.* 2012: 126), to be replaced with 'final Later Stone Age' and so on.

This is not the place to rehearse the intricacies of archaeological debate: they are at least as complicated as debates on classifying Bushman languages. Classifying Bushman languages, though, has proven to be an easier task, as by and large all experts agree on the relationships. The important thing to remember is that Bushmen have been around for a very long time. Like anyone else, they have evolved both biologically and culturally. Bushmen today are part of a very long, and continuing, strand of this evolutionary trajectory and are neither more nor less advanced than any other people.

Bushmen Today: Things Get Complicated

There are more than 200 ethnic group names in the literature, and many of these names are synonyms. For example, there are at least twenty-three labels for the !Xoõ, and one of these, ≠Hoã, is also the name for *another* small group (Traill 1974: 9). The 'Eastern ≠Hoã' are not just the eastern branch of the ≠Hoã; they are an entirely separate group who do not speak !Xoõ at all, but a language related to Ju/'hoan. The title of Traill's short monograph *The compleat guide to the Koon* deliberately makes fun of such absurdities through the ironic assumption of 'completeness', the archaic spelling 'compleat' for 'complete' and the usage 'Koon' instead of '!Xoõ'. There can, of course, be no *complete* guide to the !Xoõ. Indeed, almost any other ethnic group name could be substituted for ! Xoõ. As Gertud Boden (2014a: 241) argues, 'a lot of further research is needed on how kin categories are applied by people in trans-cultural, poly-ethnic and multilingual settings, not least because this would allow conclusions for ethnographic analogy and the reconstruction of transformational processes in the distant past'. This statement too suggests a complexity that the use of generic labels like !Xoõ, Ju/'hoan or Naro tend to hide. The concept of *process* here is important because San did not just pop up as !Xoõ, Ju/'hoan or Naro: they acquired these identities as they evolved and interacted, as very small groups of hunter-gatherers across very large territories.

What does it mean for anthropologists to insist on labels such as hunter-gatherer? Bushmen are generally presumed to be hunter-gatherers, but in a post-hunting-and-gathering world, the label is a false one. Generations have grown up alongside herders, and many former hunter-gatherers now herd their own livestock. Other changes in subsistence, such as in the River Bushman case, make classification difficult. The 'River Bushmen', as their collective name hints, are fisherfolk as well as hunter-gatherers. We know that changes in lifestyle affect the ideology of being a hunter-gatherer, and as James Woodburn (1982: 439) pointed out for the net-hunting Mbuti, such subtle changes in subsistence technique can have profound consequences. Woodburn suggests that hunting with nets should deny a people inclusion in the category of 'immediate-return' economic system because hunting with nets requires a greater degree of cooperation than hunting with bow and arrow.

Population figures today are complicated for a number of reasons. Are we counting only first-language use? Self-identity? What about people of mixed ancestry? Among Bushmen, these are undoubtedly in the majority. These issues have all been touched on, especially in Chapter 2, but they continue to be ever-present in Bushman studies, and this is worth a bit of final reflection here. Actually, it matters little that their groups are very small or that that their history represents only a tiny fraction of humankind's presence on earth (see Lee and DeVore 1968). As Lee and DeVore pointed out, hunter-gatherers in general and Bushmen in particular are very special: they represent a way of life lost to nearly all of us, but nevertheless one highly significant in our evolutionary history. It remains: 'the most successful and persistent adaptation man has ever achieved' (Lee and DeVore 1968a: 3).

Further Reading

Here and in Chapter 1, I have cited material by Christopher Henshilwood, Francesco d'Errico, Ian Watts and Curtis Marean. They and their co-authors are responsible for a great deal of writing on early symbolic culture, and for the last couple of decades the literature has been growing rapidly. Therefore, a bibliographical search on these names is always worthwhile.

The key texts in archaeology are the books by Mitchell (2002) and his co-authored one with Barham (Barham and Mitchell 2008). In rock art studies (which we shall also explore in the next chapter), the leading figure is David Lewis-Williams, and the best text is probably his *Believing and seeing* (Lewis-Williams 1981). This, along with several others (some texts, co-authored), describes the symbolic meanings of rock art. Beyond these, the great classic in the broader field of archaeology, 'The Stone Age cultures of South Africa' (Goodwin and Van Riet Lowe 1929), is certainly still worth a read, not least because the authors rejected the tendency of the time to assume that African and European classifications should be the same. It is, of course, especially good reading for archaeologists.

4   Discovery and Destruction of the /Xam

Thanks to the pioneering work of the Bleek family, the /Xam were the first Bushman group to gain fame. This period of research began in 1870, in South Africa, with the leading publication occurring some years later (Bleek and Lloyd 1911). The emphasis was on language and on folklore. Subsequent work on tiny groups such as the /'Auni, ǂKhomani, //Xegwi and N//ŋ (sadly, all now long gone) pretty much completed the ethnographic understanding of 'Southern Bushman' culture.

This chapter will cover these groups. I will attempt to discuss their importance in light of the subsequent growth of Bushman studies in the late twentieth century and in the twenty-first: I am thinking here of work by Andrew Bank (2006), Shane Moran (2009), Michael Wessels (2010) and Mark McGranahgan (2015). The focus is divided between the /Xam and other groups. The /Xam may have shot to fame in the nineteenth century, but in the last decade or so have achieved great notoriety thanks to a resurgence of academic interest, and possibly because the new motto of the Republic of South Africa is in the /Xam language. The /Xam lived near Calvinia in the Great Karoo region, in what is now the Northern Cape Province of South Africa. Their fame is both tragic and fortuitous: the first /Xam to acquire such fame were cattle thieves who were transported south to work on the breakwater for Cape Town harbour. The move was fortuitous in that their incarceration was at the Bleek family home. There they were invited to tell folktales, and later a few individuals even returned voluntarily to work for the Bleeks again. Their legacy was the Bleek and Lloyd Collection, which is part of the J. W. Jagger Library of the University of Cape Town.

Writings of the Bleek Family and Those Who Followed

Wilhelm Bleek (pronounced [bleɪk] or 'blake') was the first great ethnographer of the Bushmen. He was a German linguist who settled in South Africa. While Bleek, along with his sister-in-law, Lucy Lloyd, did manage to retrieve much linguistic data, the fate of the /Xam was nevertheless sealed. Historian Nigel Penn (1996) has documented the plight of the /Xam, who regularly killed livestock in the Cape interior. At the same time, and through the early eighteenth century, the Dutch ancestors of the Afrikaners regularly killed game animals on which the /Xam depended. In 1774, a so-called General Commando tried to destroy any vestige of Bushman resistance. Bushmen were hunted and eventually starved, and over the next nearly 100 years the destruction of /Xam society was almost complete. Linguist Anthony Traill (1996) had a slightly different take on these events, and he emphasizes internal changes within /Xam social organization. Either way, the /Xam as we know them were headed for destruction.

Bleek was born in 1827 and died young, in 1875. After his death his work was continued by Lucy Lloyd and later by his daughter Dorothea Frances Bleek (called 'Doris' by the family), who in the early 1920s became the first ethnographer to do field research with Bushmen. She was only two years old when her father died, and her early work was with Naro along the border of what later became Namibia and Botswana (D. F. Bleek 1928). Later she also worked in Angola and in eastern Africa. Ill health had led Wilhelm Bleek to abandon any attempt at African exploration, which had been his initial plan. He turned instead to assisting the controversial Anglican bishop John Colenso in working on a Zulu grammar. He also served as librarian to Sir George Grey, Governor of the Cape. Grey accumulated a vast private library in Cape Town, and later a similar one in New Zealand, where he also served as governor. In 1857 Bleek acquired the help of some twenty-eight /Xam prisoners altogether, of whom three were particularly helpful. They worked in the garden of his house in Mowbray, a suburb of Cape Town. More importantly, they were his language teachers and story-tellers there until his untimely death (see Spoor 1962; Barnard 2007a: 24–7).

Bleek's interest in language was mainly due to an incorrect assumption that the key to its origins may lie within languages such as /Xam, supposedly spoken by 'primitive' peoples. However, Bleek (1869: 56–7) was aware of a close connection between language and thought, and he sought to move his studies away from concerns with similarities between animals and humans towards this more definitive interest. Subsequent research by others was with even tinier groups, such as the /'Auni, ≠Khomani, //Xegwi and N//ŋ. The only substantial ethnography remaining among Southern San was that of the !Xoõ of Botswana, who as the northern-most Southern Bushmen will also be treated in the next chapter. The designation 'Southern Bushmen' is the traditional appellation for the groups resident mainly in South Africa, plus the !Xoõ. The majority of Bushmen in Botswana are Khoe-speaking and called 'Central'. Those generally located farther north, in south-western Botswana and northeastern Namibia, are called 'Northern'. One further twist here though: the Eastern ≠Hoã, whom we met briefly in the previous chapter, are a 'Northern' group who live in the south. They are nothing to do with the Western ≠Hoã, who actually speak a !Xoõ dialect.

All the Southern Bushman groups are today linguistically extinct, but their descendants are still there. The latter are the nomadic sheep-shearers of the Great Karoo (see De Jongh and Steyn 1994; De Jongh 2012), known as the *Karretjie Mense* or Donkey Cart People. Their language today is Afrikaans, and they now communicate though cell phone technology. The cell phone is ideal for them, as they are entirely nomadic and depend on telephone communication to organize sheep shearing activities. If anything justifies their inclusion in the category Bushmen it is their extreme poverty. This, along with the nomadic lifestyle (rather more nomadic than that of traditional San), is no doubt one of the reasons that they do think of themselves as retaining much that their /Xam-speaking ancestors held dear. Much in Michael de Jongh's accounts concentrates on the activities of the children, who largely lack inclusion in the educational system. Their prospect for the future is probably much like that of their parents and their ancestors. Although the /Xam are no longer with us, the *Karretjie Mense* today do lay claim to the title 'First People' of South Africa (see De Jongh 2012).

Figure 4.1 illustrates the locations of some Southern Bushman groups. Those presumed linguistically extinct are written in italics. All these groups were diverse, as well as distinct. What they mainly have in common is the fact that they were not Central or Northern groups. In some cases, and especially in the case of those I have labelled N//ŋ (meaning 'eland'), very little is known. These Eland People are the group written about by the late Patricia Vinnicombe (for example, 1976). They were the rock painters of the Drakensberg, and they seem to have revered the eland: the animal that they repeatedly painted on the rocks. Their rock art seems to have preserved their memory for future generations. I strongly suspect that if Bushmen have been in existence for 150,000 or 90,000 years (Behar *et al.* 2008), then they will have spoken a great many languages. The languages that have been left in the last couple of centuries are but the tip of the iceberg.

As one might imagine, /Xam is a rich and complex language. Although no-one today can truly speak it, a handful of linguists have tried to resurrect it. The folkloristic record, thanks to *Specimens of Bushman folklore* (Bleek and Lloyd 1911), is indeed very good. This work gives the /Xam original on the left-hand side of the page and the English translation on the right. There are also writings on /Xam grammar by Bleek's daughter, Dorothea (D. F. Bleek 1928/29, 1929/30), which are invaluable for anyone trying to learn /Xam. That said, the language does seem to be rather difficult. In Wilhelm Bleek's time scholars believed that all the world's languages were related. Possibly, at some deep level they are, but in general we do not make such assumptions these days.

For those linguists who emphasize language difference, languages are classified according to degree of complexity. At the simplest level, *isolating*

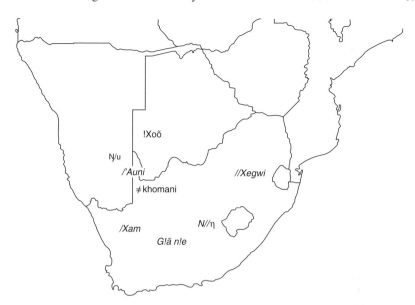

Figure 4.1 Major Southern Bushman groups of past and present
(Groups of the past are indicated in italics)

languages, like the different dialects of Chinese, tend to have more unbound
morphemes than other languages. The next level up in complexity is of
inflective or *synthetic* languages like Latin, and to a degree English. Here
bound morphemes are common: for example, the sound [z] in the word
'dogs' has no meaning it itself, but in the word 'dogs' the [z] makes the
meaning plural. More complex still, *agglutinating* languages like Hungarian,
and to some extent the Khoe languages, use bound morphemes to a greater
degree. *Polysynthetic* languages, such as the Inuktitut (Inuit) dialects, do this to
an even greater degree, such that individual morphemes are virtually meaningless in isolation (see for example, Sapir 1921: 127–56). Meaning here is
dependent on context.

What is important is this notion that, not only were Bushman languages
presumed to be related to each other, but that learning about them would lead to
a deeper understanding of all humanity. Although today we do not accept such
ideas, nevertheless this search for human origins is in a way present in much of our
thinking, and it accounts for a great deal in the nineteenth-century imagery in the
background to Bushman studies. Andrew Bank (2006) explains, in his wonderful
and detailed monograph on the Bleek and Lloyd Collection, that this is why the
/Xam were so important. Whether Wilhelm Bleek was a 'racist' for his assumption

that Bushman languages were (and are) inferior to other languages is rather beside the point. He did believe that, as did nearly everyone at the time (see also Moran 2009). Probably many in the general public today still think this way. However, as Michael Wessels (2010: 177), yet another commentator, has put it, 'It has increasingly been recognised that the /Xam materials are a product of both the intellectual milieu of Victorian Cape Town and of /Xam culture itself.' Certainly, they *are* a product of /Xam culture, and others have noted the difficult style when compared, say, to that of the Naro. The Naro have lived alongside white as well as black peoples for more than a century (see Guenther 1986: 25–7; Hewitt 1986: 235–46), and this has had its effects too.

Much the same explanation, the search for a deeper understanding of humanity, can be given to why /Xam folklore was regarded as significant. /Xam folklore is intrinsically interesting, although it does take some readers a bit of effort to get used to it. Although Bank does employ the terms, I hesitate to use the word 'myth' or 'mythology' here because the distinction between 'myth' and 'folklore' is unknown among any Bushmen. These two genres, myth and folklore, seem to blend seamlessly. There is little discernible difference between a tale about how the universe came to be and about the origin of a custom. Whether about trivialities or about metaphysics, all 'stories' (*huane* in Naro) use metaphor, trickster figures, and so on to express a kind of truth. The title of Bleek and Lloyd's (1911) monograph, in a way, expresses this: *Specimens of Bushman folklore*. Likewise, so does Mathias Guenther's (1989) *Bushman folktales*, which is a collection of narratives, of all kinds, from both the /Xam and the Naro. It includes several versions of the same tale: for example four different versions of the well-known story 'The Moon and the Hare and the origin of death' from the Naro, with two versions of the same tale from the /Xam. As that title implies, this is an explanation of death revealed to Bushmen through a mythology involving the violation of taboos. It also explains the hare's lip. Here the word 'mythology' is perhaps appropriate, for these texts are 'mythological' by most any conventional definition. Unlike Lucy Lloyd though, Guenther gives only the English translations. 'The Moon and the Hare', incidentally, does seem to be of Khoekhoe origin and was also recorded among the Khoekhoe by Dorothea Bleek. Folklore does seem to travel well among southern African groups. Similarly, we find 'Adam and Eve' and 'The Tower of Babel', albeit with Khoisan twists, among several Bushman groups.

Guenther's (1999) second book on Bushman folklore was *Tricksters and trancers*. Here he steps more firmly into a sophisticated treatment of the anthropology of religion, including the trance dancing that characterizes communication between Bushmen and the spirit world. At least one of Wilhelm Bleek's informants, //Kabbo, was, it seems, skilled in this art. *Tricksters and trancers* is more revealing of the intricacies of Bushman religion, whereas his

Bushman folktales is a more straightforward account and similar to *Specimens of Bushman folklore*. It is also similar in its use, somewhat irrelevantly, of a biblical style much as Bleek and Lloyd had used. For example, Guenther (1989: 25) records the /Xam text 'hold thou strongly fast for me the hartebeest skin', while Lloyd in one of her notebooks gives us: 'These things they are those which, we who (are) ill, we are finished, our thoughts ascending, leave us, while our bodies, our bodies [*sic*] are those which are in (or lie in?) the earth' (see Lewis-Williams 2000: 38–9). This is, of course, neither true /Xam usage nor nineteenth-century English, just awkward grammar.

Of the /Xam narrators, //Kabbo was the one Bleek and Lloyd thought the best. My vote (and Guenther's), however, would go to /Haŋ≠kass'ō, the creator of at least the noun phrase in what became South Africa's national motto. These two narrators, and some of the others, did seem to have preferences through the stories they chose to tell. //Kabbo was probably a medicine man, and he seems especially to have liked narratives concerning magic and tricksters. /Haŋ≠kass'ō had a more dramatic style that is easily accessible to the Western mind. A third of the major narrators was Dia!kwain, who favoured dialogue in his narratives. He seems to be the one favoured by Roger Hewitt, who wrote his PhD thesis on the works of Bleek and Lloyd. David Lewis-Williams (1981: 27–8) estimates that //Kabbo was responsible for 3,100 pages of text in the records of Bleek and Lloyd, /Haŋ≠kass'ō can be credited with 2,800 pages and Dia!kwain with 2,400 pages. In all, there were six main narrators, mainly male, and a few others who spoke these stories from time to time.

As Guenther (1992) points out, witchcraft is 'not a Bushman thing'. Yet in the texts of Bleek and Lloyd it seems to be quite common. Guenther found out in his field research that witchcraft and sorcery are also present among the Naro, but they are absent among other groups including Ju/'hoansi and G/wi. I also found witchcraft among Naro, although it was generally attributed to outsiders. In other words, outsiders inflicted witchcraft on Naro people. Still this does imply a belief that it exists, even if Bushmen do not practise it. Guenther attributes the idea of witchcraft and of sorcery to incipient delayed-return economies (see Woodburn 1980, 1982). It is possible that these were developing among both /Xam in colonial times and possibly among Naro. In a sense what Guenther is saying is that a benign cosmology 'protects' against witchcraft whereas a fatalistic one does not. He suggests this after examining a number of hunter-gatherer world-views and contact situations, and the general point is certainly worth consideration: witchcraft apparently occurs as a result of culture contact.

More Books about the /Xam

A number of important books chronicle the story of the /Xam. Let me take some of them in chronological order and reflect just on a few of the papers in each. The first one is on the /Xam collectively and on writings about them (Deacon and Dowson 1996). This is based on a conference held in 1991 on the Bleek and Lloyd material. It contains a number of attempts to decipher cultural information about the two main groups of /Xam: those of the Flat Bushmen and of the Grass Bushmen. Both are represented among Bleek and Lloyd's informants. My second choice here is a magnificent and splendidly illustrated book edited by Pippa Skotnes (1996), *Miscast*, which along with Skotnes's (2007) equally well-illustrated text *Claim to the country*, was a landmark achievement. The third is a collection of /Xam stories edited by David Lewis-Williams (2000). The fourth (Tomaselli and Wessels 2015) adds another dimension: how *we* represent *them*. There are, of course, a growing number of such texts, but let us stick with these.

In *Voices from the past*, Janette Deacon (1996: 253–6), herself an archaeologist, tries to locate the details of huts and the site layout of a camp from the 11,000 pages of text provided by Bleek and Lloyd from the archives of the Bleek and Lloyd Collection. Deacon had better luck both from the written sources and in archaeological excavations in the Flat Bushman case. Each Flat Bushman site hut had a fire that was used for warmth, cooking and signalling to neighbours. /Xam prepared arrows, resin and poison for hunting. Their hunting lifestyle had largely ended by the early 1870s, but some traditions remained. For example, a special hut was built for a girl to use during her first menstrual period. This is common throughout southern Africa, and we find such huts today in many parts of the subcontinent. Like herding groups such as the !Ora (Korana), the Flat Bushmen covered their huts with grass mats to protect them from the east wind. For this reason too, the normal camp layout seems to have been linear rather than circular. There are also examples of this among other Bushman groups, including the Ju/'hoansi whose archaeology was studied in the 1970s by John Yellen. However, it may be suggesting too much for gender divisions (male and female sides of the hut) to be expected among the /Xam: there is no mention of this by Yellen (1977) among the Ju/'hoansi, though there is a passing reference to this by Elizabeth Marshall Thomas (1959: 49). Such divisions are common among Bantu-speaking groups, but these differ markedly from group to group. It all depends on from which side the orientation is described (see Kuper 1982: 140–56).

Another article in *Voices from the past* is Mathias Guenther's (1996) paper on the contextualization of /Xam oral literature. This may seem like a futile effort, given the distance in time between Bleek and Lloyd and the present, but here it is a worthwhile effort. It betokens a general shift in folklore studies towards moving from an emphasis on the texts themselves towards one that stresses performance factors. The reason the texts exist at all is that they were important to the /Xam, as the site of their cultural existence and cognitive awareness. The /Xam came from two different parts of the northern Karoo: the

Strandberg, home of the Flat Bushmen, and the Katkop Mountains, home of the Grass Bushmen. The two groups are united by kinship, but they are 240 kilometres apart. Most of the tales have a traditional ring, but contemporary elements (such as disputes among ethnic groups) are also there. There are also differences among the narrators in their skills and in their points of emphasis and their creativity. Hewitt (1986) makes these points too in his lengthier treatment of the topic in the text based on his PhD thesis.

Lewis-Williams (1996) takes on a similar theme in his chapter. There is, he says, a tension between structure and performance in the myth on which he concentrates. His chapter reveals elements of /Xam cosmology, as well as a relation between myth and ritual. This, of course, is also prominent in rock art studies, Lewis-Williams's main area of interest. Lewis-Williams's (2000) collection of folktales, *Stories that float from afar*, is pretty much straight from the mouths of the /Xam with little editorial intervention. Fifty-six *kukummi* (/Xam folktales) are presented, and all are numbered. Lewis-Williams (2000: 47) presents this brief introductory statement and description of the first tale: 'The Bleek-Lloyd Collection contains more accounts of distress than joy; the final years of the /Xam were indeed tragic. The first text (*Kum* 1) captures this all-pervading sense of death. It provides a fitting introduction to the texts that follow.' This first story, told by //Kabbo, is divided into twenty-one stanzas. It reads in part:

> When a Bushman dies,
> he goes to this place.
>
> An old man wastes away and dies;
> he goes to this place.
>
> An old woman becomes lean;
> her flesh vanishes away;
> she dies;
> she goes to this place.
>
> A little child who is very small dies;
> it too goes to this place … .

(Lewis-Williams 2000: 49–51)

The tale goes on, with similar repetition, describing death by arrow, death by knife, death by dagger, and so on, and finally death through warfare. Repetition is very common in San stories. 'Death on the hunting ground' or *Kum* 2 is also by //Kabbo. It is by far the longest and continues along these lines too, although in a less poetic style (see Lewis-Williams 2000: 52–77).

Some of the stories have introductory notes by Lewis-Williams. For example, *Kum* 31 (Lewis-Williams 2000: 174–205) by //Kabbo is called 'The first /Xam man brings home a young lion', and it was told over several days. There is some dispute between the narrator and his wife and other relatives over whether this is a lion or a dog, and the text does reveal some complexity in deciphering meaning in such a tale. Taken as a whole, the texts make clear the close relation between animals and humans, the significance of kinship, the concern with 'the Early Race', the impact of daily life and its relation to /Xam belief and cosmology. The classic concerns in folklore are there too, like stories of the Moon and the Hare, as well as the Mantis. The Mantis is not merely an insect but a God-like figure to the /Xam. There are different possible interpretations. Lewis-Williams (1980: 20) once wrote that '/Kaggen [the Mantis] neither is nor is not a praying mantis'. I prefer the opposite: /Kaggen means both 'mantis' *and* 'God'. It is the same in many Bushman languages. For example, among the Naro, *n!adiba* is the word for 'sky' in its secular sense, but it also means 'God'.

Another work, this time by an actor and writer, is Neil Bennun's (2005 [2004]) award-winning *The broken string*. This chronicles the history and folklore of the /Xam and presents extraordinary insight into the lives of individual /Xam, or /Xam-ka !ei (as he prefers to call them), and of members of the Bleek family. This is a favourite of mine because, although not by an academic, he does capture the ethos of /Xam culture well. The book tells of the Early Race, /Kaggen the Mantis, sorcery, rain, death, rock art and much more. Over the last decade there has been a very considerable interest in how Bushmen are represented to the outside world. Not all chapters in the book edited by Tomaselli and Wessels (2015), *San representation*, quite fit this mould, but several do. For example, the chapter by Mark McGranaghan (2015) discusses representations of alterity in the Bleek and Lloyd corpus. The !Ora (Korana) are not simply other people who come into contact with /Xam. They have attributes as a people, and these need to be understood as the /Xam see them. /Xam individuals reflect on negative characteristics such as greed, and these are expressed in metaphorical comparisons.

Let me take just one more, this time from Lauren Dyll-Myklebust (2015). She explored the narratives on development that she encountered in her study of the establishment of the !Xaus Lodge. Bushman and Khoekhoe spirituality merge with Christian notions to create unique conceptions of power relations, all in a framework emphasizing indigeneity. As one of her informants puts it, when it comes to social development, 'We all have power.' Certainly, this suggests there may be hope for the future, if not for the /Xam then at least for Bushmen in general.

The Environment and Social Structure of the /Xam

In classic anthropological monographs it is customary to begin with a description of the environment. The environment of the /Xam was a harsh one, though not as extreme as the environments farther north in the southern Kalahari. Strictly speaking, /Xam country is part of the Great Karoo of South Africa. The environment was dry. More specifically, southern Africa in general has dry (southern hemisphere) winters and wet summers. The exception is in fact the far south of the continent, which has the reverse. In other words, in Cape Town it rains in the winter, and Calvinia is similar, with around 20 mm of rainfall per month from March until August. According to Wikipedia, the average winter temperature is about 10°C, and lower in the nearby mountains. The average summer temperature is around 22°C, though this figure masks the huge variation throughout the day. It can be over 40°C during the heat of the day, and below freezing at night.

Cape Town averages around 20 mm of rainfall in March, rising to 93 mm in June and falling to less than 20 mm in November. The fluctuation in temperatures though is much less. The pattern throughout most of eastern Africa is a much drier winter, with rains coming in the summer. There are areas where it is utterly dry most of the year, in most of Namibia for example. There are also areas of greater rainfall, notably towards the interior of the continent, but the climate of southern Africa is pretty predictable. What is more important is the availability of surface water: this is very scarce in the Central Kalahari Game Reserve, but more plentiful elsewhere. In general, the farther south one is within the interior, the dryer it gets.

The social structure of the /Xam was undoubtedly affected by their association with other groups in the Great Karoo, notably Coloured people and Griqua, Khoekhoe and Afrikaners. Ethnic groups are real only in the sense that their reality lies in the minds of those who believe in them. As we shall see later especially in reference to Naro and Ju/'hoansi, there is really nothing of permanence in ethnicity. /Xam is an ethnic construct just like any other. Nevertheless, there is a /Xam folklore: this is made up of the tales that are understood as such by both folklorists and by /Xam themselves. Folklore varies greatly across southern Africa, and indeed across Africa in general. Yet the same tales often belong to several groups: this is why, for example, Guenther's (1989) work reads so well. It is poly-ethnic or multicultural in its meaning and its representation. Part of the multilingualism implicit here is no doubt related to the fact that folklore seems to travel well across ethnic boundaries. The specific language that most people speak as a first language does not, apparently, inhibit this.

Folklore is so obvious a focus because this was a key interest of both Wilhelm Bleek and Lucy Lloyd. Thanks mainly to Bleek's daughter Dorothea (D. F. Bleek 1931 to 1936) and to Roger Hewitt (1986), we can also say a good deal about other aspects of /Xam life. We know that the word /Xam, or /Xam-ka-!kui, means 'Bushman' in general and that /Xam-ka-≠kak-ken refers to any Bushman language. /Xam lived a semi-nomadic existence in bands of between eight and thirty people. They owned their own waterholes, and families occupied separate summer residences and winter ones. Food gathering was the job of women and children. Hunting was in the hands of men, and hunters used their own arrows (rather than lend them to others, as those farther north do). /Xam poisoned their arrows with vegetable matter. They also practised trapping and fishing.

The inheritance of property seems to have been in the male line, although group membership cold pass bilaterally or be acquired through marriage. The /Xam were generally monogamous, and post-marital residence was ambilocal. Female initiation ceremonies were held, but apparently not male ones. As is common among Bushmen, the female ceremony was carried out at a girl's first menstruation. During initiation, water was rationed, and this applied also to members of the initiate's family. Even after initiation, the girl was forbidden to eat some foods or to mention some species of animal except by 'respect names'. The taboos continued until the girl married, and other taboos were also in place at any time with regard to menstruation generally. Again, much the same is true across San society. Music and dancing were common aspects of /Xam social life. Mainly, it was male members of society who took the lead, although some dances involved the women. Dancing was common after hunting and during the rainy season, and this practice also occurs generally among Bushman groups. Specialist medicine men diagnosed and treated illnesses, and trance curing was common. It was believed that medicine men could become birds or wild animals. And yet again, this belief is common.

Not that much is known about /Xam kinship. This, I suspect, is mainly because the interests of the Bleek family lay mainly elsewhere. Dorothea Bleek (1924) recorded a set of relationship terms, although there seem to be too many inconsistencies to make that much of them. What we can say, though, is that the terminology seems to be essentially descriptive. In other words, there are few generic terms like 'cousin', but there are also a number of specific referents like 'mother's brother's daughter'. There is also a tendency to use sibling terms instead of these to refer to cousins. A little more detail can be found in Barnard (1992a: 94–5), and there is possibly an inference of joking between grandparents and grandchildren (Hewitt 1986: 28). The latter is entirely to be expected and is the norm among all other San peoples. Descriptive terms are also the norm among the //Xegwi and /'Auni peoples (Barnard 1992a: 96–7).

One final thing: grandparents are very important. It is often is very difficult to get across to people in the West the fact that *parents* are not the most important relatives to a child. Among San, it is usually *grandparents* who are significant. This is partly to do with joking relations, but it is also to do with childrearing (or grand-childrearing) practices and name relations. To be named after a grand-parent is normal, even where this is not technically the practice. In other words, when it comes to kinship we must forget about what we think we know, and learn to think a little more like a Bushman. Kinship is exceedingly important in Bushman societies, not only in determining identity but also in identifying one's place within the community. This is partly due to the universal nature of the kinship systems. A person who is called a 'sister', for example, is treated as if a real sister. Her status is *real* in the sense that her classification is even played out through the incest taboo: to have sex with her is like having sex with one's own sister. We do not know for certain the extent to which this was the case with the /Xam, but the principle does hold true for all Bushman societies that have been studied. This became clear in the 1950s, the modern era for Bushman studies (see L. Marshall 1976: 201–86).

Southern Bushmen, Van der Post and 'Clicko'

The /Xam are not the only Bushmen in the Republic of South Africa. Other groups have included the /'Auni and the ≠Khomani and the Bushmen of Lake Chrissie. Virtually all of them have died out, and certainly there is now no record of their kinship systems. The /'Auni and ≠Khomani live on the very northern edge of the Kalahari and have been studied by several anthropologists and linguists. The //Xegwi were the subject of a short monograph by E. F. Potgieter (1955). He calls them simply the Batwa, a word used in several Bantu languages for Bushmen. They inhabit the Province of Mpumalanga, between Pretoria and eSwatini (Swaziland). There are very few left, fewer than 100, and most speak siSwati (Swazi) as their first language. Beyond the South African border, there are also the Mountain Bushmen of Lesotho, whom I have called N//ŋ. This is the group described in the monographs or rock art by Patricia Vinnicombe (1976) and Marion Walsham How (1970 [1958]). The description Mountain Bushmen is accurate because these Bushmen did indeed inhabit the inhospitable high ground of the Maloti and neighbouring areas until the early twentieth century. They are gone now, but school children in Lesotho have learned to appreciate their skills as artists. N//ŋ meant eland, and the eland symbolizes power, potency and any number of similar concepts.

Recently there has been a resurgence of interest in linguistic studies. Partly, this is to do with the endangered status of many Bushman languages. It is no accident that former President Mbeki chose to put South Africa's motto in /Xam, a 'dead' language that no one in South Africa can speak but which nevertheless epitomizes South Africa's importance as a cradle of all human-kind. Most non-Bushmen know, if not the writings on the /Xam, then *about the /Xam,* through the writings of Sir Laurens van der Post. Van der Post's *Lost world of the Kalahari* and *The heart of the hunter* (1958, 1961) are supposedly about Bushmen in general, although the travelogue about his wanderings through Naro, G/wi and Ju/'hoan areas of the Kalahari is in fact built around texts collected by 'an old German professor'. This is, of course, Wilhelm Bleek. The six-part television series *Lost world of the Kalahari* was aired on the BBC in 1958 (see also Barnard 1989). It was the second most-watched television programme in the United Kingdom in the 1950s, beaten in viewing figures only by the coronation of Queen Elizabeth II three years earlier.

An earlier generation had already experienced this too, through the efforts of the showman variously known as Guillermo Farini or Gilarmi A. Farini (real name, William Leonard Hunt), who exhibited 'Earthmen' as a missing link between apes and humans in the 1880s. These 'Earthmen' travelled to Europe, while later Ringling Brothers and Barnum & Bailey Circus displayed 'Clicko the wild dancing Bushman'. There were indeed several other 'Bushmen' exhibited through the nineteenth century, and 'Clicko' was actually not a Bushman anyway but a !Ora (Korana) from the Cape. 'Clicko' was born in the late 1860s or early 1870s and died in New York in 1940. His extraordinary life has been documented by the historian Neil Parsons (1999, 2009).

Rock Art of the San

The /Xam were not the only painters or engravers, but their significance as artists has been considerable. Rock art has been part of the history of /Xam studies since Bleek's time, and it remains significant. Some have argued for a line of diffusion from Europe to South Africa (see Willcox 1984a, 1984b: 3–4), though to me this seems unlikely. Rock paintings have been dated to at least 27,500 BP at Apollo 11, so a separate southern African origin seems most likely. This is especially true if we accept the recent notion that Apollo 11 was painted at 80,000 BP (see Vogelsang *et al.* 2010). By comparison, rock art in Australia may date to 28,000 BP or (some say) much earlier, and in Europe to 35,500 BP. There is rock art across the globe without any clear evidence of diffusion or migration with the techniques associated with it.

The significance of Bushman art revolves around two debates: first, the relation between art and mythology or religion, and secondly, disputes among experts on who came first, the painters or the engravers (also called the sculptors). Wilhelm Bleek (1874: 13) captures the essence of the former when he writes:

The fact of Bushman paintings, illustrating Bushman mythology, has first been publicly demonstrated by this paper of Mr. Orpen's; and to me, at all events, it was previously quite unknown, although I had hoped that such paintings might be found. This fact can hardly be valued sufficiently. It gives at once too Bushman art a higher character, and teaches us to look upon its products not as the mere daubing of figures for idle pastime, but as an attempt, however, imperfect, at a truly artistic conception of the ideas which most deeply moved the Bushman mind, and filled it with religious feelings.

Joseph Orpen (1874) was among the first to see the beauty of Bushman art as well as the first to understand its importance in showing the relation to Bushman mythology. These were established in his 1873 expedition to climb in the Drakensberg.

Lewis-Williams has written an enormous amount on this. Lewis-Williams's books (for example, 1981; 1983; 1990; 2002a; 2002b; 2010; 2015; Clottes and Lewis-Williams 1998) are just a few samples of this magnificent corpus. His articles and his edited volumes (for example, Lewis-Williams 2000; Dowson and Lewis-Williams 1994) add to this. *Inside the Neolithic mind* (Lewis-Williams and Pearce 2005) continues where *The mind in the cave* (Lewis-Williams 2002a) left off. And finally here, *Deciphering ancient minds* (Lewis-Williams and Challis 2011) returns directly to the folklore and mythological material in Bleek and Lloyd. Lewis-Williams frequently invokes these texts in his attempts to interpret the art on the rocks, and his understanding both of the original texts and the rock art is incomparable (Figure 4.2).

Historians would argue over who got to South Africa first, the painters or the engravers (see Lewis-Williams 1981). Stow (1905), especially in his map, facing page 563, suggested that the painters migrated down a southerly route through what later became Namibia, while the engravers (whom he called the sculptors) came into South Africa to the east. We now know that this is unlikely: the most prominent display of engravings is at Twyfelfontein in present-day Damara territory (see Dowson 1992). Stow died young in 1882, after many years of research on rock art of the Cape. He was a geologist by trade, and his writings were later published through the efforts of historian George McCall Theal. As Schapera (1930: 208) writes, 'The literature on this aspect of Bushman culture [pictorial art] is voluminous.' It has grown exponentially since Schapera's time, although the debate on painters versus engravers has rather died down. The emphasis today is certainly on the relation between myth and art.

Nowhere is this more true though than in Siyakha Mguni's (2015) book *Termites of the gods*. Mguni covers rock art from several countries, including South Africa, Lesotho, Botswana, Namibia and Zimbabwe. Janette Deacon says in the cover blurb:

This book has the potential to change the public perception of San rock are as a relatively trivial pastime and replace it with convincing evidence that many images and themes are in fact based on sophisticated religious symbolism that permeated all aspects of San life over thousands of years. It is a milestone in rock art interpretation because it focuses specifically on the complexity of one particular theme, the elusive formlings, which have challenged rock art specialists for decades.

Formlings are oddly shaped images in either paintings or engravings. As Mguni (2015: 15) puts it, 'The term is neither German nor English, but a

Figure 4.2 Rock engraving

nominalisation of the word "form" using German grammar.' It was coined by
the German prehistorian Leo Frobenius in the early twentieth century, and it
refers to a variety of shapes and embellishments found in southern African rock
art. The greatest concentration of these is in the Matopo Hills of Zimbabwe.
Some say these are purely decorative or abstract; others, such as Mguni, say
they are symbolic. He sees them as termite nests and argues their metaphorical
associations with bees and honey, with plants, with animal fat and with things
associated with potency.

Of course, we have no way of knowing for certain, but his arguments do
seem plausible. They also do indicate a unity in Bushman religion, in spite of
many differences in detail among the groups. To me this is the most interesting
thing. There is essentially a single Bushman religion, and it has been around for
a long time. It is more collectivist than individualist, and Bushmen often
disagree in points of detail. For example, the exact number of gods does not
matter, for 'the God', in a sense, is not a countable entity. African religions

more generally may possess a degree of vagueness as well as a focus on what is practical (see J. Morris 1994: 118–47), and this seems to be truer in the case of San than in other parts of Africa. How many religious entities there might be depends on context: in other words, on what one is trying to explain. Even rock art suggests this, as one recent analysis of San myth implies (Lewis-Williams 2018). In a sense then, there is one Bushman religion, and 'nuggets' (Lewis-Williams's word) of it are found among all groups.

Legend of the Lost City

One of the most bizarre stories of southern Africa concerns the legend of the lost city. This was hinted at several times by Farini, especially in his book *Through the Kalahari desert* (Farini 1896). It was also the subject of searches by numerous expeditions from the 1930s onwards, including by the South African military. In 1967 an intriguing book by John Clement of the Kalahari Research Committee appeared. Clement always capitalized the words Lost City. He concludes his monograph with the words, 'Like all legends, that of the Lost City will be a long time a-dying, and doubtless there will still be some who are disinclined to let the matter rest in spite of all the contrary evidence. And possibly this is just as well, for there is something rather sad about the destruction of a legend' (Clement 1967: 150). As this implies, he did not believe that the Lost City existed, but he put its purported existence down to two things: misinterpreted natural phenomena and Bushman mythology. Farini, no doubt, had a hand too.

I suspect that no Bushman in 1896 knew much about any city, let alone a 'lost' one. Obviously, such imagery is more important in the European imagination than is any San mythology. Farini's 'ruins' were supposedly a city, thousands of years old, or possibly a place of worship or the burial grounds of some ancient people. All these are, of course, ridiculous assertions, though generations of (white) people believed them. What is interesting to me about all this, and indeed the parallels in South African fiction, is that Bushmen are forever caught up in white people's mythology as much as in their own. If there were a lost city, perhaps it was Great Zimbabwe (see for example, Beach 1998). Still, I doubt it. Some wanted such a city to exist, and they wanted it to be one created by whites, or perhaps by Phoenicians, rather than by Iron Age Shona. There was no expectation that there was a lost city of the Bushmen.

Further Reading

At present, there is a wealth of material on the /Xam: new research articles are still being written (for example, De Prada Samper 2017). Other recent works include books by Bank (2006), Moran (2009), Wessels (2010), Hollmann (2004) and Bennun (2005). There is also a good deal of information in Skotnes (1996, 2007) and Deacon and Skotnes (2014). The latter also includes several essays by the main contributors to Bushman ethnography. Equally valuable is Bank (1998), whose scope is different: it concerns the construction of Khoisan identities through time. For readers interested in literature and poetry, there is also Helize van Vuuren's (2016) monograph *A necklace of springbok ears* and the extensive work of folklorist Sigrid Schmidt (2013a, 2013b). Schmidt is the great expert on Khoisan folklore.

Further detail on ritual, including both the medicine dance (also called the trance dance or healing dance) and female initiation rites, is contained in Chapter 7. The entire collection of Bleek and Lloyd's work is available at *The digital Bleek and Lloyd*: http://lloydbleekcollection.cs.uct.ac.za.

5   The !Xoõ and Their Neighbours

If Bushman studies begins with the Bleek family, our modern interest begins later. Many would point to the Marshall family and still later to Richard Lee and the Harvard Kalahari Research Group. However, another way to look at it is geographically, and it is to this view that we now turn. Going from south to north, the next major group to be covered is the !Xoõ. The !Xoõ of Botswana (as we shall see, they are also known by many other names) are the northernmost of the 'Southern Bushmen'.

The ethnography was originally an MA thesis by 'Doc' Heinz and dates from the 1960s, but it is of very high quality. The thesis is quite lengthy, at least for its time. Since then Gertrud Boden has worked with this group, as well as with other groups, and she has provided material on social change especially in the fringe areas of the !Xoõ region. !Xoõ are perhaps less well known than the /Xam, but their existence points to the wide historical extent of the 'Southern' Khoisan language family. In addition to the !Xoõ, other groups are present, including the N!aqriaxe: the [q] in this word is a voiceless uvular stop, produced at the back of the throat between [k] and [ʔ]. In fact, N!aqriaxe sometimes call themselves !Xoõ. This is not because they do not know who they are, but because the word seems to be so widely used! Other peoples are present too, though the others all speak related languages. !Xoõ and southern groups generally are certainly not numerous, but they are widely dispersed. They are also quite interesting in that they have been able to resist attempts at resettlement and to some extent social development. At the same time, they inhabit a particularly harsh area of the Kalahari and have been subject to extreme poverty because of it.

In the late 1960s H. J. Heinz set up a project among them at Bere in Botswana. Both development and anthropology were new to him. His previous work had been in parasitology, and that had led him to the !Xoõ in the first place. 'Doc Heinz' wrote his doctorate on his parasitological work, but his master's thesis (published as Heinz 1994 [1966]) became a classic in San studies. Indeed, although now dated, it remains about the finest master's thesis on any Bushman group. One of the first things Heinz did was to introduce a teacher, Liz Wily, and she set about to teach, among other things,

Hunter-gatherer ideology

(Sharing is valued and widely extended)

The immediate consumption and sharing of food	Is the appropriate social behaviour
The accumulation of food	Is antisocial and selfish behaviour

Non-hunter-gatherer ideology

(Accumulation is valued; sharing is rare outside the family)

The accumulation and storing of food and property	Is the appropriate social behaviour
The immediate consumption of food	Is antisocial and selfish behaviour

Figure 5.1 Sharing versus accumulation
Source: Barnard 2017: 85

geography. This proved to be a great hit with the pupils, although none of them expected to travel beyond their local area. More problematic is the assumption that kids will acquire useful knowledge through a Tswana-based curriculum taught by Tswana teachers. Tswana teachers do not share the key values of their pupils: sharing and the principle of egalitarianism. These are deep values, and they depend on a structural opposition to the notion of accumulation. In essence, hunter-gatherers value sharing, and non-hunter-gatherers value accumulation (see Figure 5.1). The long battle between Heinz and Wily, each driven by ideological premises, was divisive both for the two protagonists and for the !Xoõ themselves (see Barnard 2007a: 70–2). Wily was said to espouse Marxist or even Maoist principles, and Heinz capitalist ones.

Studies of the !Xoõ

The most significant studies of the !Xoõ have been by their chief ethnographer, H. J. Heinz (for example, 1994 [1966]), and by the linguist Anthony Traill (for example, 1994). Both produced a number of papers, respectively on !Xoõ religion, settlement patterns and social change and on phonetics and phonology and other linguistic matters. The 'classic' !Xoõ are those of Bere and once studied by both Heinz and Traill. More recent ethnography includes also the work of Gertrud Boden (for example, 2014a, 2017), a kinship specialist who has worked both with !Xoõ along the Namibian border and with Kxoe in the far north of Namibia.

Yet there are also groups of !Xoõ in nearby areas of Namibia, including highly deprived ones living in 'the corridor'. This is the area within Namibia that lies just off the Botswana border. Boden (2007) has produced a splendid monograph on the traditions of these people. In fact the !Xoõ are called not just '!Xoõ', but by some twenty-three different tribal labels (Traill 1974: 9). Boden refers to them as 'Nohan. Every place name seems to describe another 'people', whereas the !Xoõ seem to be just as unified a group as any other. Their dispersal does not necessarily indicate diversity but rather, possibly, their distrust of strangers.

I have referred in the chapter title to the *neighbours* of the !Xoõ. These are, in fact, a people who speak a different language. Both groups sometimes call themselves ≠Hoã. Until the early 1970s, this caused some confusion (see Traill 1973), but it is now known that what was once called Eastern ≠Hoã is not just the dialect of a group of ≠Hoã (who live in the east), but an entirely different language. The Eastern ≠Hoã are generally referred to today just as ≠Hoã. They are a *Northern Bushman* group who speak a language that is otherwise spoken only in the south. In other words, it is a distant relative of Ju/'hoan in the 'wrong' part of the Kalahari. Presumably they migrated to the south a few centuries ago. As Boden (2007: 8) says, 'Phonetically, Taa [that is, !Xoõ] is one of the most complex languages in the world. It has more than 120 consonants and more than 40 distinct vowel qualities.' Confusingly, Taa is the generic label for the !Xoõ dialects of what is today called the Tuu language family. The !Xoõ of 'the corridor' are squeezed between several other groups, some with cattle and others without, but many still cling as much as they can to their traditional livelihoods and traditions.

There is also some tantalizing cultural material in Traill's (1994: 186) dictionary: for example, the definition of *sōo*, 'the ritual feeding for example of an initiate or to prevent illness. The person feeding the initiate waves the food in a circle above his own head while repeating the retroflex noisy click [!!] and then passes it backwards under his opposite arm to the person being fed.' There is, though, no further cultural context given. There is further material in the posthumous trilingual dictionary (Traill 2018), which adds Setswana to !Xoõ and English. This will be of interest primarily to linguists, thanks to additional work added and explained by Hirosi Nakagawa (Traill 2018: 1–36). Boden's (2014a, 2017) recent work on kinship among Taa-speakers in general reveals some further puzzles beyond the ones I noted for !Xoõ a few years earlier (Barnard 2016c). The latter relates mainly to the use of terms for cross-cousins. Boden notes further that the two dialects among the 500 Taa-speakers in Namibia and several dialects among the 3,000 Taa-speakers she estimates for Botswana have several differences. Many of these relate to contact with other languages. It is not even known if the varied names for all these languages do, in fact, bear much relation to dialectal differences.

In this chapter and in subsequent ones I shall try to stick as closely as possible with the format of traditional ethnographic accounts. The classic four areas were pretty much always economics, politics, kinship and religion. These in general followed the usual description of geography and the environment and preceded a final chapter on 'social change'. Other themes were added as appropriate, for example gender and folklore. Geographically, the Kalahari is a desolate place, but it varies considerably from south to north. The southern Kalahari is the driest part. The northern Kalahari, such as the area inhabited by the Ju/'hoansi, has more water. Areas such as Ghanzi ridge, where the Naro live, are 'wet' although this is mainly because of extensive underground water supplies. This enables cattle production on a large scale (see Russell and Russell 1979). Other areas, such as the CKGR where the G/wi and G//ana have traditionally lived, lack surface water and have very few boreholes. The !Xoõ have a harsh environment, not as tough as the far southern Kalahari but tougher than that of the Ju/'hoansi. The complexities of settlement patterns in the Kalahari are illustrated in Figure 5.2. The three different models there refer to some of my earlier writings, where these were first raised. In the case of southern groups (c), their pattern has been affected by the fact that they are even less territorial than the !Xoõ. It seems that a threshold of abundance is required before 'normal' human rules kick in. In this they resemble not humans, but Kalahari antelope (see Cashdan 1983).

This said, we should remember that when we talk of settlement we are talking of processes, as much as patterns. The reason that Bushmen are so good at handling settlement is that millennia of experience has taught them how. Sophistication in one sphere may not imply sophistication in another. Bushmen may not display much refinement in material culture, but they do show an advanced superiority in grammar and other forms of verbal expression. People are interested in what is important to them, not necessarily in what is important to us. As Claude Lévi-Strauss (1968b: 351) once put it:

[A]ll this complicated theory was clearly conceived and invented by native sociologists or philosophers. Thus, what we are doing is not building a theory with which to interpret the facts, but rather trying to get back to the older native theory at the origin of the facts we are trying to explain. After all, we know that mankind is about one or two million years old, but while we are ready to grant man this great antiquity, we are not ready to grant man a continuous thinking capacity during this enormous length of time. I see no reason why mankind should have waited until recent times to produce minds of the caliber of a Plato or an Einstein. Already, over two or three hundred thousand years ago, there were probably men of a similar capacity, who were probably not applying their

(a)

Naro	Ju/'hoansi	G/wi and G//ana	!Xoõ
Most water Least territorial			Least water Most territorial

(b)

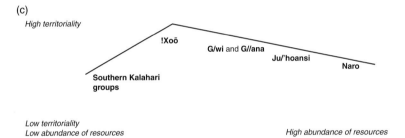

	Dry season Aggregation	Dry season Dispersal
Wet season Aggregation	**Naro**	**G/wi and G//ana**
Wet season Dispersal	**Ju/'hoansi**	**!Xoõ**

(c)

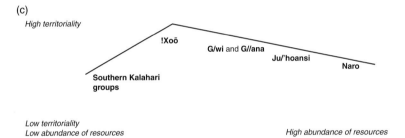

Figure 5.2 Kalahari Bushman settlement patterns: three models
Source: Adapted from Barnard 1986: 51 (a, b); 1992c: 142 (c)

intelligence to the solution of the same problems as these more recent thinkers; instead, they were probably more interested in kinship!

They still are, if only in the Kalahari. The Kalahari is not really a desert in the sense that many imagine. Rather, it is a dry, sandy and dusty plain, very dry in the south (within South Africa) and becoming gradually better with surface water available in a few places. These are mainly on the limestone ridge north of the !Xoõ, where the Naro are the main Bushman group. Heinz (for example, 1972) always maintained that 'man is a territorial animal'. This no doubt coloured his views on territoriality, as he

Figure 5.3 !Xoõ running

painted the !Xoõ as living in relative isolation and within clearly defined band territories. These territories were separated by strips of no-man's land lying between them, and the bands were to some extent groups that shared a common dialect. It is difficult for an outsider to understand this, and perhaps especially so for me as I speak (or at least once spoke) only Naro. This language is widely spoken as a lingua franca in western Botswana, and I used it with !Xoõ informants not infrequently. Yet this means, among other things, that I am not able to assess which !Xoõ dialects are which. I am not even certain that many !Xoõ can either, and both Heinz and I employed Naro interpreters (Figure 5.3).

Heinz published a rather strange autobiography, co-authored with the aptly named Marshall Lee (Heinz and Lee 1978). This is mainly an account of his affair with Namkwa, a Bushman woman with whom he later fathered a child. She eventually proved to be highly entrepreneurial, and with the acquisition of cattle by the !Xoõ, she acquired most of the herd. Among his other works is an account of male initiation, in which Heinz's (1978) own initiation is taken as the example. This earned him derision for speaking publicly about such events, and also condemnation by at least one !Xoõ. Certainly, Heinz himself urged caution in discussing it, although he did note that by 1978 the facts were already in such a distant past that they might by then become known. I do not know whether this secret material is open to public scrutiny now, but I shall resist the temptation. The situation, it seems to me, is similar to that in Aboriginal Australia, where what might be revealed remains taboo.

Heinz's thesis remains one of the best pieces of work on social structure. It is weaker on things like religion and folklore. Perhaps these were simply not in Heinz's area of interest. Yet nevertheless, we should be grateful for all the detail he does give on things like initiation and use of the land in this particularly dry part of the Kalahari. Whether his interest in territoriality yields truth or not is open to question.

!Xoõ Kinship and Social Structure

I have written on the peculiarities of !Xoõ kinship before (Barnard 2016c; see also 1992a: 74–5). The difficulty presented is in the word for cross-cousin. A cross-cousin is termed, in effect, a step, extended or classificatory 'child'. That is, the word is ⊙*aa !au*. This word *!au* seems to mean 'avoidance' (to be afraid of) in the technical kinship sense. That is, a person one 'fears', may not marry or have sex with. However, this notion has now been debunked! According to Boden (2014a: 171), the forms given by both Traill and Heinz 'turned out to have been erroneously documented for "cross-cousin" in East !Xoon during recent fieldwork'. There does seem to be an East/West difference here, as in the western dialect at least, we find 'parent of a child-in-law' or 'parent of a married couple' [*sic*], and usages in the Taa language family (that is, specifically in !Xoõ) which resemble those in /Xam and N//ŋ. Usage here is more than simply poorly recorded; it is incorrect. It seems to be the case that 'friend' and 'cross-cousin' are equated. It becomes all the more complicated if we take in loan words like *dzalai* (from Kgalagadi, apparently also meaning both 'cross-cousin' and 'friend'). And we find the same in N!aqriaxe or Eastern ≠Hoã (these are identical), where both *ši-m'zale* and *kyxoõ* are recorded as 'cross-cousin'. The same terms also mean 'grandchild' and 'father's sister' (see Gruber 1973). A person is normally named after a grandparent or someone of that category.

In all these languages we find similar terminology structures. I have argued in the past for the fact that these are early in the prehistory of kinship forms (Barnard 2009), and I hold to this. This is especially true of !Xoõ and N!aqriaxe, more than for the terminologies of South Africa. The parallel/cross distinction and the equation of grandparents and grandchildren seem to be the key. This is probably more important than the fact that a cross-cousin and a friend are classified together. Indeed, we find similar usages in South America, for example, among the Trio of French Guiana and Suriname (see Rivière 1969). The idea is that a cross-cousin is 'joking'. However, among the !Xoõ, cross-cousins are *not* appropriate for marriage. Heinz (1994 [1966]: 177) puts it this way:

Cross-cousins marriages [in addition to parallel cousin ones] are likewise forbidden. Thus a union with one's father's sister's daughter or mother's brother's son is forbidden because of the fact that one can play with one's father's sister and mother's brother places the child of either in an avoidance category. This applies equally to marriage with one's father's sister's son or mother's brother's daughter.

The phrasing here may be awkward, but the meaning is clear. What Silberbauer (1981: 143–9) called the principle of congruency holds true. This means that an avoidance partner's avoidance partner must be 'joking', while a joking partner's avoidance partner will be 'avoidance'. It does not actually hold true in this instance for the G/wi (with whom Silberbauer worked), but for the !Xoõ here it does. Generations alternate between the category of cousins and that for parents/children: this is common in Bushman societies.

Among other aspects of social structure, there are many. In his thesis Heinz (1994 [1966]) identifies among these the family, the extended family, the band, the 'nexus' or 'band nexus' (what I have termed the 'band cluster') and secondary groups (including age groups: children's play groups, adolescent groups and so on). Let me take each in turn. After dealing very briefly with the harsh environment, Heinz (1994: 49–71) turns his attention to the family. Although no demographic data are included, he notes that both polygamy and polyandry are found. This is rather unusual among Bushmen. Families normally reside together, and this seems to be the case with polygamous families. Although a whole family will generally share a fire, there is a division between the sexes, with young girls often staying close to their mothers and boys over ten years old sleeping beside the men. Unlike among the Ju/'hoansi, there is little formalization of sleeping arrangements. A man's wife's sister (his 'little wife' and potential spouse) may sit anywhere including in-between the husband and wife. Men have more authority in the household, although this is not exercised in a dictatorial manner. The exception is in cases of adultery or negligence in watching over children. Here corporal punishment is permitted. Heinz goes into a good deal of detail on family life, and he also gives a number of examples. Boys become independent from their parents at about the age of fifteen, and girls presumably upon marriage – about the same age (Figure 5.4).

While the family is important, the smallest territorial unit is larger than that. This is the band (Heinz 1994: 71–98). Bands are made up of groups who hunt and gather together. These may not quite literally be territorial, but nevertheless men are expected to hunt on the same side of the camp in which their home is located. !Xoõ own property individually: this includes trees where water is found, for example. Even a man's son is *not* permitted to drink from it without permission. Such rules seem to be stricter than in other Bushman groups, and this may reflect either the fact that they truly are stricter or simply Heinz's (1972) personal obsession with ownership and territory. Bands break up on occasion, and, as in other San societies, when someone dies the entire camp is

Figure 5.4 !Xoõ woman with child

vacated. That is because of a fear that the spirit on the dead person may remain in his or her hut.

Larger than the band is the band cluster, or nexus (Heinz 1994: 98–115). Unlike the band, the band cluster is not a political unit. However, it is territorial in the sense that it has recognized boundaries. Everyone knows to which territory they belong, and they are separated by areas of no-man's land. Heinz equates the unit with what is sometimes called a 'tribe' or a 'people', or in !Xoõ, a *miate*. These also have labels: for example the people of Taketswane are called the 'people that follow the eland' and the people of Kang the 'people of the south'. The size of these units is variable. Generally, there are no more than seven bands per band cluster, and the number is usually between two and seven. Both ritual authority (such as the timing of male initiations) and political authority are vested in the headman of a band cluster, and these powers often differ. Band clusters are often centred around boreholes, where meetings take place, and the boundaries between them are often dialect boundaries. The band cluster truly is the main territorial unit, and membership can change upon marriage. Fighting within the band cluster is not uncommon, and participants usually side with members of their own band.

Secondary groups include those define by age and by gender (Heinz 1994: 117–45). Puberty at least used to be especially important to the !Xoõ. There have long been ceremonies associated with it: the female initiation ceremony and the male one. The former is individual and occurs at the time of a girl's first menstruation, and the latter is or was collective. As in other Bushman groups (G/wi, Naro and Ju/'hoansi), the female ceremony is based on the idea of the 'Eland Bull Dance' (conventionally spelled with upper case letters). The girl's grandmothers, or more generally older women, are in charge, and the male eland, the symbol of potency for these and other Bushman groups, has a key role. Heinz does not give much detail, but it seems to me that a great deal is held in common among Bushman groups: food taboos, avoidance by men, gifts, tattooing and so on.

The collective male ceremony normally take place when boys are about fourteen years old. Heinz was himself initiated in this way. Although there is no special time of aggregation, men tend come together between April and July. The early part of this period coincides with the Kalahari truffle season. Generally there are often no initiations during drought years. The initiation organizer is called the *tshoma* (Heinz records the word as *chomma*, although a glance at Traill [1994] suggests that [tshoma] is the more likely pronunciation). He is normally the oldest or most experienced man of the band. He decides who is to be initiated and who is not. Initiation involves dancing as a group, food and other taboos, instruction in behaviour, tattooing and the telling of secret things.

As in other Bushman groups, bride service is practised for up to three years before marriage (even for a headman), and there are wedding ceremonies. Heinz (for example, 1994: 207–12) often compares details of !Xoõ life to that of other groups, including particularly the Ju/'hoansi and ≠Au//eisi (≠X'au//'eîsi) to the north, and he notes differences in both natural environment and acculturation. Heinz does note that the duration and intensity of the rainy season is a factor in territoriality. He also notes differences between 'wild' and 'acculturated' groups in terms of what is borrowed and what is not. The band cluster is important, and through it education is carried out. Taboos remain significant too, not only in kinship but also in things such as initiation rituals. He later did decide to write on male initiation for the International Conference on Hunting and Gathering Societies, which was held in 1978. This was on the grounds that the practice had, by then, virtually died out. However, that material has never been published. It was therefore, he presumed at the time, safe to write on it. That conference, by the way, was later called 'CHAGS *zero*', when the acronym came into use. That was in 1988, with 'CHAGS 5'.

The one thing that is missing from Heinz's account is religion. The notion appears occasionally, such as where he mentions 'God' (*Gu/e*) in passing, but there is no discussion. Presumably this is because his intension was just the recording of social organization.

The N!aqriaxe or Eastern ≠Hoã

As I have said, the Eastern ≠Hoã are not just a ≠Hoã group who live in the east. They are a very tiny group of *Northern Bushmen* who live in the south. Since they all speak other languages too, it is difficult to estimate their numbers. Brenzinger (2007: 189) says there are perhaps 200 native speakers, but this figure may be rather high. I have also heard a figure of around 50. In any case, with a colleague I did once survey schoolchildren from the Kweneng district and found that *none* of them claims this as their first language. The language in question is N!aqriaxe, otherwise known as Eastern ≠Hoã. It was 'discovered' by Traill in 1972 (see Traill 1973).

N!aqriaxe, Eastern ≠Hoã: it does not matter. People do not speak to their children in this language at all, and nearly all N!aqriaxe are married to non-N!aqriaxe and speak the other language instead. That said, I once did collect a few interesting items of vocabulary with this group, and linguists have done much more (for example, Gerlach and Berthold 2014). What these linguists have found is that not only the terms themselves, but also spatial conceptualizations are shared across language boundaries: grammar, it seems, has a spatial basis too. But for me the most extraordinary thing is that, in 2011, I encountered a N!aqriaxe man who could speak languages in five different language families. He could speak perhaps eight or nine altogether and certainly spoke N!aqriaxe (in the Kx'a family), G/wi and G// ana (in the Khoe-Kwadi family), one or more dialects of !Xoõ (in the Taa family), Kgalagadi and probably some Tswana (in the Bantu family) and Afrikaans (in the Indo-European family). This ethnographic fact was of interest to me, on theoretical grounds, because such a scenario was undoubtedly very common in the prehistory of language (Barnard 2016b: 38–45). Monolingualism is what is unusual, even today throughout much of Africa. If we are counting linguistic abilities, the servant of the Secretary to the South West Africa Administration is reputed to have spoken nine languages and to be able to 'mix a good cocktail' (Gall 2001: 133).

It is hardly surprizing that kinship terminologies are not well recorded. However, we are fortunate here. Jeffrey Gruber (1973) and later Gertrud Boden, in several papers, recorded these within Southern African Khoisan kinship systems (Barnard and Boden 2014). They did uncover some interesting material, including diachronic material on the shifting nature of Bushman kinship patterns. Additionally, in recent work Linda Gerlach and Falko Berthold have been delving into such matters with the remaining N!aqriaxe individuals. The late Jeffrey Gruber had already found that N!aqriaxe or Eastern ≠Hoã used Kgalagadi terms for cross-cousins and had apparently ceased use of any earlier terms for these relatives. This clearly indicates a high probability of intermarriage and multilingualism among the population. I have seen this too at Bere and elsewhere in the western Kalahari with mixed population groups. My suspicion is that this has been the norm for millennia.

We know that Neanderthals, Denisovans and modern humans interbred, and the same must have been true within our own species (see Sion *et al.* 2018).

It is interesting also that kin terminology structures, like language itself, have a tendency towards regularization. It does seem that languages become more and more complex in grammar, before reverting to simplicity through forming pidgins and then effecting creolization (see McWhorter 2011). This seems to be the case even with small populations, although when a husband and wife speak different languages this must test that theory. Rather than imagining any pure bunch of Bushmen, we should accept that their 'natural' state is indeed in mixed groups. Of course this does not mean that any cultural or linguistic entity does not recognize itself as *real*, but rather that such a reality when seen in the long term is ever changing. The very existence of a group like N!aqriaxe is fascinating precisely because it does test such theories. As we shall see later, it is the same with Naro, who are a much larger population, and to an extent also with Hai//om. What is so sad is that all these peoples are so impoverished and likely to remain so for some time to come.

I have mentioned before that Traill (1974: 9) remarks on the absurdly large number of labels to designate !Xoõ. I doubt that there are any more such peoples, but it is at least possible that new groups and new languages are yet to be discovered. How different these are from 'known' peoples is anyone's guess. In fact, according to research from 1996 by linguists Chris Collins and Jeffrey Gruber (2014: 17–20) there is a nearby language called Sàsí that is mutually intelligible with N!aqriaxe. Neither Sàsí-speakers nor N!aqriaxe-speakers had known of each other's existence until members of these groups were introduced. Both use the term ≠'Amkoe for 'person', although nobody has yet suggested that this should be the term for the language of both groups. Collins and Gruber (2014) prefer the term ≠Hòã (actually, with a *double* low tone mark) in their grammar of this rather complex language.

An Alternative View

Throughout this chapter I have characterized !Xoõ society through what may be termed the standard model. This assumes a characterization of units such as *bands* and *band clusters*, each within a hierarchical framework of lesser and greater dialect areas. Beyond this we find areas of no-man's land and places beyond those, with a Hobbesian mistrust of strangers and of people who are 'different'. I suspect that this is much like the vision that Heinz had of the !Xoõ and their neighbours. But is this view correct?

Let me suggest that it is perhaps not. It may well be correct for the !Xoõ, but it is an unlikely model with which to explain the social structure of many other groups. In particular, it does not explain the way of life of the N!aqriaxe or of human evolution in general. We get hints of this in two sources: first what we know of the N!aqriaxe and secondly, on a more theoretical level, what we know about human sociality more generally. This latter insight comes out especially in an intriguing paper by Canadian anthropologist Helga Vierich (2015). She studied the Kua (or Kūa or Kúa), a group who live in the Kweneng district, south of the !Xoõ and in fact very near the N!aqriaxe. She speaks of this multilingual people not as living in *bands*, but rather as existing within over-lapping *networks* of individuals. She argues that this arrangement fosters the extension of cooperation beyond kin groups, avoids inbreeding and so on. In short, it has evolutionary advantages that the one described by Heinz does not. Which model better describes our ancestors at Blombos Cave or other archae-ological sites is open to debate, although my present, optimistic view favours Vierich's. Humans are adaptable creatures, and it matters very little that we live in small groups and marry our kin. Languages die and are reborn time and time again. As long as we speak lots of them, languages adapt too.

Further Reading

The classic is Heinz's MA dissertation, written in 1966 and eventually pub-lished in 1994 (Heinz 1994). On kinship systems, the best source is the work of Gertud Boden (see Barnard and Boden 2014). Of the other groups mentioned in this chapter, very little is known. They were already dying out when first encountered and in any case the temptation to accept assimilation must have been very strong. If ever there were an example of living on the cultural edge, the N!aqriaxe, ≠Hoã (or ≠'Amkoe) must be it. All we can say is that they remain true San or Bushmen.

Linguists seem fond of changing labels: even the current and now univer-sally accepted term for 'Northern Bushmen', *Kx'a*, dates only from 2010 (Heine and Honken 2010). The complexity of all these languages calls for thought, if not new research, by anthropologists as well as linguists. Language itself pretty definitively evolved and diversified within southern Africa. For this reason, if no other, the southern African region is an obvious candidate for more collaborative work on human evolution.

6   G/wi, G//ana and the Central Kalahari

The Kalahari Basin area of Botswana remains one of the richest ethnographic regions of the subcontinent. The G/wi (also spelled /Gwi, /Gui, G/wikhoe and so on, and of course also spellings with a vertical rather than a slanted line in the click) are probably the second most famous of Kalahari groups. The pronunciation is the same regardless of whether either the 'g' or the click goes first: the 'g' simply indicates that the click is voiced or pre-voiced. According to Hirosi Nakagawa (pers. comm.), the correct pronunciation should be [g/ui]. Only the Ju/'hoansi are better known than the G/wi, and in both cases ethnic identity may indeed be fluid. The G//ana are nearly as well known, and their language is also nearly the same. G//ana are also known as G//anakhoe or G//anakhoena (*khoe* means 'person', and the *-na* makes it plural).

This chapter focuses on the groups who live in the vast but sparsely populated Central Kalahari Game Reserve (CKGR) in the interior of Botswana. The leading ethnographer of the G/wi was the late George Silberbauer, originally a South African, who was there in the 1950s and 1960s. He later did visit the Ghanzi district again but did no further field research. His research interests from the 1970s had turned to Australia, where he had settled. Several Japanese anthropologists have also worked with G/wi and G//ana, and they tend to see them essentially as one group, the 'Central Kalahari San' or 'Central Kalahari Bushmen'. The differences between G/wi and G//ana are negligible. Indeed, some G//ana claim part-Kgalagadi ancestry for their group. And as we shall see later, we know that Naro are probably part Naro and part Ju/'hoan, and that there is very little, if any, difference between Ju/'hoansi and their southern neighbours, who call themselves ≠Au//eisi (or more correctly, ≠X'au//'eîsi). Several distinguished Japanese ethnographers worked with G/wi and G//ana, and some still work with them. Part of the purpose of this chapter is to provide interpretation of the work of Japanese ethnographers in light of Silberbauer's earlier study.

In truth, there are some differences in the details various writers discuss, whether because of historical change, because of different theoretical concerns or because of individual interests. Early interests in settlement, kinship and economics have given way to specialized topics like ethnicity, but also to anxieties over the long-running dispute between the government and NGOs over who owns the CKGR. Essentially, the ultimate cause was simply the name 'game reserve'. Silberbauer's intention in employing that phrase had always been to allow traditional hunting. He never suggested that that right be denied to the CKGR's inhabitants. The CKGR has seen, in theory, an increase in development opportunities provided by the government, while ironically groups to the east of the Reserve gradually, and perhaps unwittingly, become more like the Tswana majority of the country. One thing at issue is the recent dispute over land and water rights, settled recently in court in 2005, yet in a way that enabled both sides to claim victory.

A few of the eastern groups will be considered briefly in this chapter too, partly in relation to their transition to 'modernity' – albeit a modernity of impoverishment and low social status.

Ethnography of the Central Kalahari Game Reserve

The Kalahari Basin is the region with the most disputed claims and counter-claims by its inhabitants and the government of Botswana. These have tended to focus on rights to land and to water, and the area is practically the driest of any in the Kalahari. Only the far southernmost part of the Kalahari, along the South African, Namibian and Botswana border area, is drier. It is also less inhabited than most of the rest. Still, several major Bushman groups all live in this area. We might think of it as having a population of about 3,000. That is the figure estimated by Silberbauer (1981), who spent the years 1958 to 1965 partly there and partly in the district proper. The district in question is the one called variously Gantsi or Ghanzi. The latter is the older, and the more Tswana-like spelling Gantsi was only introduced by the Botswana government in the 1970s. The former has never gained complete acceptance, and both spellings occur in the literature. Incidentally, the word Ghanzi (although, of course, not the spelling) is Naro in origin.

The number of inhabitants of the CKGR is far fewer than 3,000 now: many moved to areas to the east of the Reserve. Many others were resettled by the Botswana government west of the Reserve. This was since the 1990s, and it is hardly surprising given the paucity of surface water there. The availability of water has been reduced in recent years, and the number of boreholes east of the Reserve has increased (see, for example, Hitchcock 1978). Silberbauer author-ized the first borehole when he was District Commissioner, and he used to take the pump away with him each time he left. For ease of comparison, remember that the CKGR is slightly larger than Switzerland (which has a population of about 8.5 million). 'Far fewer than 3,000' is by comparison a very tiny population.

Other ethnographers include the Argentinian amateur Carlos Valiente-Noailles. I say 'amateur', but he did write a two-volume doctorate on gender relations among the G//ana (Valiente-Noailles 1994). He lived in Switzerland for several years and practised as a lawyer in Argentina. He has written a general ethnography of this group and commented on what we call them (Valiente-Noailles 1993: 1–13). Rather than using the term Bushmen, Basarwa, San, N/oakhoe, hunter-gatherers or traditional or former hunter-gatherers, he has long held a preference for 'Kua' (with or without an accent). This is the preferred term in that part of the Kalahari and means the same thing. He has also written interestingly on customary law (*//née//né*) as it applies to Bushmen and how it differs from law (*moláo*) among the Tswana and Kgalagadi (Valiente-Noailles 1993: 125–8). He has also written extensively on, among other things, the seasons and the lack of water (1993: 31–82) and on Kua religion (1993: 187–210). His general ethnography of the area is detailed and extremely well illustrated with professional photographs.

The majority of ethnographers of the Central Kalahari groups, however, are from Japan. These include Jiro Tanaka, Kazuyoshi Sugawara, Kazunobu Ikeya and several others. The efforts of those in the Japanese tradition are discussed in my *Anthropology and the Bushman* (Barnard 2007a: 62–5) and in greater detail in the monograph by my former student Hiroaki Izumi (2006). Tanaka was trained at Kyoto where there has been a long tradition of primatological studies. This had been instituted by Kinji Imanishi, who worked with Japanese macaques at a time just after the Second World War when Japanese people were forbidden to travel abroad. When things loosened up, others were allowed to travel. The first here was Junichiro Itani, who worked with Pygmies. The idea in the Kyoto tradition was that macaques and chimpanzees were mirrors on humanity and that through comparison one could work out what it means to be truly human. Humanity in nature was, in a sense, the theme of the tradition. Tanaka started with pastoralists in eastern Africa, before moving on to work with San. Following Tanaka was Sugawara, who had also studied primates before he took to working with San. (The label 'San' is generally preferred in Japan.) We shall explore the work of these researchers later in this chapter.

Finally, a handful of others have ventured into the central Kalahari. Most prominent perhaps have been Americans Elizabeth Cashdan and Robert Hitchcock and Canadian Helga Vierich. Cashdan (for example, 1984, 1986) worked particularly with the G//ana, while Hitchcock (for example, 1987) and Vierich (for example, Vierich and Hitchcock 1996) worked in development in various parts of Africa. Hitchcock's studies have been particularly significant in establishing the long downturn in social development trends for Bushmen, both in the specific areas where he has done field research and more generally throughout the Kalahari. Cashdan (1987) worked to the northeast of the CKGR, along the Botletle River where, she argues, trade began. There San (presumably mainly G//ana or Deti) traded as pedlars. They would sell milk, berries and firewood to their neighbours, whose goods were often too far away to access easily. In contrast, those on the Nata River tended to engage more in generalized reciprocity. The Botletle area is where population density has been increasing, and this has been a factor in these changes in subsistence pursuits.

Living without Water

Cashdan's area of research lies mainly beyond the CKGR, and is served by seasonal surface water which can accommodate cattle. The CKGR, in contrast, has no permanent source of water. G/wi and G//ana settlement is therefore constrained by this and by the availability of plant foods. The presence of game meat is rather less of a problem, because the Reserve has an abundance of game. In recent years, goats have been introduced too, although of course this is illegal in a supposed 'game reserve'.

The CKGR can be divided into three or four main zones. In the north is an area of dune woodland, with a smaller north-eastern area composed of mopane forest. Across the centre is a band of grassy plains. In the south there is a band of savannah thornveld. To the far southeast, there is another tiny patch of dune woodland (Silberbauer 1981: 37–50). Rainfall is very erratic, but in essence there is a southern summer wet season and a winter dry season. The average rainfall is about 392 mm per year (see, for example, Tanaka 1980: 19–21). It is much the same in other parts of the Kalahari, although the settlement patterns depend on whether ground water is present or not. Traditionally, G/wi tended to aggregate in the wet season (around November or December) and migrate, roughly once a month, from water resource to water resource. They would then disperse as family units around July (Silberbauer 1981: 245–9; see also Tanaka 1976). When tsama melons are available, migration tends to be from melon patch to melon patch. When none are present, inhabitants simply move from location to location, exploiting whatever is available (see Figure 6.1). This phenomenon has also been demonstrated by several Japanese researchers, particularly by Jiro Tanaka (for example, 2014).

Tanaka's work is important because he is able to show the long-term effects of times of drought and times of plenty through nearly fifty years of work with the G/wi and G//ana. In truth, Tanaka's research was actually carried out over a slightly shorter period than fifty years, from the beginning of his studies in 1966 to the publication of the Japanese edition of *The Bushmen* in 2008. Although he began research as an individual, from the early 1980s he has been part of a team of researchers, touching on ecology, traditional social structure, social change and the devastating effects of resettlement. Silberbauer's work pretty much ended at around the time Tanaka's started. Still, this means that we have a documented period of research covering the

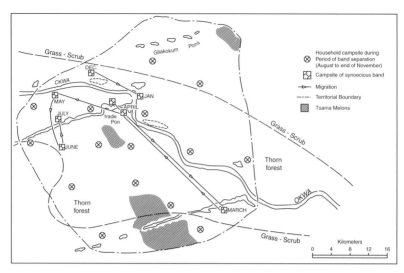

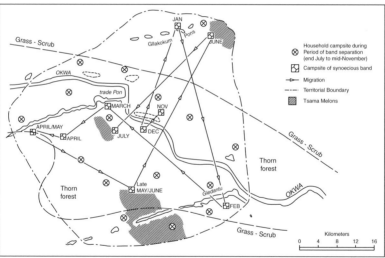

Figure 6.1 Traditional G/wi settlement patterns: poor and good tsama seasons
Source: Silberbauer 1981: 246

entire time from the late 1950s up to the present. It is worth stressing that Figure 6.1 represents supposedly 'traditional' settlement, and that some changes seen since then have been dramatic.

Among changes, the period covering the run-up to Botswana's independence in 1966 was one of relative drought. After seven years of drought, there followed roughly seven years of plenty. When I arrived in Ghanzi in 1974, there was again a period of relative plenty. I did not quite realize it at the time, but the cycle of years of drought and years of plenty was normal. This precarious existence continued, and with the drought years of the early 1980s a generation of children was growing up without the knowledge their parents had had in how to live by hunting and gathering. I exaggerate slightly, but this was to have its effects on the attempts at resettlement that followed. That said, G/wi, G//ana and other hunter-gatherers do tend to come off better than their cattle-herding neighbours. Pastoralism is more difficult to maintain as a lifestyle than hunting and even gathering. This is why we can assume that foragers, including the Central Kalahari Bushmen, have been in their present locations for a very long time. As Tanaka (2014: 5) put it,

Some archaeologists pointed to a possible migration from East Africa 10,000–12,000 years ago through a comparison of stone tools, but the possibility of such a major ethnic migration has now been ruled out. This is because hunter-gatherer life necessarily limits people's movement to gradual migration that involves shifting a hunting ground by a short distance in search of game, whereas pastoralists may embark on a major migration over thousands of kilometers in journeying to a new pasture. It is more appropriate to think that the stone tool-making technology itself was transmitted from East Africa during that period.

Ikeya (2018) notes there have been remarkable changes in Central Kalahari settlement patterns between the 1930s and the 1990s. Some of these changes have been due to forced resettlement, but certainly not all of them. A great strength of Japanese approaches has been the emphasis on detailed documenta-tion, including that of the introduction of livestock into the Reserve. There has also been a significant increase in desertification near the settlement at Xade. This in part is due to the rising human, as well as livestock, habitation.

Other Aspects of G/wi and G//ana Social Life

While southern groups were very important in the history of Bushman studies, their significance has been vastly eclipsed by the ethnography of the G/wi, the G//ana and the Naro, as well as comparative studies of other groups such as the Shua (Hietsware). All of these are Khoe-speakers, and they share many cultural similarities. Although Silberbauer led the way, it is probably not really an accident that many of those who came on the scene later were Japanese anthropologists. The Japanese language happens to share the usual word order of SOV (subject, object, verb) with the Khoe languages, including G/wi and G//ana. Also, Khoe languages, just like Japanese, use postpositions rather than prepositions. That is, Japanese-speakers may find it slightly easier to speak G/wi or G//ana than do English-speakers. In contrast,

Figure 6.2 G/wi man with 'guitar'

Ju/'hoan, like English, has the word order SVO (subject, verb, object) and uses prepositions. I would not read too much into these similarities, but they are probably worthy of thought (Figure 6.2).

A major, if probably not yet widely read, source on the G/wi and G//ana is an 'encyclopaedia' of culture and society edited by Tanaka and Sugawara (2010). This tells of the numerous expeditions undertaken by seven anthropologists, two linguists, a geographer and an economic historian from 1967 to 2010. All of them are Japanese. Its intended audience consists of G/wi and G//ana who have learned English, the people of Botswana generally and, of course, scholars. Since the time of Silberbauer, a number of new ethnographers have come on the scene. The first was Jiro Tanaka (1980), whose book *The San* tells a slightly different story from Silberbauer's. An interesting review of Tanaka's book by Silberbauer (1982a) comments on the diversity of approaches in their accounts. Indeed, one could be forgiven for thinking they were writing about two different peoples. This is not to suggest that either account is mistaken, but rather to highlight the fact that ethnography can be a very subjective genre. Silberbauer's account emphasizes his own more ethereal ecological vision, whereas Tanaka's is more deliberately objective and makes little attempt to get inside the mind of a G/wi. This comes out too in Silberbauer's (1981: 259) diagram illustrating his 'model of a socioeconomic system'. The idea is that the 'cognitive scan' mediates between the scientific environment and the vernacular one.

The band seems to be central to G/wi social organization. We can see this in settlement patterns, which also emphasize the availability of water, and in the local politics governed by the seasonal alternation of aggregation and dispersal. As Silberbauer (1981: 167–8) explains,

G/wi bands are both open and egalitarian communities … The problem in band politics is to combine that autonomy with band solidarity and retain cohesion in the polity. This is an aspect of a larger problem: The G/wi must steer a mid-course between making band life attractive enough to draw the members together but not so attractive as to prevent their drawing apart again. A centralized, hierarchical structure with specialized personnel and roles would be unable to function when the band separates.

Given that dispersal is an ecological necessity, the social order is maintained. This is the key to the functioning of G/wi society, as indeed it is of virtually all hunting-and-gathering communities (see also Silberbauer 1982b). However, Silberbauer (1996: 62–3) does make the important point that it is adaptability that is crucial to hunter-gatherer lifestyles, not the rigid maintenance of a single way of living. He points also to flexibility in things like religious belief (1996: 52–4). G/wi, it seems, are rather more prone to such changes than are Ju/'hoansi. I have long felt that Silberbauer's (1981) *Hunter and habitat* is the finest of all Bushman ethnographies, but his 1996 paper surpasses even this. Decidedly, he warns against too rigid a definition of the idea of the 'hunter-gatherer', and the transition between G/wi life in the 1950s to that of the 1960s shows this.

The essence of G/wi and G//ana life is found in practices like sharing, cooperation and egalitarianism generally. This is shown in every ethnography. For example, when large game is killed there are strict rules to determine who takes what. The first division is among those who participated in the hunt. The man who did the killing takes the hide and also the back tendon. He makes implements from the tendon. The senior man, especially the father-in-law, normally receives the head. The families divide the meat, and close relatives, friends and visitors all receive meat. Other things, such as clothing, household goods and ornaments, are also shared (see, for example, Tanaka and Sugawara 2010: 108). Since 1984 it has been possible for children to go to primary school, for seven years, at Xade. Older children sometimes attend junior high school in Ghanzi, and G/wi and G//ana seem to value education at least as much as children elsewhere. How much this might affect traditional practices though has yet to be seen. Certainly, the values of hunter-gatherer peoples may be changing, a point made by several recent commentators (see Sugawara 2004: 118–26). Of course there are also differences in ethnographic approaches in Japan and the West, as Sugawara (2004) has also emphasized.

There does seem to be some disagreement among specialists on things like exact species names for watermelons. I have frequently described tsama melons, as watermelons are known in Setswana. Yet as writings by Silberbauer (for example, Silberbauer 1981: 265–70) and by Ikeya (2000: 71–2; Tanaka and Sugawara 2010: 130) show, life is a little more complicated than it seems. Silberbauer (1981: 94) notes that the classification of plants is sometimes more discriminating than that of scientists. Ikeya (2000: 71–2) adds that there are different kinds of wild watermelon, one he calls *kaan*, which ripens at the start of the rainy season, and another, *//nan* (*n//an*), which ripens a little later. The rainy season is roughly December to March, and the dry season April to November. The former fruit rots quickly, and the latter does not and can be stored. There are also several varieties that can be cultivated, and these days they often are deliberately grown. In addition, they have different names in the G/wi and G//ana dialects. Yet, in other respects, these two dialects are virtually identical.

G/wi and G//ana Kinship

G//ana kinship is basically the same as G/wi, though both are very different from the kinship systems of the /Xam or of the Ju/'hoansi. There are, however, similarities between systems like that of the !Xoõ and the Khoe-speaking groups (G/wi and G//ana, Naro, Eastern Khoe Bushmen and 'River Bushmen'). All these latter ones, like that of the Khoekhoe, make parallel/ cross distinctions. Parallel cousins are classified as 'siblings', whereas cross-cousins are considered more distant. Cross-cousins are potentially marriage-able. As far as is known, the kinship system of /Xam emphasizes instead proximity to ego, and the Ju/'hoan system is not that much different in this from /Xam.

However, it has an imaginary notion of proximity in that Ju/'hoan name-sakes are treated as if actual relatives of the grandparent category. We shall explore that later in the discussion of Ju/'hoan kinship. The important thing here is to differentiate parallel and cross systems like G/wi and G//ana from lineal and collateral systems like /Xam and Ju/'hoan. That said, there is some ambiguity about /Xam, since kinship studies were only in their infancy at the time of the Bleek family's research. Even Dorothea Bleek (born 1873, died 1948) might have got this wrong. Silberbauer (1965) was, as it happens, also prone to mistakes is his early recording of G/wi kinship. Yet Silberbauer's mistakes were corrected in his later work (for example, 1981). Like virtually all other Khoe-speakers, G/wi and G//ana distinguish joking relatives from avoidance relatives. Joking relatives include grandparents, cross-uncles and aunts, cross-cousins and the reciprocals of all of these. One may literally and figuratively 'joke' (*!ao-kjima* or *!ao-tama*) with them, whereas others are classified as avoidance or more literally 'feared' (*!ao*). The latter include parents and parallel uncles and aunts and their reciprocals. One is meant to show deference to them or not sit too close to them, and so on. In short, one may sit close to and ultimately marry cross-cousins, but not people one calls siblings. Likewise, joking is fine with grandparents and grandchildren, but not with parents. If there is an extreme avoidance relationship, it is, of course, in-laws (especially a man's mother-in-law).

Naming is complicated among many Bushman groups, though not among G/wi and G//ana. Among G/wi and G//ana, people are generally named after significant events, and names tend to be unique to the individual. Nevertheless, 'universal kinship' is practised: in other words everyone in the entire society is 'kin'. I came up with this idea during my early fieldwork. Perhaps the label is not the best, but that is what I called it and the label has stuck. Hunter-gatherers very commonly have such systems everywhere, perhaps the most famous being that of the Ju/'hoansi as made famous by Lorna Marshall (1976: 201–86). In such systems there are no 'non-kin', and in the absence of name relationships, close friendships are used instead: my best friend is my joking relative, and his or her joking relatives are my own. His or her avoidance relatives are my avoidance relatives. This is how it works for G/wi and G//ana. Of course, this can cause some inconsistencies in classification, but generally what Silberbauer has called the law of uniform reciprocals works instead (see Silberbauer 1981: 144–5).

Marriage is possible at a very young age, at the time of Silberbauer's fieldwork between seven and nine for a girl and between fourteen and sixteen for a boy. There are no marriage ceremonies, although there is a transition marked by the use of 'in-law' terms. There is initial uxorilocality, as long as ten years, and this is normally accompanied by bride service. Generally, the entire group takes part in educating the young girl, and divorce is easy for either party (see Silberbauer 1972: 304–21, 1981: 142–66). One interesting phenomenon noted particularly by the Japanese ethnographers is the *zaã-ku* relationship (the -*ku* suffix simply means 'each other'). This is an adulterous relationship that is not stigmatized, but in fact accepted as normal. The same term is used for early sexual relations between adolescents, and triadic relationships are actually not uncommon. G/wi and G//ana do not seem to worry about the potential for children to be born from such unions, although there is a notion that female bodies are impure and that a contagious 'dirt' may cause illness (see Tanaka and Sugawara 2010: 73–5; Ono 2014; Tanaka 2016). Indeed, there are many taboos related to sex and sexual conversation among Khoe-speaking groups, and Japanese ethnographers have begun to comment extensively on these taboos and the social relations that give rise to them (Figure 6.3).

Figure 6.3 Young G//ana man playing mouth bow

Fortune and Misfortune

The notion of 'God' is expressed in the concept N!adima. He is the Creator, and N!adisa (the same word, in the feminine gender) is his wife. According to Hirosi Nakagawa (pers. comm.), these are loan words from Naro. The 'correct' designation of the god is 'G//ama' or phonetically, [g//ámá]. Not that much is said about these beings. Silberbauer (1981: 73) records a few snippets, like the notion that snakes have 'a hatred of man', a hatred given to them by N!adima. Otherwise, N!adima seems remote and not that much spoken of. He is nevertheless significant as the creator of the universe and particularly of the G/wi environment. He is also responsible for setting the sun, moon and stars on their celestial paths.

Valiente-Noailles (1993: 187) refers to //gamá, who is the same being, and this alternate use of different labels is common among Bushmen. In some usages, //gamá appears to be the devil or the spirits of the dead, who in Naro, for example, are called *g//aũa-ne*. The usage may seem strange, but remember that the position of the click viz. the 'g' (indicating voicing) is simply a matter of the ethnographer's preference. It also does not much matter whether these are Kua, G/wi or G//ana, as religion is one thing that pretty much all Bushmen agree on. There is a male high god, who is married to his female counterpart.

Communication with the deity is through myth and in dreams. Valiente-Noailles (1993: 201) also speaks of the soul or ≠*oee*. This was placed in every human at the beginning of their lives. Some say it lives in the heart and is present even before birth. Interaction also occurs through the spirits. This is especially true in the medicine dance, which again is one thing all Bushmen share. In essence, the spirits are evil, although in the medicine dance their presence is employed to do good. All ethnographers agree (see, for example, Silberbauer 1981: 175–7; Valiente-Noailles 1988: 235–43).

The medicine dance is *the* ritual for all Kua or Bushmen, and invariably it involves women providing singing and hand-clapping and men dancing in a circle around them, or sometimes off to the side. Women dance too among some groups and occasionally cure. Curing is done by the healer placing his hands on the body, and it does not matter whether a person is perceived as ill or not. Anyone can receive treatment, even ethnographers. Yes there is some variation, but in the dozens of medicine dances I have witnessed there has been a great deal of uniformity. Whether among G/wi, G//ana, !Xoõ, Naro, Ju/'hoansi, ≠Au//eisi or Hai//om, it is almost exactly alike. Settlement patterns, territorial practices, diet, initiation rites and language are extremely diverse across the Kalahari, but religion is always much the same. This is true regardless of specific beliefs, like how many gods there are: that is flexible. It depends on how one wants to count the deities (see also Barnard 1998b).

Sometimes it is difficult to establish when a custom just is a custom and clearly to be associated with an ethnic group, and when its existence reflects more the predilections of an ethnographer. It is well known that Heinz (1972), for example, regarded territoriality as an issue, but when is this an issue for Bushmen in general and when a reflection specifically of a !Xoõ concern? He does not make this quite clear. If there is a G/wi equivalent, it is probably the idea of the 'bad omen' or, in G/wi, *ziu* (Tanaka and Sugawara 2010: 5–6). As far as can be ascertained, there have been no bad ethnographers among the G/wi or the G//ana, and even Silberbauer's (1963, 1965) earliest works were later corrected in points of detail. The differences of opinion are as common among these Central Kalahari peoples themselves as they are among their ethnographers. To some extent, the same is true elsewhere, as evidenced, for example, in the 'debates' once held among Ju/'hoansi for the benefit of their ethnographers as well as among the Ju/'hoansi themselves (Blurton Jones and Konner 1976).

Valiente-Noailles, it must be said, is an amateur ethnographer, but one with a competence that rivals many professionals. A different sort of amateur, also competent though quite different in style, is Gene Waddell (2018a, 2018b). He is an amateur historian, especially of architecture. Let me quote (Waddell 2018a: 24): 'By 2017 few if any Bushmen continued to rely entirely on hunting and gathering for their subsistence, but they had continued to do so longer than any people on earth, and they had continued to long enough to provide the best available evidence for how all other peoples had lived 50,000 or more years ago.' The date is quite correct, and the sentiment pretty accurate. This self-publishing amateur makes a profound comment that is at least worthy of thought. One of the reasons that Bushmen are important is that they have survived for such a long time. I would only add that their survival is, at least in part, because of their intense spiritual knowledge, which is always flexible and open to debate and to new interpretations.

East of the G//ana

East of the G//ana lies the area where the Rev. Samuel Shaw Dornan did field research in the early twentieth century. Although he reports on a number of groups, his main work was with the Hiechware or Shua who live near Francistown and Serowe. Dornan's (1917, 1925) work is vague by modern standards. Dornan (1917: 37–8) suggests that Bushmen and Pygmies 'were probably originally the same people' or (1925: 46) that Pygmies are 'substantially the same people as the Bushmen'. His lengthy account *Pygmies and Bushmen of the Kalahari* (1925) is full of comparative material, mainly on *other* peoples: Tswana, Khoekhoe, Griqua and so on. This seems to be because he had a strong belief in the fact that, through miscegenation, many peoples are interrelated. He also believed that Bushmen had been driven south through the expansion of the Bantu-speaking populations. Their languages, therefore, diffused across the African continent. We now know that virtually none of his suppositions here are true: yes there has been much miscegenation, but Bushmen have not mainly been driven out of their lands. Nor have their languages much diffused, and certainly Bushmen are not related to Pygmies. Nor are they simply different because of environmental factors.

However, it is true that Bushman groups do stick to their own territories and practise a gender division in food acquisition. The most accurate parts of Dornan's account seem to be the sections in which he discusses family life and housing, music and dancing, the spirit world and totemism. Totemism (Dornan 1925: 161–2) here is especially interesting, since it is so rare among Bushmen. Dornan claims it is in its infancy, and this may be somewhat true. It does no doubt exist, although conceivably it is borrowed from neighbouring groups. Dornan (1925: 200–1) also comments on the hideous wars against the

Dutch, when in the ten years between 1786 and 1795, 2,700 Bushmen were killed and 700 imprisoned, compared to 270 whites killed. In the same period, it was estimated that 600 horses, 3,500 cattle and 77,200 sheep were taken. It is no wonder therefore that attempts to 'civilize' the Bushmen at that time met with such little success.

Another person to work with eastern groups was Elizabeth Cashdan (for example, 1987), who studied trade and reciprocity among G//ana and neighbouring groups in the 1970s and later developed ideas in evolutionary ecology and evolutionary psychology. On the Nata River in the early 1980s, Cashdan (1987: 167–93) discovered extensive networks of food circulation between compounds. This was exchange in generalized reciprocity, and it occurred between Bushmen and cattle herders as well as between Bushmen. In contrast, groups along the Botletle tended to engage in balanced reciprocity. Later too, Helga Vierich and the late Susan Kent worked in the Kweneng district with related groups. Kent's material is much more reliable than work by Dornan and others. I am thinking here especially of her articles in the edited volumes on cultural diversity and ethnicity (Kent 1996, 2002). Vierich's material is equally revealing. She writes (Helga Vierich, pers. comm.) of Richard Lee persuading her to work with the virtually unstudied groups in the south-eastern Kalahari:

I expected to find people literally ensnared by the dominant Bantu-speaking tribal groups of Botswana, as this was an area of contact for over 500 years. Instead I found a vibrant and tenacious set of people, speaking at least three Khoisan languages, whose hunter-gatherer economy still supplied the majority of food for most of them, and who had welded, out of long contact and persuasive persecution, a unified ethnic identity. I settled on a detailed study of the Kua, one of these language groups.

So, all in all, we know a great deal about the Central Kalahari Bushmen and their southern neighbours. Yet we are still constrained in this knowledge by social change. It has been many years since 'traditional' was *really* traditional: since the 1960s in most parts of the Kalahari there has been no stagnation but a progress of sorts. That is, people who live there, whether they call themselves G/wi, G//ana or Kua, have in this timeframe, and possibly before, been subject to rapid change. This does not make them any less Bushmen because culturally they live by the same rules. Egalitarianism, a keen sense of family, universal kinship, but with a sense of anarchy, and so on still govern their social interactions. The 'environment' here must include also changes brought about in more recent decades by attempts at resettlement in New Xade. What the future may bring for these people, especially now with even further environmental pressures due to decades of drought, is anyone's guess. My money is on a retention of tradition but with a positive feeling for change. Ultimately, San society is governed by a tremendous ability to adapt to circumstances, and this is probably as true now as it has been in the past.

Further Reading

Works on the G/wi include Silberbauer's (1965) *Bushman survey report*, as it is customarily known (officially, the *Report to the government of Bechuanaland on the Bushman survey*). His 1973 Monash PhD thesis was later updated and published as *Hunter and habitat in the central Kalahari desert* (Silberbauer 1981), which is a truly excellent ethnography. Another important, and equally excellent, work of his is his chapter in *Hunters and gatherers today* (Silberbauer 1972).

Works by Japanese writers include monographs and other writings by Tanaka (1980), among others. Tanaka's (2014) *The Bushmen* tells of the fifty years of research that he and is colleagues have put into the study of these people. Importantly too, Tanaka and Sugawara's 'encyclopaedia' contains 152 pages of material on G/wi and G//ana society. There is also a 'Supplementary Issue' of the Japanese journal *African Study Monographs*, edited by Akira Takada (2016). This contains several papers in English by Japanese writers (and one German) on residence, hunting (including commercial hunting) naming, ecological knowledge, sex, kinship and grammar.

Finally, an interesting take on Bushman studies is to be found in *Bushmen* (Waddell 2018a, 2018b). These are self-published books in the Amazon list. There is very little new material in it, just lots of quotations, notably on G/wi and Ju/'hoansi. These are the fourth and fifth volumes in a series on Aboriginal peoples of the world. Especially interesting is the material on sources (Waddell 2018a: 98–159), which to some extent echoes my *Anthropology and the Bushman* (Barnard 2007a).

7 Naro

'Central', 'Northern' or Unique?

The Naro (formerly spelled Nharo or Naron) are the main group I worked with, from 1974 onwards. They are also the group studied by Mathias Guenther. I say *Central, Northern* or *unique* here in reference to their linguistic classification.

Naro is a Khoe or 'Central' language, but two recent genetic studies (Pickrell *et al.* 2012; Pakendorf 2014) have shown that it is highly likely that their original language was, like Ju/'hoan, a Kx'a or 'Northern' one. When I first learned of this, as a result of an 'endangered languages' project I was on at the time, it caused me concern. Yet on reflection, it need not have. My work on human origins taught me that such things are *normally* unstable. 'The Naro' a thousand or a few hundred years ago were *not* a stable population of about a few thousand, as they are today. They numbered far fewer, and they were almost certainly multilingual. Also, their kinship system, and such, is actually the product of evolutionary development. These things put together explain a great number of facts: why they use the Ju/'hoan naming system and how this affected the Khoe kinship terminology they developed, the existence of specific customs like *xaro* (*hxaro*) and *kamane* exchanges, and so on. In other words, ethnic groups are not stable entities at the outset; they *become* stable. Indeed, they explain a great deal in the prehistory, especially in the linguistic prehistory, of southern Africa as a whole.

The Naro: Who Are They?

Naro, as I say, are also known as Nharo or, as Dorothea Bleek (1928) called them, Naron. The *-n* is a plural indicator. Apparently, locals (especially on the Namibian border) sometimes also refer to them as //Aikhoe. The Naro are the people on which I wrote my PhD thesis (Barnard 1976). Mathias Guenther (1973) also did his PhD on the same group, and Dorothea Bleek (1928) worked with them in the 1920s. Her short work (only sixty-seven pages, of which about nine are actually devoted mainly to other groups) was the first ethnographic monograph on any Bushman people. Guenther (1986: 1) put their number at 5,000 in Botswana and 4,000 in Namibia, although I suspect that the number within Botswana was and is considerably higher.

Other Naro ethnographers include Hendrik Steyn (on economics), Hessel Visser (on language), James Suzman (for his undergraduate work) and, most recently, Jenny Lawy. Each of us has concentrated on rather different areas of Naro country and on very different topics. These groups and a few other groups of eastern Botswana will be discussed in this chapter. The so-called River Bushmen, who inhabit the Okavango swamps of northern Botswana, will be treated in Chapter 10. Linguistically, all these peoples are quite similar. That is, they all speak Khoe languages. Linguistically they are, like the G/wi, G//ana and other 'Central' groups, related to the herders. This does not necessarily mean they have ever had livestock, but they may have. Some of their vocabulary does suggest this, or at least that these groups had a knowledge of herded animals a time long time ago. In other words, Naro and perhaps some other peoples seem to have undergone sound shifts that suggest this as a possibility. We simply do not know.

However, none of us could have foreseen the big problem. These are a people who once, very probably, spoke a language closely related to Ju/'hoan (a Kx'a or Northern language), but who went through a dramatic shift from speaking that language to speaking a Khoe one. This language shift was perhaps a millennium (or more) ago, and it affected other, smaller, Khoe-speaking groups too. The shift from Kx'a to Khoe was almost unique to Naro and to their closest relatives, like the Ts'ao or Ts'aokhoe (north-eastern Naro) and possibly the ≠Haba. The latter group is uncertain because linguists classify their dialect as *not* that closely related, although it does share some of the features mentioned below. Certainly, it has always seemed very similar to me, and in the past I called Naro, Ts'ao and ≠Haba together 'Western Khoe Bushmen'.

There is an interesting story to be told here, and one with a lesson for prehistorians. The recent genetic studies by Brigitte Pakendorf (2014) and by Joseph Pickrell and his team (Pickrell *et al.* 2012) suggest that ancestors of the Naro were originally speakers of a Kx'a language who shifted to using a Khoe one. As I suggested earlier, the label *Kx'a* actually only dates from 2010 (Heine and Honken 2010), but the idea is rather older. It stems from the work of Dorothea Bleek (1929). Far from being an unsurmountable problem, the revelation of language borrowing explains a great deal of ethnographic detail. I have hinted at some already, but at least four points are obvious:

(1) why the Naro have a Ju/'hoan-type naming system,
(2) the custom of *xaro* or *hxaro* (which they call *//'ãe*, used in Ju/'hoan as a verb),
(3) the notion of *kamasi* (Ju/'hoan) or *kamane* (Naro) and
(4) the fact that their kinship usage has Ju/'hoan-like terms instead of the ones found in virtually all other Khoe languages.

Let me take each in turn.

(1) The naming system is not just about the names, but also about the custom of using them to extend kinship through rules of namesake-equivalence. This, in theory, is done indefinitely. For example, if my name is John, then anyone else named John is my 'grandrelative', and I call his sister as if she were my own sister. Also, I cannot marry her for that would create an incestuous relationship. It would be as if I were marrying my own sister. Even some of the names themselves are found in both the Naro language and in Ju/'hoan.

(2) *Xaro* or *//'āe* is a pattern of gift-giving of non-consumable property. This overlies a set of rights to use each other's resources. For example, I give you my digging stick, and the two of us share rights to hunt in each other's territory. The spelling *hxaro* is very common, but in fact is incorrect. There is no *h* in the word, but rather just a velar fricative, *x*. Its discoverer, Polly Wiessner, has recently changed from the spelling *hxaro* to the spelling *xaro*. Ju/'hoansi use the noun *xaro*, but Naro know only the verbal form *//'āe*, which is also used in Ju/'hoan.

(3) *Kamasi* is the Ju/'hoan word for bridewealth (and among Naro, also childbirth prestations). In Naro it is used with the Khoe suffix *-ne* rather than the Ju/'hoan one, which is *–si*, in short *kamane*. Bridewealth is actually rather unusual among hunter-gatherers generally, but it is practised by both Ju/'hoansi and Naro. Much more commonly bridewealth is found among herders of cattle, sheep and goats, whether in the Kalahari or elsewhere. This may hint at changes in lifestyle among some Khoisan peoples, but that is not my point here.

(4) The 'missing' kinship term of Naro is *n//uri-* or *//nodi-*, found in nearly every Khoe language to mean cross-cousin, cross-nephew, cross-niece, grand-child, etc. Naro, like all Khoe languages, has this concept but uses Kx'a terms instead. Kx'a languages make linear/collateral distinctions, whereas Khoe ones (including Naro) make parallel/cross distinctions. Instead of *n//uri-* or *//nodi-*, the Naro language uses *tsxõ-* or *mama-*, terms which are most likely borrowed from a Kx'a dialect, possibly an extinct one. These are used, though, in the Khoe manner, that is, simply instead of *n//uri-* or *//nodi-*.

When I first tried to explain the peculiarities of Naro kinship (Barnard 1988a), I thought I had everything cracked. Later, when these facts from genetic studies came to light, everything really did fit together. The lesson is that we must not think of early Naro as the group we known today as 'the Naro', but rather as a very small, mixed group of multilingual hunter-gatherers in which the Naro language eventually won out (see also Barnard 2014). No doubt much the same could be said about many other San groups throughout history or prehistory. I mention that the Naro use the same naming system as the Ju/'hoansi. Naming is very important both to Naro and to Ju/'hoansi, and we know that the Naro use a large but sill finite set of names: 138 male names and 91 female names, according to Hessel and Cobi Visser (Visser and Visser 1998: 225–7).

History changes not only the nature of groups, but also their very existence as groups. Fredrik Barth (1969) and his colleagues showed this in the 1960s through their famous edited collection *Ethnic groups and boundaries*. This was based on a conference held in Bergen two years before. Ethnic groups, it was argued, are not stagnant, but fluid in nature. This transpires via individual action or, in the case of the Naro, through language shift. For these Naro this was likely to have been effected through intermarriage between speakers of a Kx'a dialect and speakers of a Khoe one. In such an instance, one language becomes dominant, as indeed does one kinship system. Then stability occurs. It is not just individuals who move between groups, as Barth as his colleagues maintained, but entire groups. Their existence is altered. This kind of ethnic-group shift may be more common among very small groups like the Naro and their hunter-gatherer ancestors. The ancestral population may indeed have been only a few families, and possessing not only different dialects but several distinct languages. Events like this may be relatively rare in the annals of ethnography, but plainly they do occur.

Another example is the shift from Aasáx (literally 'hunter's mouth') to Maasai in Tanzania recorded by J. C. Winter (1979). That case is similar in that it involved a small population of hunter-gatherers, but actually quite different in that the shift seems to have involved an entire population *becoming* a new ethnic group. The Aasáx acquired the age organization, the kinship system and so on of the Maasai, and in so doing eventually lost their identity as a distinct group. This shift can be dated quite firmly to the 1890s and to the Rinderpest epidemic that swept through eastern and southern Africa at that time, whereas the Naro shift was certainly several centuries earlier. We know this for the Naro because the Naro language evolved to what it is today quite separately from other Khoe languages. That is why the kinship term *n//uri-* or *// nodi-* does not occur in Naro. My more general point is that the Naro language shift is not totally unique, but similar to events elsewhere. In Chapter 9 we shall find another example, that of the Hai//om, who probably once spoke another Kx'a dialect and shifted to another Khoe one, specifically to Khoekhoe (Khoekhoegowab): the language of the pure, that is, without agriculture, herders of southern Africa. There is as yet no genetic evidence for this, but given their location and various cultural factors, not least their hunter-gatherer lifestyle, it seems pretty definite as well as fairly recent. There are also linguistic clues, as in the sound shifts that differentiate Khoe languages. If a language *keeps* an earlier form, it will not have undergone the shift later, so we look for that as our clue (see Westphal 1971).

Further Facts about the Naro

The leading ethnographers of the Naro have been Dorothea Bleek (1928), daughter of Wilhelm Bleek, in the 1920s, H. P. Steyn (for example, 1971), Mathias Guenther (for example, 1979a, 1986, 1989), beginning in the 1970s, and me (for example, Barnard 1978; 1979a). My work also began in the 1970s and was in different parts of Naro country. Dorothea Bleek was a general ethnographer, though she shared her father's particular interest in language. Her brief period of field research was centred at the border post on the Namibian side, at a location called Buitepos (which means border post). She was only two years old when her father died, and six when four Ju/'hoansi or !Xun arrived to work with her aunt, and eight when the Bushmen left (see Weintroub 2014: 156). Guenther's work focused initially on the lives of the Naro as 'farm Bushmen' and later turned to their interest in religion, folklore and art. He has also done significant work on /Xam folklore (for example, Guenther 1989, 2014a). My own concern has mainly been with kinship and with settlement patterns. In terms of settlement, the Naro are unusual in that they live in a relatively wet part of the Kalahari. This is not so much because of rainfall but because of a plentiful supply of underground water resources.

As we saw in Chapter 5, I once compared Naro to !Xoõ, G/wi and Ju/'hoan populations (Barnard 1979a; see also Barnard 1986). This was specifically in regard to differences in settlement patterns. I found that micro-environmental differences create radically different patterns of settlement. The !Xoõ have the least water and have traditionally lived a fairly precarious existence, in small, isolated units. In relative terms, they are *permanently dispersed*. The Naro, on the other hand, are (or can be) *permanently aggregated*. In between, we have the G/wi and the Ju/'hoansi. G/wi have traditionally aggregated in the wet season (that is, in the southern spring and summer), around waterholes, and later in the year migrated from one patch of tsama melons to the next. Ju/'hoansi have traditionally done the opposite, in a way. They aggregate at permanent waterholes in the dry season, and disperse as family units as seasonal water becomes available. G/wi cannot do this because they have no permanent water resources at all, and they sometimes would leave the Central Kalahari Game Reserve to find water among their neighbours to the east. Of course these patterns of settlement have been disrupted by drought and by forced resettlement in recent times, but they were well recorded in the ethnography of Silberbauer (1981: 191–257), among others.

In recent years Guenther's main interest has been in Naro religion. However, he also once commented on Naro territoriality and on territoriality among other hunter-gatherer groups (Guenther 1981). The Naro are not particularly concerned with land and territory, and certainly less so than reported among the !Xoõ. It is, though, sometimes difficult to separate an ethnographer's true interests from his or her ideological attitudes. Heinz (1972) was always the key proponent of the view that hunter-gatherers are territorial. He is supported in this by his colleague Irenaeus Eibl-Eibesfeldt (for example, 1975), who also worked with the !Xoõ. They believed this simply because humans are 'naturally' territorial. Guenther rejects the notion that all hunter-gatherers are necessarily so, and looks instead to specific factors that lead to this. Moreover, Guenther rejects the assumption of territoriality on the grounds that it contradicts the idea of fluidity and open, non-aggressive behaviour. Such behaviour characterizes Naro society particularly, although it is also common with hunter-gatherers more generally. The Naro are not aggressive; nor are their territories divided by sharp boundaries with strips of no-man's-land between them. That view, of strips of no-man's-land between territories, is reminiscent of the reports of !Xoõ social organization by Heinz. Rather, Naro move freely between campsites, and this practice occurs both because of a sense of freedom and also in response to internal disputes. Such internal disputes are indeed not uncommon among Naro, but they have nothing to do with territoriality.

According to Guenther (1986: xi), of the 55,000 Bushmen in southern Africa 'at present' (that is, in the 1980s), 'probably no more than 3,000 are still hunter-gatherers'. Of course, the exact definition of 'hunter-gatherers' is debateable. H. P. Steyn (1971), of the University of Stellenbosch, conducted several years of research among Naro in the late 1960s and early 1970s. His focus was on economic life in the western Ghanzi district, and he reports splendidly on the routine activities most ethnographers are hardly aware of. Hunting and gathering are still practised but punctuated with long periods of inactivity, and individuals come and go as they choose. According to Steyn (1971: 281):

The typical daily activities of Bushmen in the villages can be described as follows: The early morning is spent socially round the fire with others. Gradually, these gatherings start to break up as people busy themselves with tasks of a personal nature. Men may scrape and cure skins, repair metal traps and trap discs, sharpen scrapers or spears, cut digging sticks, repair skin bags and cloaks with an awl and sinew, play musical instruments, roll fibre into a rope to be used for making snares, scratch thorns from the soles of their feet, sleep in the shade or lie talking idly. If tobacco is available, talking and smoking are synonymous, the pipe being passed round the circle, including women and the older children.

This sounds very like typical hunter-gatherer behaviour to me.

Game includes a great variety of animals: eland, kudu, wildebeest hartebeest, gemsbok, springbok, duiker, steenbok, warthog, porcupine, hare, ground squirrel and so on. The distribution of meat is quite precise, and this is normal among most all Bushman groups, although it can be altered according to personal preference (see Steyn 1971: 308–9). A foreleg goes to the parents of the hunter, assuming they live with the group. The hunter's brother receives a hind leg. His parents-in-law get a hind leg and part of a foreleg; and his grandparents, the heart, liver and head. If these relatives live elsewhere, the hunter may keep these parts. The important thing is that *everyone* gets a share, no matter how small the share is. Plant food is less widely shared. This is quite normal for all Bushman groups too. The seasonal cycle is also fairly typical, although Steyn is unusual in describing not an idealized primal pattern but a realistic, up-to-date version: after the spring rains, the western Naro tend to live in the bush. Then they seek water-bearing melons, and when these are gone they spend the remainder of the year in close association with Kgalagadi pastoralists or alternatively staying on Coloured-owned farms (Steyn 1971: 315–18). Steyn's description here obviously refers to the area in western Botswana where he worked. This part of the Kalahari is mainly inhabited not by whites but by their relatively poor, mixed-race relatives. Although the area around Ghanzi is mainly dominated by white-owned farms or cattle ranches, the area to the west around Xanaxas (/Xanagas) was designated as Coloured by the British colonial administration. The reason why both areas are there at all is to do with Cecil Rhodes's plan to stop German expansion from South West Africa (modern Namibia) into what is now Botswana. That was in the 1890s. As for the names of the places, these reflect ever-changing occupation by different ethnic groups. Steyn worked mainly around Kalkfontein and Tshootsa, just south of the Trans-Kalahari Highway. His work, though, predates construction of the highway.

Naro social organization should hold no surprises. Naro are divided into bands or *tsouba* (in the singular), and the largest territorial unit is the band cluster territory or *n!usa*: what Heinz called a nexus. This seems to be a dialect area, and these are named. Ownership of the band's territory is vested in everyone who lives in it, although of course the Botswana government recognizes instead the freehold rights of the farmers. In the Naro view, God gave the land of the band cluster to the 'Oldest Parents' (*Kaiem G//odzi*), that is, the ancestors, both male and female, to look after in perpetuity. Bands are rather more fluid in duration and composition than the clusters, and a few months' residence is normal before one calls a band their own. The size of a band is anywhere from eight to over forty people, and sometimes more than one group will share the same waterhole. Indeed Guenther points to groups of up to 150, in other words similar in size to bands reported by Passarge (1907: 31–2) during the Rinderpest epidemic in the late nineteenth century. Certainly farm labour is important for the many Naro who do such work (see Guenther 1979a), although traditional hunting and especially food gathering is equally important. The Peace Corps volunteer Gary Childers (1976) reported subsistence at 28 per cent for food gathering, 38 per cent farm labour and payment in kind, along with food sharing at 8 per cent, herding one's own livestock at 7 per cent, cultivating, craft-making, hunting and leather work at lower percentages. I suspect that all these figures are difficult to establish, but the gist is clear. Naro maintain a rather mixed economy.

The use territory is actually rather complicated. In *Hunters and herders* (Barnard 1992: 235–6) I discussed territoriality and pointed out that only the Naro and the !Xoõ have band clusters. Both these groups exercise territorial exclusivity for these. However, Naro family organization is not territorial, whereas !Xoõ family organization seems to be highly territorial. Ju/'hoan family organization is not associated with territory, but G/wi and G//ana social organization is *temporarily* so associated. In between, we have the band level. G//ana and Ju/'hoansi have overlapping band territories, whereas G/wi territories are more exclusive. Both Naro and !Xoõ bands do seem to be largely territorial. I suspect that these territorial dynamics reflect very specific environmental factors and that seasonality is very important. Individuals move about, and the flexibility allowed reflects this. 'Naro' here is to be taken as Naro in a traditional setting, but even this is hard to separate from the fact that life on farms is different from traditional Naro life.

In Naro custom, the headman is simply the oldest male member of the group, and his wife is the headwoman. These roles are perhaps less significant that they once were, and status (and especially status-seeking) is frowned upon in Bushman society generally. Further detail is contained in other sources (especially in Guenther 1986: 169–214; Barnard 1992a: 137–44), but the key point is that visiting by families is very common, and social structure depends on this degree of flexibility. When disputes arise, it is easy for groups to divide. Perhaps this is related to the fact that Naro generally live on farms, in other words, on what is in fact other people's land. However, this is similar to the situation with other San groups. Although relatively well off for San, Naro tend to be unemployed. To some extent the politics of this seems to be breaking down: I have seen this at Hanahai, a government settlement scheme occupied at least since the 1970s. There, marked social boundaries have appeared in the last few decades, and these social boundaries have taken on a territorial dimension (Barnard 1986: 49–50). There are differences too in the kinds of settlement that Naro occupy, a point made in our further comparative study, by me for the Naro and by Widlok for the Hai//om (Barnard and Widlok 1996).

Naro Religion

The details of Naro religion have been well recorded, especially by Mathias Guenther. He worked mainly at D'Kar, the site of a mission station northeast of Ghanzi. Ironically, Naro seem to have had beliefs not entirely different from some Christian notions. Monotheism has always been the norm among Bushmen in any case, as it is more generally among hunter-gatherers: a point made long ago by Father Schmidt (1929; 1939).

There is, and has always been, a strong belief in God, who is called N!eriba, N!ariba or N!adiba (see, for example, Guenther 1979b). These differences in orthography are not significant and reflect only the choices of individual ethnographers. And as Guenther implies, we should never be too quick to take everything at face value or just to create 'a chaotic jumble of unclear utterings' (1979b: 126).

The name of the deity is also sometimes given as Hiseba, sometimes translated as 'the Lord'. Guenther remarks that virtually every individual he spoke to has a different version of beliefs about him and a different set of understandings of Naro myth. There are also differences between eastern Naro, where Guenther worked, and those living in the western Naro area. And there are differences between Naro influenced by Christianity and those living more independently. N!adiba is the creator god, and his enemy is G//ãũaba or G//ãwaba, a devil figure and trickster. The latter appears in the medicine dance, usually in the plural (g//ãũane). The suffix -ba is simply the masculine singular, and the –ne, common gender plural. My decision on when to use upper case and when to use lower case reflects my sense of what might seem sensible if I were speaking Naro. (For the sake of consistency in my own writing, I have altered the spellings here slightly from Guenther's.)

Actually, and Guenther does note, it is all rather more complicated than this. Let me quote Guenther (1979b: 107):

In some accounts //Gãuwa is associated with the sky, usually a lower region than that inhabited by N!eri, in others with the earth, in a third (the one perhaps most common) with both realms. In this latter account, the way in which he manifests his association between the celestial and the earthly realms also differ widely, ranging from mystic, pantheistic oneness of //Gãuwa with earth and sky, to mechanical movements between the two realms. The most graphic account of mechanical movement is descent from the sky by means of invisible spider's fibres and lateral motion across the lower regions of the sky and the earth's surface along an intricate network of invisible fibres that span the entire veld like a vast spider's net.

Let us call him G//ãũaba. He often assumes human form and plays tricks on people, especially on Afrikaans-speaking ranchers. His moral qualities are ambiguous, since he is both good and evil, though in fact not purposely either! Many such beliefs about N!adiba, G//ãũaba and the spirit world occur through-out southern Africa. The idea generally is that these beliefs allow a playful quality and not one of awe or fear. There is a separation between the everyday economic concerns of the Naro and their spiritual understandings, a point made both by Guenther (1979b) and by me (Barnard 1988b). And in a sense, there are similarities here in ritual.

Naro possess two clear rituals: the medicine dance and the Eland Bull Dance. The former is probably the more important and certainly the most widespread. It occurs across southern Africa, and is broadly similar everywhere. In it, women clap and sing, with complex rhythm and counterpoint. They sit at the main fire of the band with children, and are often densely seated. Men dance round the group. One or more will enter trance, and in this state can cure others present. Curing involves placing one's hands on each person in turn. The ill receive more of this than others, and special attention is paid, for example, to pregnant women. Fundamentally curing is a man's role, although among Ju/'hoansi women sometimes perform at medicine dances. There are breaks between songs. Each song lasts a few minutes longer than the average pop song, and the entire performance can last all night. Sometimes though, it simply fizzles out, such as when nobody at all goes into trance. This is not that uncommon. More rarely, medicine dances happen in the case of serious illness or an unusual event. I witnessed the last once among Naro. An elderly woman became possessed by a spirit, and the spirit had to be exorcized. The presence of spiritual entities is normal, but this was unusual. When in trance, the medicine man or men either draw out sickness from the bodies of those present and send them to the spirits or take on the spirit from within. In other words, explanations differ. In this case of spirit possession, once the medicine man removed the spirit through trance he ceased to do anything else. The camp simply returned to normal.

Views differ radically concerning what is actually happening in a medicine dance. I have attended perhaps about forty of these, mainly with Naro but also with other Bushman groups. Often these do not really get started. Some trance performers claim that 'medicine' (*tsoo*) boils inside their bellies and that this is what brings the trance on. Others say that an evil 'spirit' (*g//ãũaba* or *g//ãũasa*) has entered their body. Some claim that their own spirit does battle with an alien spirit outside the dance circle. In short, there are several possible explanations, though this really matters very little to Naro. Commonly medicine dances are held at full moon or simply when a lot of people are gathered in one place. Their existence is essentially for curing, although they are not normally performed specifically to cure a single individual. Medicine dances are often as much entertainment as curing, although importantly they *both* cure and entertain. They enable medicine men (or very rarely, medicine women) to go into trance. This gives them a certain prestige in Naro society. I once saw such a man swallow nine hot coals in succession to aid the 'boiling' in his stomach. Feeling 'hot' inside, he was able to move around the dance circle and to cure each person individually. Importantly, no one is excluded: whites, blacks or Bushmen, well or perceptively ill, everyone receives treatment. Sometimes some receive a little more, for example, a pregnant woman. Medicine dances begin with women clapping and singing. Then one or more men gradually go into trance. Physiologically, they shake, and their blood pressure rises. Both the medicine dance and female initiation occur in a dance circle, and the direction of the dancing does not matter.

Further detail can be found in my 'Nharo Bushman medicine and medicine men' (Barnard 1989b) or in Guenther's work.

The latter ritual is the Eland Bull Dance. The Eland Bull is not a real eland but a male human who symbolizes the presence of the eland. In turn, the eland is a representation of male sexuality. The late Michelle Rosaldo once enlightened me as to what might be going on here. Maleness is envisaged as the act of chasing the female, whereas feminine nature is seen as the reverse: the woman is chased by the man. It is not, as in post-foraging societies, a simple matter of 'nature' versus 'culture', but a slightly different embodiment of gender relations that is being portrayed. Put simply, women are celebrated as sexual objects, just as men are epitomized as hunters (cf. Collier and Rosaldo 1981). However, this is not to undermine the egalitarian nature of Bushman society that easily accommodates this seeming reversal, and it is played out too through the existence of bride service. Yes, gifts are given at marriage and at childbirth, but service is also expected: a man must hunt not only for himself and his children, but also for his parents-in-law. This seems to enhance the stability of Naro society.

In the Eland Bull Dance (Barnard 1980: 117–18; Guenther 1986: 278–81), each girl is initiated individually at the time of her first menstruation. Typically, the girl's grandmother or someone of that status is in charge. This is not as odd as it may seem since 'grandrelative' is of a close joking category. Periodically, they dance around the outside of the hut and the fire. They sing a different tune than in a trance dance, and as they do this they lift their skirts behind them. A 'grandfather' chases after them in dance step, with his fingers above his head in the sign of an eland in hunting sign language. Her grandmother typically presents a gift to the initiate at the end. After the ceremony, the girl is free to take lovers or to marry. There is, in fact, little difference between taking lovers and marriage. Naro used to hold male initiation ceremonies too (D. F. Bleek 1928: 23–5), but these have disappeared or simply evolved into forms of hunting magic. Those ceremonies involved group initiation, with ritual tattooing, and they lasted for a period of a month. Today, only the tattooing remains. In principle, men who bear the tattoos (between the eyes) are meant to see their prey better.

Perhaps the crucial thing about the Naro is that their ideology of existence is so different from ours. In one sense, they are just people, exactly like you and me. However, there are subtle differences. I have already remarked on sharing as an ideology, and this propensity to value this social attribute seems to be typical of nearly all hunter-gatherers. Another attribute is the value placed on followership. This is because followership implies that the community is the focus, rather than self-interest and a sense of public service (as in the West). Yet another is universal kinship, where everyone in society is 'kin' and no-one is 'non-kin'. I discovered this among the Naro early in fieldwork, but it does seem to be a general principle that differentiates hunter-gatherers from other sorts of people (see Barnard 1978, 2017).

Naro Kinship

In my youth I commented extensively on Naro kinship. This is not the place to review that literature. However, let us look again at Naro kinship in reference to its position as one kinship system of a Khoe-speaking people. The most notable thing in this regard is the 'missing' kinship term *n//uri-* or *//nodi-*. Its place is taken by other terms, especially *tsxõ-* or *mama-*. These two words are grammatically different, in the sense that *tsxõ-* takes a possessive prefix and *mama-* does not. Otherwise, they are virtually interchangeable. Both indicate members of the 'grandrelative' category.

In *Hunters and herders of southern Africa* (Barnard 1992), there were many diagrams of relationship terminology structures. In this book there is only one, Figure 7.1. Part of the reason for this is that such structures are simply not that common in anthropology any longer. They, and the theoretical ideas they involve, are no longer fashionable. They have been replaced by new theoretical developments in the discipline, for example in the work of Janet Carsten (2000, 2004), following earlier work by David Schneider (for example, 1984). The phrase 'relationship terminology' (rather than 'kinship terminology') is used here partly in deference to such alternative theoretical positions, although these are not necessarily consistent with my own position. They do make some sense though, in view of the fact that Naro kinship is predicated on the notion of name relationships in addition to kinship proper or 'real kinship'.

Figure 7.1, in fact, represents a *basic structure*. Things are different when a person's category is disrupted because of the rules of namesake equivalence. For example, if my sister is called Tsebe, then anyone else who bears the name Tsebe is also regarded as my 'sister', and I call her that and treat her appropriately. To have sex with any 'sister' would, of course, be regarded as incest. Bear in mind too that these terms generally take the prefix *ti-* (meaning 'my'), and all except *mama, au* and *ai* require suffixes to indicate number and gender. For example, *mama-ba* and *mama-sa*, for cross-relatives, *au-ba* for father and *ai-sa* for mother. Someone else's father or mother is referred to respectively as *sau-ba* or *sau-sa*. William McGregor (2014) found strikingly similar configurations among Shua near the Makgarikgari Pans, north of the Tshwa and G//ana. Siblings are referred to by the junior term, *!uĩ*. In other words, a brother and sister, two brothers or two sisters are *!uĩ-ku* ('siblings to each other'). Beyond this, the Naro classify everyone as either 'joking' (*g//ai* or *!au-tama*, 'feared-not') or 'avoidance' (*!au*). In practice, Naro universal kinship is worked out through

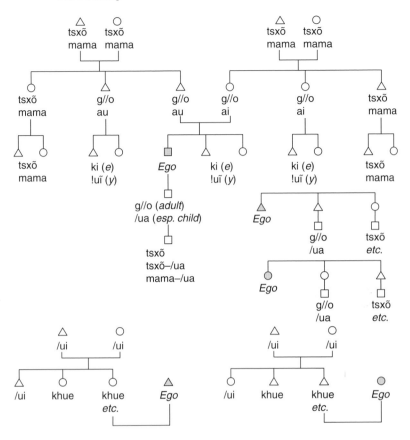

Figure 7.1 Naro relationship terminology
Source: Barnard 1992a: 149

rules of namesake equivalence. The older person classifies the younger, and the kin link remains for life (Figure 7.2).

The Naro exchange marriage and childbirth gifts, which they call *kamane*. This word seems to be the same in the singular and the plural. Briefly, the ideal set of gifts is a steenbok, given from a husband to his in-laws, with the skin going to his wife. She uses it to carry the first-born and any other children of the couple. Other close relatives also receive gifts. *Kamane* are distinguished from *abane* (ordinary gifts), and the latter involve particularly the gift of non-consumable property from a man to his wife's grandmothers. This is required as a gift in order for a man to claim 'ownership' (as they say) over his wife. The same transaction also found in *xaro* (abstract noun) or *//'āe* (verb) exchange.

Figure 7.2 Making maize meal

This is the gift of non-consumable property from anyone to anyone else. It can be *anything*: a man once asked me for my vehicle, and Polly Wiessner (pers. comm.) reports similar requests among the Ju/'hoansi. More typically though, it is a hat or a digging stick. There is no marriage ceremony otherwise, and divorce is easy for either party.

I could, of course, go on about Naro kinship for some time (see also Barnard 1982, 1992a: 145–53, 2014), but probably this is enough (Figure 7.3).

Central, Northern or Unique?

In answer to my opening question, the Naro are, of course, all three. To me, they embody all that is interesting about Bushmen in general and about 'culture'. Neither culture nor society can be taken as a given. These things

Figure 7.3 Making arrow heads from fence wire

are moulded by individuals but certainly not on purpose. Their existence highlights one of the vagaries of evolution and is a consequence of both evolution itself and culture contact. Contact cannot be planned, but nor is it necessarily a one-way transition. I suspect the Naro did influence the Ju/'hoansi or their ancestors, but mostly Naro grew out of a constellation of Kx'a and Khoe-speaking groups that existed centuries ago. The revelation that they once spoke a Kx'a language gives great insight about them and also about Bushmen in general.

Finally, the language shift the Naro, and the Hai//om, went through may not be as unique as we might think. Over the last 50,000 years many San groups could have seen similar changes, with varying degrees of impact not only on language but on culture as well. The very fact that Kalahari hunter-gatherers have been here for tens of thousands of years, and are still here, certainly suggests that they have been able to adapt (Figure 7.4).

Figure 7.4 Naro boys by fire

Further Reading

The two main ethnographers of the Naro are Mathias Guenther and myself. Among Guenther's important publications is a general ethnography of the Naro (Guenther 1986). My own papers are mainly of kinship (for example, Barnard 1982).

I should mention that Hessel Visser, a missionary linguist who works with Naro, has published a rapid succession of Naro-English/English-Naro word-lists. The standard orthography for Naro is his, but he is very unusual in including only the Nguni-derived click symbols **c** for /, **x** for // and **q** for !. He adds a **tc** for ≠. This click is non-existent in Nguni languages. Nguni languages are those found mainly on the east coast of South Africa (Xhosa, Zulu, siSwati and so on). However, his most recent, fourth edition (Visser 2001) does also give both standard Bushman orthography and the new version. In this book I include only standard Khoisan, as recognized by the International Phonetic Association. To do otherwise would render much of this book very complicated indeed, since the use of standard Khoisan is so widespread and Nguni symbols confined to Naro alone. All ethnographers do retain traditional Khoisan usage. However, in the next chapter I do follow the lead of the relevant linguist, the late Patrick Dickens (1994), who did use the standard Khoisan forms in his click symbols.

Cambridge University Press re-issued both *The Naron* and its companion volume *Comparative vocabularies of Bushman languages* (D. F. Bleek 1929) in 2011. However, the latter still contains a confusing error. All the languages are referred to in code; on page 3 the Naro language is listed as C1, and the Tati language recorded by Dornan (1917) as C2. These are in fact *reversed*: Naro is C2, and Tati is C1. They are correctly given in Bleek's (1956) posthumous Bushman dictionary. The Tati group is the one whose ethnography was later recorded by Dornan (1925).

8   Ju/'hoansi or !Kung

Classic San

The !Kung of the Botswana/Namibia border area, who are now generally called Ju/'hoansi, are the most studied and the best known of all Bushman groups. Yet they are certainly not the only Bushmen in the Kalahari. This chapter will outline the important ethnography of Lorna Marshall, Richard Lee, Megan Biesele, Edwin Wilmsen and several others, with the focus being on settlement and band structure, kinship, ritual and religious belief, among other things. Many debates have emerged on the significance of this work. For example, have the Ju/'hoansi been isolated as hunter-gatherers, as supposedly claimed by Lee (1979) and others, or part of a larger political economy of the Kalahari, as Wilmsen (1989) maintains? Does this tell us anything about the 'original affluent society' as described by Marshall Sahlins (1974: 1–39), or not?

I shall also touch briefly on other !Xun- or !Xũ-speaking groups, such as !Xun proper in the north and the ≠Au//eisi or ≠X'au//'eîsi in the south. Indeed, are the latter actually Ju/'hoansi, or are they a separate group? This depends on ethnic perception: the language is the same, but many individuals consider themselves as belonging to different groups.

On Maps, and Why the Plural Ending?

In this book I have a number of maps. These mainly draw the boundaries around nation states. An alternative, which I remember from my youth, is instead to indicate *rivers* (or dry river beds) rather than boundaries. This was the method of the eminent linguist Ernst Westphal. He used to keep dozens of such maps on his desk, ready to fill in migration routes, locations of ethnic groups or whatever was required for students or colleagues as the need arose. Rivers, of course, are central to migration, and they offer a different perspective. There are other possibilities: elevation, vegetation and so on.

However they got there, Figure 8.1 illustrates the main Bushman groups of northern Botswana and Namibia. Some groups, such as the Hai//om, are undoubtedly of mixed origin. Others, like ≠Au//eisi and Ju/'hoansi are either very closely related or identical.

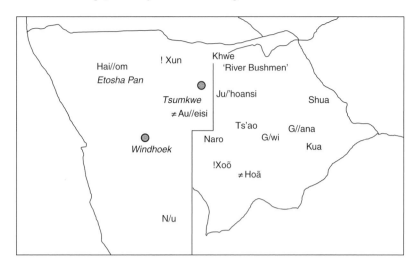

Figure 8.1 Bushman groups of northern Botswana and Namibia

The famous !Kung Bushmen are now generally known as Ju/'hoansi. Ju/'hoansi is their own preferred name. Lorna Marshall always called them !Kung, but like nearly all of their ethnographers today I shall refer to them as Ju/'hoansi. Their name means simply 'real people', and some Ju/'hoansi use the term *Ju/'hoansi* to mean *all* Bushmen. The leading ethnographers are actually quite numerous: more than a dozen anthropologists have worked with this group since the early 1950s, and newer ones seem to appear every year. For this reason and because of the prominence of some of their ethnographers, like Marshall and Lee, they are extremely well known. Lee's (2013) account is among the most readable and is the most easily accessible, and I recommend it to all who are unfamiliar with the group.

For some reason, it has become conventional in anthropology to refer to the Ju/'hoansi by the plural form in their own language. The -*si* is the plural indicator. Happily, this is not the case for other groups, or we would have *Naron, G/wikwena* (G/wi people, literally 'people of the thorn forests') and so on, or for that matter, *G/wikxwisa*, the G/wi language, feminine singular, etc. (see Silberbauer 1981: 1–2). We could also have numerous singular, dual and plural, as well as gender-specific variants. The International African Institute's (1933: 479–80) nine-point recommendation on the spelling of 'African tribal names' does not seem to apply to the Ju/'hoansi. That recommendation, on the general elimination of African prefixes and suffixes, was approved by the National Executive in London and stood through colonial times, the independence of African states, the Second World War and countless other potential upheavals. Therefore, I shall follow convention and use Ju/'hoansi for the people, but Ju/'hoan for the language or for a single person. There are some exceptions, however: in some of his work, Richard Lee simply drops the -si, and Biesele occasionally does this too.

Towards the end of the chapter, I will also touch briefly on other Kx'a-speaking (Northern Bushman) groups. These are the people who live north of the Ju/'hoansi. Those who live to the south of the Ju/'hoansi call themselves ≠Au//eisi (≠X'au//'eîsi). Here I have given the spelling ≠Au//eisi, which is a fairly common usage, whereas ≠X'au//'eîsi is more correct phono-logically but not widely known. The usage !Xun, rather than !Xũ, simply follows the current trend for representing a !Kung nasalized -u with the symbol -un. So, in short, we have !Xun in the north (Angola and the far north of Namibia), then Ju/'hoansi in the middle (northern Namibia and north-western Botswana) and ≠Au//eisi in the south (Omaheke Region of Namibia and Ghanzi district of Botswana). In *Hunters and herders of southern Africa* (Barnard 1992a), I called these groups, respectively, !Xũ, Zu/'hoãnsi and ≠Au//eisi and used !Kung as the overall term for the three.

Even before modern anthropology, a plethora of writers passed either through !Kung country or nearby it, if only on their way to the Okavango or the Zambezi farther north. Among them were Sir James Alexander, Sir Francis Galton, Charles John Andersson, James Chapman, David Livingstone, Thomas Baines and Siegfried Passarge. The last is implicated in the infamous Kalahari Debate (see Barnard 1992b), and I shall explore the essence of that debate later in this chapter.

Studies of the Ju/'hoansi

Beginning in 1950, Lorna Marshall, Richard Lee, Megan Biesele, Edwin Wilmsen and many others have all worked with this group. I described the efforts of Lorna Marshall, an amateur ethnographer, and the professionals who followed in *Anthropology and the Bushman* (Barnard 2007a: 53–65). The general focus of ethnography has been on settlement and band structure, kin-ship, ritual and religious belief, among other things. The focus of my own work, particularly *Hunters and herders* (Barnard 1992a), has been on kinship, but I shall leave that mainly to the side here.

More important has been the ethnographic findings and on the debates that have emerged. Sahlins's (1974: 1–39) famous reference to 'the original affluent society' is well known in anthropology and does ring a chord to every anthro-pology student in the English-speaking world. Ironically his essay was actually written in France, where the phrase is not 'the original affluent society' but the French '*la première société d'abondance*', literally 'the premiere society of abondance' (Sahlins 1968). In light of this, it is interesting that James Suzman

(2017) entitles a semi-popular book on the Ju/'hoansi *Affluence without abundance*. Suzman also prefers the term 'Bushmen', rather than San, which is relatively unusual among specialists on ≠Au//eisi and Ju/'hoansi. It also contradicts his earlier use of San in the Regional Assessment of the Status of the San in Southern Africa, an EU-funded project whose results were published in 2001 (Cassidy *et al.* 2001; Felton and Becker 2001; Robins *et al.* 2001; Suzman 2001a, 2001b). The findings of these studies were detailed and cited a vast array of literature, and they were often critical of all the governments concerned. Both the South African, James Suzman, and the Canadian, Renée Sylvain (1999), worked in the Omaheke Region of Namibia, where a mixed population of ≠Au//eisi coexists with Herero and other groups. The impact of Herero settlement there, in what had before the War of 1904–1908 been Herero territory, cannot be underestimated. This is particularly true in that Herero keep cattle and Ju/'hoansi generally do not.

The two leading ethnographers are Lorna Marshall and Richard Lee. I rely here primarily on the fourth edition of Lee's (2013) *The Dobe Ju/'hoansi*. I regard this as the definitive source. Lee covers not only the ethnographic work of his own, but also a good deal of the material collected by his colleagues. It is important to note that the Ju/'hoan ethnographic literature is vast. It amounts to literally tens of thousands of pages, plus commentaries by non-ethnographers. This chapter can only be but a brief summary of that vast corpus. Even within anthropology Ju/'hoansi tend to dominate the ethnographic reports. As I have suggested, things like *xaro* and the naming system are not particularly common among Bushman groups. Most groups do *not* practise *xaro*, and the Ju/'hoan naming system occurs only among the Ju/'hoansi and neighbouring peoples, like the Naro and their immediate neighbours, Ts'ao or Ts'aokhoe and ≠Haba. Other groups have different naming customs.

Among recent writers on the Ju/'hoansi, Bradford and Hillary Keeney (2013) have done interesting work. They are both specialists in spiritual healing. I say 'recent writers', but their earliest work in Bushman studies dates from 1995. Much is on the popular (or populist) side, but it is intriguing nevertheless for what it reminds us of the lost spirituality of the Western society (for example, Keeney 2002, 2015). As they put it (Keeney and Keeney 2013: 76), 'A search for the "correct" interpretation of Bushman stories misses the point.' Here they are following Biesele (1993) and several other ethnographers both of Ju/'hoansi and of other groups in their concern with flexibility in interpretation. Keeney and Keeney emphasize the transformation of society between the First Creation and the Second Creation. The latter marks separation and then the reincorporation of individuals, not only in stories but also in things such as the medicine dance and female initiation. In essence, they begin with the Second Creation, which defines 'normal time'. First Creation harks back to a time when there was no death and animals and people were one. This was the time of the prevalence of *n/om*, the spiritual force that is virtually undefinable. We shall return to *n/om* later, but first let us take on more mundane matters.

Environment, Settlement and Politics

Lee (2013: 42–3) writes: 'My first full day of fieldwork had already taught me to question one popular view of hunter-gatherer subsistence: that life among these people was precarious, a constant struggle for existence. My later studies were to show that the Ju/'hoan in fact enjoyed a rather good diet and that they didn't have to work very hard to get it.' In fact, he estimates that only twenty to thirty hours in subsistence activities are required per week. Of course there is variation through the year. October, and the end of the dry season, is said to be particularly difficult, but even then there is an abundance. The food inventory consists of 106 edible plants (including the highly nutritious and abundant mongongo nut): fruits, nuts, berries, edible gum, roots and bulbs, greens and melons. Reliance on meat, however, would be much more precarious.

The seasonal cycle is divided in five seasons (Lee 2013: 31–8). The first is the spring rains. This is October and November, which is a time of lightning displays (among the most brilliant in the world) and light rainfall. The second, December to March, is the main rainy season. This is a time of major animal migrations, and groups are widely dispersed among waterholes. Then there is a brief autumn period, in April or May, when there is plenty of food, including mongongo nuts. The cool dry season follows and lasts until late June. The spring begins around August, and at this hotter time game animals are both sluggish and abundant. Droughts are common, but in good times there is little need to fear a lack of food. Ju/'hoansi vary their habitation according to need. In the wet season people are scattered and occupy hamlets as small as about three huts, or sometimes rather more. In the dry season (May or June to September or October) they tend to live near permanent sources of water in groups of twenty to fifty people, or eight to fifteen huts. Common today are villages beside cattle posts. Former migratory lifestyles have given over to these more permanent settlements, and the pattern today (and to some extent since around 1970) has been to occupy an area around a Tswana or Herero village. San living this lifestyle place their huts in a crescent by the entrance and facing the cattle, whereas the traditional pattern favoured a circle with no livestock in the vicinity.

As readers may have noticed, the traditional Ju/'hoan seasonal cycle, in terms of aggregation and dispersal, is nearly the opposite as that of the G/wi. This is because the G/wi have no surface water at all in the dry season, and the Ju/'hoansi have relatively ample supplies. There are other, more minor differences: G/wi dispersals are as family units, and Ju/'hoan dispersals as larger units (see Barnard 1979a; Cashdan 1983). The seasons are the same; it is the supply of water that creates these differences. In other words, each group maximizes their use of water, and their seasonal cycle is dependent on its availability. In a sense, politics among the Ju/'hoansi works very well indeed. As Richard Lee (1990: 237) has put it: 'Foraging societies organized in bands can function very well in groups of twenty-five to fifty with economically active members working two to four hours a day. Simple farmers can be seen to operate along similar lines. Doubling the population to 100 begins to introduce logistical problems. Who is going to hunt and gather where?'

These numbers may seem arbitrary, but this is precisely what Lee found out in his input–output analysis in the early 1960s and confirmed in later work. Marshall (1976: 308) concurs: 'The !Kung live in a kind of material plenty . . . '. They use what is available, give fairly freely and generally want for nothing. Of course drought can be a problem, but lack of time is not. The constraining factor is the availability of land, as well as water. Hunting and gathering activities require large territories for the population size. They do not need lots of people. On the contrary, as Lee implies, a larger population would require a social organization that is ordered and hierarchical. This is why 'primitive commun- ism' can work for Bushmen in a way that it could not in other forms of society.

Beyond environment and settlement in the narrow sense, there is the subtle detail of how close one can sit next to someone and when to talk and when to listen. These, of course, are defined culturally. It depends too if in kinship one is a joking partner or an avoidance partner. These are not about literal joking or avoidance, but about kin categories (see Marshall 1976: 201–51). A Bushman camp is open and one can see almost everyone else who is present, but as one observer has stressed, speaking to someone sitting at another fire would be like entering a conversation with someone at another table in a restaurant. The rules about when to speak and when to stay silent are perhaps a bit more complicated. I have seen among several Bushman groups a tendency to talk more than one might expect in the West. It seems not to matter if anyone else is listening.

On the other hand, among some other hunter-gatherer populations, notably among the Mbendjele in central Africa, remaining silent for long periods of time is quite acceptable. Their choice of means of expression is interesting. According to Jerome Lewis (2009: 236–7): 'They mix words with sung sounds, ideophones expletives, whistles, signs hand signals, gestures, vocabulary from other people's languages, animal sounds, and other environmental sounds, sometimes in a single speech act.' I have not seen this among Ju/'hoansi, but it would not surprise me, in spite of the difference in environments. Certainly, among other desert-dwelling Bushmen there are elements of this in their speech patterns.

The definitive source on politics are the relevant chapters in Lee's (1979) *The !Kung San*. There is also an essay by Lee (1990) on 'primitive communism', which, he argues, is the form politics takes among the Ju/'hoansi. Like most hunter-gatherers, they practise minimal politics and have little time for authority figures, either within Ju/'hoan society or among others. Ownership of land is communal, and vested in a *n!ore* (Lee 1979: 333–69). *N!oresi* (the plural of *n!ore*) are traditional territories. They are also named groups, and there is evidence that in the past, that is, in the nineteenth century, they were exogamous. Kinship seems to have been more important then, whereas today it is land that is important. Groups are no longer exogamous, and one may inherit membership in a *n!ore* from either one's father or one's mother. There is also a system whereby groups maintain reciprocal rights to hunt and gather in each other's *n!oresi*.

Both Marshall (1976: 287–312) and Lee (2013: 236–8) have emphasized the fact that sharing and cooperation are important. Lee does this under the guise of science re-discovering social equality. More broadly, for example, hunters do not shoot their own arrows: they lend them to others. The 'owner' of a kill is not the person who did the killing, but the owner of the arrow. He shares the meat both within the band and with members of other bands.

One of the most significant papers on the Ju/'hoansi is Polly Wiessner's (2014) 'Embers of society'. She noted that night-time conversations concerned mainly stories (81 per cent) and myth (4 per cent), whereas stories made up only 6 per cent of daytime conversation. The dominant topics in the daytime were economic matters (31 per cent) and complaints (34 per cent). While she warns against assuming that these statistics are necessarily typical (since, for example, storytelling becomes dominant in larger groups), nevertheless the results are revealing and possibly of evolutionary significance.

Kinship and Exchange

Joking and avoidance relations have already been mentioned. A full description of Ju/'hoan kinship is given in Marshall (1976: 201–51), Barnard (1992a: 47–53) and a number of other sources, so here I shall concentrate just on some essential features of the system.

The Ju/'hoan system distinguishes lineal relatives from collaterals, just as the English system does. However, there are a number of differences: in English kinship there are no joking or avoidance categories. The mild tendency to avoid one's mother-in-law in English kinship is nothing compared to the strict categories one finds among the Ju/'hoansi. Essentially, this involves the literal avoidance of sitting too close to an avoidance partner or entering their hut, the lack of use of names in direct address to such individuals, avoiding asking for food or even in some cases of speaking to someone. The last is typical of relations between in-laws, both among Ju/'hoansi and in many other parts of the world. In addition, the famous case of the Ju/'hoan naming system has a profound impact on kinship. People are named after their senior relatives, and junior relatives bearing the same name are treated as equivalent. For example, if my grandfather is called Dabe and I bear his name, then I call anyone else with this name 'grandfather'. I call my little sister's namesake 'little sister', and so on. This regulates incest too, in that I am forbidden to have sex with my (classificatory) 'sister', just as if she were my real sister.

All this is the same as among the Naro, except that whereas in classical terms the Naro have a bifurcate-merging 'Iroquois' system, the Ju/'hoansi have a lineal 'Eskimo' one. In a sense, the Naro have it easier, since in their system grandrelatives are already in the right category. In the Ju/'hoan system the second-born child of a given gender needs to be re-categorized. That is, when one runs out of grandparents to name a child after, one has to use uncles and aunts instead, and the generations have to be reversed. An uncle, for example, becomes a 'grandparent', and a grandparent becomes an 'uncle' (see Barnard 2014). This is only from *my* point of view and only on that side of the family. My brothers and sisters still classify them as uncles and aunts. The uncles and aunts on the other side of my family are still uncles and aunts to all of us, while the generations are all reversed as need be: uncles and aunts become grandrelatives and vice versa. If it sounds confusing, it is! It caused the Marshall family untold problems early in their field research (see Marshall 1976: 227–42). The Naro system is obviously simpler for a child growing up within it, or for the Marshalls coming into the system from the outside. As in most Bushman kinship systems, they are universal. This means that ethnographers have to learn the rules for themselves. Ethnographers are participants, and not just observers. The joking and avoidance categories are regulated through the naming system, exactly as among the Naro. Names cycle down the generations, and Ju/'hoansi claim that the names originated with the first Ju/'hoansi.

There are some disagreements among ethnographers. One obvious one is Marshall's suggestion that all cousin marriage is forbidden. I am inclined to think Wilmsen (1989: 177–80) is right on this issue, however. It is not that there is a taboo against this, but that the naming system gets in the way. This is because since grandparents and grandchildren share the same names, then the grandchildren are quite likely to be forbidden. They are often terminological 'brothers' and 'sisters'. We see similar situations among the Naro, and in these cases too, one gravitates towards marriage with cross-cousins or with more distant cousins. This indeed, as Wilmsen suggests, does happen among Ju/'hoansi. The 'cousins' in the Ju/'hoan case are of course any cousins, since there is no distinction in Ju/'hoan between parallel and cross-cousins.

Among the most interesting things to come out of studies of the Ju/'hoansi has been the *xaro* (*hxaro*) system of exchanges of non-food items. These enable and cement rights to use each other's property among exchange partners (Wiessner 1982). In her doctoral thesis (1977: xlii), she notes that this is not merely a relation between two people but involves a chain of people, each of whom is under obligation to others along this chain. This has a wider signifi- cance in environmental use and economic and social relations. A huge set of social responsibilities is involved, as the system serves to equalize the distribu- tion of property: if someone does not have a pair of shoes, she can acquire one through *xaro*. If one does not have access to good hunting grounds, he can get this by relying on a *xaro* partner. Many anthropologists seem to think this custom is widespread among San, but in fact it is fairly unique to Ju/'hoansi, Naro and closely related groups. It just seems widespread, perhaps because it is so well adapted to San culture.

All this said, in fact there is trouble afoot. Janes Suzman, in particular, argues that the system seems to be breaking down due to changes in land tenure. This is especially true around Skoonheid, his main research base: 'The loss of spatial stability as a key constituent of how Ju/'hoansi constructed relatedness to one another meant that kinship was no longer the principal means by which Ju/'hoansi claimed access to resources or property' (Suzman 2000: 119). I would suggest that kinship remains central but that its dynamics are indeed changing. I have visited Skoonheid, and it is a strange place. Perhaps it is not typical. The situation there is perhaps analogous to the of the 'farm Bushmen' of Ghanzi that Guenther (1973) has described, rather than to the more typical Naro groups whose description makes up the bulk of Guenther's work.

Spirituality

Two concepts that are crucial to understanding Ju/'hoan spirituality are *n/om* and *!aia*. Translated literally, *n/om* simply means medicine, and *!aia* means trance. Yet, it is a bit more complicated than that. *N/om* can refer to anything out of the ordinary, for example, energy or power, some special skill, or menstrual blood, sorcery, medicinal herbs or the vapour trail of a jet plane. It is said to 'boil' in the stomach, and to be a bit like fire (Lee 2013: 143–5). *!Aia* is a related concept. It is a trance induced in order to heal. Mainly men have it, but women can possess this ability too, some- times in a 'weaker' form (see Lee 2013: 145–8; Katz, Biesele and St Denis 1997: 47–62). It is said to be like death, and is sometimes loosely translated as 'half death'. Physiologically, it seems to involve a 'boiling' of medicine in the stomach, with the heat inducing rapid breathing and very high blood pressure. Those anthropologists who claim to have experi- enced it say it is like waking from a deep sleep.

These concepts are probably what are most crucial to understanding the Ju/'hoan view of the world. However, we must, of course, not forget their deities. As with other San peoples, these do not often figure as prominently as we might expect. They are there nevertheless. Deities include the Great God, Old G≠ao. This is his 'earthly name', a name also found as an ordinary name among Ju/'hoansi. He also bears seven 'divine names', some of which also occur among other peoples, such as the Naro, and some of which are the names of medicinal plants believed to grow in heaven. Perhaps the most important name, though, is G//ãua. This term (with various spellings) is found among many Bushman groups, either for the Devil or Satan or (in the plural) for spirits of the dead (see, for example, Barnard 1988b).

All the deities have wives and children. Yet, as with other groups, the definitiveness of these is not always obvious. Gods do not really seem to be countable entities. Nor do they figure much in everyday discourse. Yet the similarities across ethnic boundaries are very striking, as are ways of talking about natural phenomena. Among the !Xun or northerly Ju/'hoansi, as among the //Xegwi of South Africa and the Cape Khoekhoe, the moon is seen as a divine figure or a manifestation of the (main) deity. For this reason the term 'moon' is often capitalized. Among nearly all Khoisan groups, the moon (or Moon) is male, and the sun (Sun) is female. This is not simply a matter of grammatical gender but an expression of belief in gendered aspects of lunar and solar being.

These occur, for example, in the well-known though not very well-explained mythological tale of the origin of death. This occurs in the story of the Moon and Hare (note the upper-case designations). Essentially, the Hare's mother is found sleeping, though the Hare thinks she is dead. If the Hare had accepted the Moon's view that she was merely asleep, all would have been well. But the Moon becomes angry and strikes the Hare. This explains the Hare's lip. It also, supposedly, explains the fact that death will come to all humanity. By contradicting the Moon, the Hare brought death (Barnard 1992a: 83–4). I know this is hardly clear from this account, but such is the way of Bushman folklore: stories are often told only in part, largely because virtually everyone already knows them!

Commenting on Ju/'hoan stories, though with much wider implications, Biesele (1986: 165) has written:

Oral traditions are preserved tenaciously, but they are also preserved flexibly. They bear the stamp of the ages, of having 'been received', but they also bear the stamp of successive new individuals and of the concerns of their times. Herein lies their power as adaptive tools: they are constantly creating the present for contemporary individuals but also giving it the sanction of seamless connection with the remote past.

She goes to reflect on the implications of her comment for making evolutionary sense of the inevitable *incompleteness* of anthropologists' folklore collections. In other words, everything makes sense if we imagine it within a wider time frame, yet stop looking for linearity when there is none. I would only add that the time depth is so great that that it spans geographical locations over virtually all of southern Africa: Guenther records virtually identical myths among /Xam and Naro; Biesele among the Ju/'hoansi records nearly the same story as Vierich among the Kua. The latter has moral implications too, as it teaches children that they must not take the death of a hunted animal for granted, but respect it for giving up its life so that humans may eat (Vierich 2018a: 10). Indeed, this moral sense is characteristic of Vierich's (for example, 2018b) recent work, as she confounds the stereotypes we have learned to accept about what constitutes 'progress'. My central point here, following Biesele, is that evolution requires adaptation, and it requires flexibility too (see also Biesele 1978; Barnard 1986b).

In the past, the various Ju/'hoan groups practised both male and female initiation ceremonies. This is well recorded in early accounts by Schapera (1930: 118–22, 124–5), as well as Louis Fourie, Hans Kaufmann and Dorothea Bleek. Male initiation involved fasting, dancing and hunting magic, including tattooing. Initiates also had to avoid unmarried women. Female initiation, as among the Naro, involved an Eland Bull Dance. All these rituals, where they occur, are remarkably similar across the Kalahari. It would seem that whereas there may be great diversity in matters of use of the micro-environments that characterize Bushman lands, in matters of religious belief and practice there is a unity. This is borne out especially in a recent article by Mathias Guenther (2017). He concentrates on hunting, but his main point is that in the context of a New Animism, elements of ritual, myth, rock art and mysticism blend. This is true of the /Xam, but it is also true for the Ju/'hoansi. Lewis-Williams is also writing in this vein, in a way updating the Old Animism of the Bleek and Lloyd material to take in newer perspectivist ideas: instead of thinking like an outsider, learn to think more like a Bushman.

The distance between the 'primal time' of shamanic experience and that of San mythology is slender: the two seem to be in communication with each other (see Jolly 2002). San are flexible when they need to be. For example, the eland is very rare in the northern Kalahari, so Ju/'hoansi often substitute the gemsbok for the eland in their symbolic domain (Biesele 1993: 94–7). Indeed, Biesele's (1993) *Women like meat* and much of Guenther's work is full of discussion of metaphor within folklore. This enlivens their text, of course, but it also offers a picture of how San thinking is creative it its expression of meaning. It may also be associated with sympathetic magic (see Thackeray 2018) and even an alteration of gender (Power and Watts 1997): when females are represented as men and males as women.

There is some material published on Ju/'hoan music. For example, Emmanuelle Olivier (1998, 2001) comments on musical categories and social contexts of performance. Performance includes the use of voice with hand-clapping (for example, in the medicine dance), the use of voice alone and more rarely the use of instrument alone. As Olivier notes, the significant thing about Ju/'hoan music is that it is closely bound to sociality, symbolic behaviour and religion. These cannot be separated in their understanding, and the same is largely true for Bushmen in general. Olivier has documented this among several groups, though mainly on the Namibian Ju/'hoansi. The musicologist (and viola player) John Brearly has also done recordings in the Kalahari among a number of Bushman groups.

Putting it all together, music along with ritual, folklore and belief about the heavens are all part of a culturally rich expressive framework. It is very difficult for us to understand this, simply because most of us are not Ju/'hoansi. Of course, the Ju/'hoansi have medicine dances as well, and with creativity and the variations described by Richard Katz (1982), Megan Biesele (1993), Lorna Marshall (1999) and Richard Lee (2013: 137–53), among others. Some members of other groups, like Naro, G/wi and !Xoõ, claim that Ju/'hoansi have the best 'medicine' of all.

Peacefulness and Growing Old

Ju/'hoansi and other Bushmen are well known for their apparently peaceful nature, although this is tempered by a high degree of sexual jealousy and personal violence. They are not quite the harmless people they were once depicted as (see E. M. Thomas 1959, 2006). However, they are good towards the elderly, and age carries a great deal of respect (Rosenberg 1990).

The issue of violence is well covered in Lee's (1979: 370–400) major monograph, as well as in numerous earlier and subsequent papers and chapters (for example, Lee 2013: 121–30). In another paper, by Mathias Guenther (2014b), there is an interesting explanation for this violence. He blames it not on the San themselves but on their reactions to the intrusion of settlers, who in the nineteenth century came to dominate the San. The result was raiding and feuding among San groups. Before this, he argues, they had been comparatively peaceful. Lee (2014) in the same issue of the *Journal of Aggression, Conflict and Peace Research* is in agreement. He suggests that for the 7,000 generations between the emergence of *Homo sapiens* and the Neolithic, humans were at peace with one another. However, it is not quite clear to me, in comparing his 1979 and 2014 statements or indeed that of 2013, the degree to which it is true that Ju/'hoansi are nonviolent. Witness this comment from 1979, in response to the question 'And how many men have you killed?' (Lee 1979: 399–400):

Without batting an eye, ≠Toma, the first man, held up three fingers; ticking off the names on his fingers, he responded: 'I have killed Debe from N≠amchoha, and N//u, and N!eisi from /Gam.'

I duly recorded the names and turned to Bo, the next man. 'And how many have you killed?'

Bo replied, 'I shot //Kushe in the back, but she lived.'

Next was Bo's younger brother, Samk"xau: 'I shot old Kan//a in the foot, but he lived.'

I turned to the fourth man, Old Kashe, a kindly grandfather in his late sixtees [*sic*], and asked: 'And how many men have *you* killed?'

'I have never killed anyone,' he replied.

Pressing him, I asked: 'Well then how many men have you shot?'

'I have never shot anyone,' he wistfully replied. 'I always missed.

The prospect of old age for Ju /'hoan and !Xun-speaking groups has been the subject of several studies too, for example in Lee's (2013: 101–20) chapter in *The Dobe Ju/'hoansi*. Lee's chapter there is actually attributed to his wife and colleague Harriet Rosenberg, in recognition of the collective effort that went into it. Conversely, Takada (2015: 112–58) looks at the socialization of children farther north, among the !Xun. Here the question of survival in the changing socio-economic circumstances of !Xun and Ju/'hoan life is at the heart of discussion. At first, the nomadic lifestyle of the decades before the Second World War gave way to a more settled existence and brought closer contact with Ovambo. This was heightened through missionary influence, and differences between !Xun and Ju/'hoansi occurred. For example, !Xun children tended to be raised more by co-residing older children, and Ju/'hoan children more by adults. Dependence on subsistence by agriculture affected birth rates, family organization, settlement patterns more broadly, as well as subsistence and a host of related things. This has been well described, for example, by Marjorie Shostak (1976; 1981) in her work on Ju/'hoan childhood and growing up. This is done through the words of one Ju/'hoan woman who had lost many of her relatives through various illnesses. Shostak's work was unique in that it brought to the reader's attention not only the precariousness of living in the Kalahari, but also its advantages. Her subject, N≠isa, tells much of the story herself through her memories of lost lovers, siblings and others.

After a diagnosis of breast cancer, Shostak (2000) bravely returned to Botswana for further work with N≠isa. A recent cross-cultural study by a group of Cambridge psychologists (Lew-Levy *et al.* 2018) has also explored aspects of growing older, particularly with regard to gendered behaviour, and there is no doubt that the change in subsistence has significant effects (see also Garfield, Garfield and Hewlett 2016). How long San can continue with their egalitarian lifestyle in light of such changes is an open question. Although school teachers in the Kalahari may claim they would seek help from local Bushman healers if they needed it, still they regard the Ju/'hoansi as 'primitive' (see Katz, Biesele and St Denis 1997: 70–83). There seems to be little attempt to bridge the gap between cultures here, and much the same is true in schooling for San throughout southern Africa. It is worth further reflection with regard to the debates surrounding Kuper's (2003) *Current Anthropology* article, and indeed my own article in *Social Anthropology* (Barnard 2006). On every

continent, who is indigenous and what is indigeneity are extraordinarily difficult to define (Saugestad 2001b). One thing that seems not to be allowed is
schooling. This is ironic in that nobody in my experience appreciates book
learning as much as a Bushman does. It is not for nothing that they have as great
a knowledge of plants and animals as Western botanists and zoologists (see Lee
1979: 464–73; Blurton Jones and Konner 1976).

The Ju/'hoansi in Film

Film depictions have also been prominent, as at least one ethnographer, John
Marshall, took to film while his sister Elizabeth Marshall Thomas (1959) wrote
books, his father, Laurence Marshall, did still photography and his mother,
Lorna Marshall, wrote the classic ethnographies. John's best films perhaps are
the mainly short ones, ethnographic portrayals like *Bitter melons* or *A joking
relationship*, both made in the 1960s. Much more famous was his *The hunters*
(J. Marshall 1957), now a classic, although Marshall (2012 [1993]: 35–41)
himself later seemed to have regrets about the way in which it was done, both in
terms of filming technique and in terms of its overly romantic portrayal. That
film shows the chasing and the killing of a giraffe. The portrayal is certainly
romantic, and as Marshall later admitted it has elements of *Moby Dick* in it. It is
not true though that John killed the giraffe himself, although the giraffe did die
after having been chased for five days. The 16 mm colour film he used was
cheap at the time, and he claimed to have used about half a million feet of it
(more than 150 kilometres) in his efforts to show the Ju/'hoansi both in
ordinary activities and in larger efforts, as in his famous *The hunters*.

It could be argued that Marshall was responsible for an academic genre as
well as a theoretical perspective of realism in film studies (see also Strong
2015; Tomaselli 2017). This is especially true in his later films. It is also borne
out in Jay Ruby's edited volume *The cinema of John Marshall* (Ruby 2012
[1993]) and in a special double-issue of the journal *Visual Anthropology*,
volume 12, numbers 2–3 (Tomaselli 1999). Each contains a significant number
of articles by Ju/'hoan ethnographers, including (among others) Marshall and
Biesele, as well as critics like Tomaselli. Whatever the truth in that, Marshall
was indeed using film for the purpose of *learning* to use it. It was at first a kind
of hobby to him, although it did later become his career. The beauty is that he
was not only passionate about it but also skilled in making film and in explaining and analysing his own efforts.

A list of films on San is contained in the special issue of *Cultural Survival
Quarterly* (Anon. [c] 2002: 57). Photography has been equally important, as
work by Ilisa Barbash (2016) makes clear. She documents the Marshall
family's expedition photography, and equally its interplay with anthropology,
in the 1950s and 1960s.

The ≠Au//eisi (≠X'au//'eîsi)

In a sense we are testing the limits of the notion of an ethnic group here. ≠Au//eisi were among the first groups identified. They may call themselves ≠Au//eisi (or more accurately, ≠X'au//'eîsi). In fact, they were usually labelled 'Auen' in the early literature (the same word, with the clicks deleted and with the Naro suffix rather than the ≠Au//ei suffix). 'Auen' was the term Schapera (1930) employed. Or they were called Makoko or Makaukau by neighbouring groups. Makoko is the same word again, but with a Bantu prefix, sloppy pronunciation and no orthographic clicks. In reality, they speak virtually the same dialect as Ju/'hoansi. There really is no difference.

This reflects a story about Bushman ethnicity. The late Ernst Westphal (pers. comm.) once told me that he had played recordings of Ju/'hoansi to ≠Au//eisi: they recognized them as identical and even claimed to know the speakers. The difference between these groups would seem to revolve solely on self-perception. The spelling ≠X'au//'eîsi, preferred by Rainer Vossen, is no doubt more technically correct, but the word ≠Au//eisi is already fairly well known in the literature. At that time I wrote *Hunters and herders* (Barnard 1992a), the orthography had yet to be regularized. This was done by the late Patrick Dickens, and the !Xun (who do seem to be slightly different) had yet to attract their own ethnographer. They have since been the subject of work by Takada and others. In short, ≠Au//eisi means southern Ju/'hoansi. These are the same Ju/'hoansi reported on in James Suzman's ethnography. It may seem a trivial issue, but San are in a sense *not* all the same, and in another sense they *are* all the same.

Tsumkwe at 50

In 2010, a small team headed by Richard Lee (2013: 215–27) completed a survey of the Namibian village of Tsumkwe, near the Botswana border. They presented this as a report to the Nyae Nyae Conservancy and as a paper at the 2010 meeting of the American Anthropological Association in New Orleans. Fifty years before, the Native Affairs Department of the South African administration had dug a borehole, built a gravel road and resettled about 1,000 Ju/'hoansi. These people then lived scattered at twenty-five waterholes across 10,000 square kilometres. The administration also provided schooling, health services, a missionary and rations.

Among their findings, at the time of the survey thirty out of ninety-eight ate mainly wild foods, and about the same number ate mainly store-bought foods. Eighteen lived equally on both. More interestingly, in 1968–1969 just over half (50.8 per cent) said they liked living in the bush, and most of the rest said they did not. In 2010, 96.9 per cent preferred the bush. Their reasons were equally interesting. Food was more plentiful in the bush than in a town. The bush was quieter, and town was full of alcohol-related bickering. Town life was boring and at the same time stressful, whereas the bush was the place of cultural tradition, 'who we are as a people'. Thus two generations of life at Tsumkwe seem to have inspired a 'back to the bush' mentality. This is brought out too in the recent monograph by Salomé Ritterband (2018) *Tracking indigenous heritage*. Tourism brings in income and at the same time encourages the revitalization of tradition. In this sense, touristic performances are indeed a complement, even if a risky one, to formal schooling: 'staged authenticity' in a living museum (see Ritterband 2018: 157–236).

Lee and his colleagues are cautiously optimistic about the future. In spite of their extreme material poverty, it is still too early to tell what will come next for the Ju/'hoansi at Tsumkwe. They are a contradiction: they retain values of personal liberty, gender equality and a reverence for 'the bush'. They value both the healing dance and their newfound Christian ideology. They have made a successful transition to the mixed economy, and HIV/AIDS has not been as bad as had been predicted – partly because their diet is still a relatively healthy one. Lee's (2018) most recent study seems to bear this out. Foraging persists, and there is little sign yet of it being replaced by a market economy. That said, of course there has been trade for over a century. Lee (1998) writes, for example, of life before his own research, when Ju/'hoansi first encountered cattle and iron cooking pots. They had used clay ones before that. Life has certainly improved since earlier times, but Ju/'hoan existence remains, by their own choice, one of hunting and gathering.

A recent commentator on the Marshall family's research has been the museologist Ilisa Barbash (2016). She notes (2016: 195) that the Ju/'hoansi the Marshalls knew initially had no knowledge of or interest in photographs. Their lives were 'highly portable', but those of their descendants are very different. Whether they choose to hunt and gather or not, they now have (or will soon have) access to digital photographs. With these, they can preserve their collective memories.

The Kalahari Debate: A Very Brief Comment

This is not the place to comment to any great extent on the Kalahari Debate. However, let me summarize very briefly.

The main part of the debate was a spat between two German writers: Gustav Fritsch (1872, 1906) and Siegfried Passarge (1905, 1907). Lee (1998: 67) makes a passing comment on the debate, if only to reiterate his own strongly held position: the Ju/'hoansi are still here through *resistance* to change. The debate was resurrected by Edwin Wilmsen in the late twentieth century, and it still continues. Essentially, Fritsch held that Bushmen lived in small bands and in relative isolation from the outside world. Fritsch (1880) also believed that Bushmen were Africa's original race, living *prior to* humans, and that they were incapable of ever learning a European language. Passarge saw great diversity among them and heavy contact and influence from Bantu-speaking herders. Fritsch's side later became labelled as 'traditionalist', and Passarge's as 'revisionist'. Of course, it is more complicated than that, and there have been a great many commentators through the years (see also Barnard 1992b, 2007a: 97–111). The best commentary though is by Robert Gordon (1992). It does pre-date the debate proper, but certainly it sets the scene on what was to come. It also attempts to convey the stark reality of militarization in the face of differing images of 'the Bushman' in the 1980s and 1990s.

The modern form of the debate was ignited by several publications, the most significant of which was Wilmsen's (1989) *Land filled with flies*. This portrays a revisionist picture: Bushmen are not only in contact but subservient to their more powerful neighbours. There really are no 'real' Bushmen any longer, the story goes, and there have not been at least since the 1890s when Passarge recorded the devastation caused by the Rinderpest epidemic. This viral disease affects cattle. It swept through eastern and southern Africa at that time and affected not only cattle but also wild animals. The modern form of the debate, sometimes called the Second Kalahari Debate, was played out mainly through the journal *Current Anthropology* (for example, Solway and Lee 1990; Wilmsen and Denbow 1990; Lee and Guenther 1991, 1993). Among these articles, for example, is Lee and Guenther's (1991) 'Oxen or onions'. The title refers to what is written in the journal of Swedish explorer Charles John Andersson, who had such bad handwriting that the word 'onions' could not be deciphered. Did the nineteenth-century Ju/'hoansi possess cattle? Or does the reference refer rather to Kalahari onions? The word is 'onions': Wilmsen misread Andersson's rendering. He also misread a map, which places Andersson much nearer Ju/'hoan country than he actually was. Which side won? On these specific points, it is difficult to conclude that the traditionalists have the upper hand. On the general point though, the jury is still out.

Wilmsen (2003) has more recently hit back with a very extensive polemic in defence of *Land filled with flies*, its maps, the details of Andersson's (see 1856, 1861) travels and so on. The debate does seem to have subsided for now, although Wilmsen and his collaborator James Denbow have plans for further work that is of relevance. The Western image of Bushmen has been moulded by such imagery for many centuries, and it shows little sign of ending (see, for example, Barnard 1998a). But let a Ju/'hoan have a final say. The epigraph in Salomé Ritterband's (2018: 7) *Tracking indigenous heritage* is from Tilxo Dabe. It reads: 'I don't want our culture to change. I want the children to know both: they must know how to read and write. And at the same time, they must also know how to hunt and how to gather.' This perhaps expresses the dilemma between seeking modernity and accepting tradition: Bushmen want both.

Further Reading

The best book on Bushmen or San is undoubtedly Lee's (1984) *The Dobe !Kung*, retitled *The Dobe Ju/'hoansi* (1983), third edition (2003), fourth edition (2013). Each edition is, of course, updated and reflects changing circumstances for this people as well as containing additional chapters and some new photographs. The fourth edition is 294 pages long, in addition to preliminary material. There is also a more succinct, and now dated, version within Bicchieri's book *Hunters and gatherers today* (Lee 1972).

Among other sources, I recommend Marshall's (1976) *The !Kung of Nyae Nyae* and her (1999) *Nyae Nyae !Kung beliefs and rites*. These are classics, and the latter supplements the former with excellent material on Ju/'hoan religion, much of it previously published in the journal *Africa*. The best recent book is Biesele and Hitchcock's (2011) *The Ju/'hoan San of Nyae Nyae and Namibian independence*. This is particularly good at bringing up to date issues of leadership, as well as social development in independent Namibia. Another interesting text is Suzman's (2017) *Affluence without abundance*, which is recent and describes well the dilemma its title suggests. For anyone requiring the details of subsistence, rainfall or demography, there is Lee's (1979) *The !Kung San*.

There is a special issue of *Survival International Quarterly*, vol. 26, issue 1 (Lee, Hitchcock and Biesele 2002a) that deals with many groups but concerns mainly the Ju/'hoansi. Several articles there are written *by* Ju/'hoansi. Ritterband's (2018) *Tracking indigenous heritage* provides as excellent, forward-thinking assessment of the potential for cultural tourism in Namibia. Another interesting source is Boris Gorelik's (2017) *Rooibos*, which considers the case of boiling water in the absence of iron pots. Finally, Waddell's (2018a, 2018b) *Bushmen* has some useful quotations from various sources on the Ju/'hoansi. It is written in the past tense, but hopefully his decision to do this will prove to have been premature.

9   Hai//om
Khoekhoe-Speaking San

The Hai//om are a linguistic peculiarity. They speak Khoekhoe, the language of the herders, but they are hunter-gatherers. Rather like the Naro, they have both Khoekhoe and Kx'a 'blood' and a few Khoekhoe customs, and this explains both their origins and their peculiarities. They are also known as ≠Akhoe or, more correctly, as ≠Ākhoe. (The macron in Khoekhoegowab indicates not merely a long vowel but a change of tone in a 'doubled vowel': either high to low or low to high.)

The Hai//om or ≠Akhoe are now well understood, thanks to the work of Thomas Widlok and Ute Dieckmann. I visited Widlok in the field in the 1990s and later examined his thesis. I met Dieckmann in Namibia in the 2010s. This chapter will focus on their work, but it will also deal with its implications, for example, in the management of Etosha National Park and in dealings between Hai//om and their northern neighbours the Ovambo. The Ovambo or Owambo, incidentally, call them Kwankala or Xwagga. The Hai//om are a Khoekhoe-speaking population, and this reflects an important aspect of their prehistory. Presumably, like the Naro, they once underwent a dramatic transformation through language shift. Some aspects of their kinship practices have, in fact, retained their Khoekhoe essence to a greater extent than among Khoekhoe themselves. The use of Khoekhoe names and the transmission of these through cross-descent name lines (male to female and female to male) is an obvious example (see Widlok 1999: 194–7). These are less prominent among Khoekhoe, and many Khoekhoe no longer have knowledge of them. It is also said that Khoekhoe do like revealing them to strangers.

The two main sources on the Hai//om are the ethnography by Widlok (1999) and the history by Dieckmann (2007). The former is a straightforward ethno-graphic treatment of Hai//om life, though with a slight emphasis on economic aspects. Widlok alternates between the terms Hai//om and ≠Akhoe in his description. In the thesis on which his book is based (Widlok 1994: 16), he quotes one ≠Akhoe as saying: 'The Owambo call us "Kwankala" and some-times "Xwagga", the Boers call us "Bosman, dom Bosman", and the Damara say "Saab ge" (He is a San). But we do not like these names. "Hai//om" is a name given to us by the Nama, and "≠Akhoe" is the name that was given to us by God. These are good names.' Dieckmann's text is a history, specifically on colonial times, and it is updated with material on conservation and on the present dispute on the ownership of Etosha Pan. Dieckmann (2009) has also written a short but very useful photographic guide that includes, among other things, information on material culture and on the seasonal cycle.

Earlier material includes, among other writings, important works by the medical officer Louis Fourie (1926, 1928). Fourie's work refers to earlier customs, although some of these (like the name lines) are still in practice. Since the group is Khoekhoe-speaking, the spelling of the name reflects this fact. Thus there is an unwritten glottal stop after the click, as well as the German diphthong /ei/ before the click. In other words, one occasionally sees the group name written Hei//'om. Other variants include Heikum and Hai//'omn, where the final -*n* is a plural indicator. The slanted lines in the click symbol are generally given as verticals (rather than slanted lines): ||. This is the custom in all Khoekhoe dialects.

Why Do These San Speak Khoekhoe?

In a sense, it is simply because they have long done so. As we saw in Chapter 7 with the Naro, linguistic flexibility is not particularly problematic in a multilingual setting. If only historical data existed we might know more, but the fact is that Hai//om are, at least until the twentieth century, virtually pure hunter-gatherers who happen to speak the language of the herders. It is a relatively distinct dialect, but that is to be expected: language always changes.

We do not know whether the Hai//om, like the Damara who speak a very similar dialect of Khoekhoe, were once herders. Certainly the Damara keep cattle and sheep. The Damara are traditionally blacksmiths and servants of the Nama. They were once known as ≠Nūkhoen ('Black people') or Bergdama ('hill people'). Neither, of course, are particularly accurate and reflect ethnic comparisons and former locations of residence (see Barnard 1992: 199–213). The idea of being ≠Nūkhoen seems to have seen a resurgence in recent times, as noted in some of Sullivan's (2017) work. The idea of being 'Bergdama', however, seems to remain taboo. Their preferred name is Damara.

There were in the past a number of cultural similarities between Damara and Hai//om. These included particularly the 'holy fire' and the 'sacred tree' (see Fourie 1928: 87–8). The fire was known literally as the *hai /ais* or 'tree fire' and the tree simply as the *!hais* or 'tree' (connoting peace, or in Damara meaning the entire encampment). Fourie's orthography here, incidentally, follows the German fashion (for example, *ei-* for *ai-*); Khoekhoe spellings were only updated in the 1970s. Even now, many individuals go back to the old

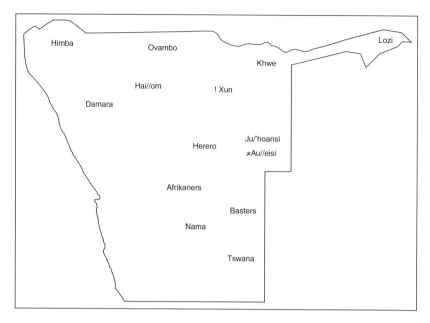

Figure 9.1 Ethnic groups of northern Namibia

orthography known through the Bible and in hymns. Fourie describes the fire and the tree of the Hai//om of Etosha at some length, and it is clear that these customs are derived from similar ones among the Damara whose territory lies to the immediate west (see map, Figure 9.1).

As the title of Widlok's (1999) book suggests, the Hai//om live to a great extent on mangetti (the Herero name for them) or mongongo nuts (the Tswana name). This nutritious nut (or bean) is often cited as the quintessential bush food, particularly for the Ju/'hoansi. In fact though, the group Widlok worked with live inside a particularly rich mangetti grove. The nuts are ubiquitous there, as well as nutritious: to them it is like a Garden of Eden. However, mangetti do not grow all year round. The peak season is April, and theoretically Hai//om could live just on these nuts. However, they prefer to travel north to exchange them with Ovambo for millet and other things. Obviously, Hai//om are San, but they share a great deal culturally with Damara, with Khoekhoe and with the Bantu-speaking Ovambo with whom they trade. To a great extent this trade is seasonal, with Hai//om often living with Ovambo in the winter dry season, and more independently in the summer wet season. This flexibility, though, is subject to circumstance.

Further Cultural Ambiguities

Male initiation ceremonies are similar to those of other Bushman groups, even if female ones differ. Male initiation is characterized by seclusion and tattooing, but females underwent some seemingly strange customs similar to those of the Khoekhoe. These included the denial of fire and the touching of each boy's testicles through a hole cut in the thatch. The idea was to prevent future infections as a result of menstruation (see Fourie 1928: 89–91). The same customs are also reported for the Khoekhoe. There are also similarities with the use of 'great names' that pass from father to daughter and mother to son. These alternating or cross-descent name lines are unique to Khoekhoe-speakers: Hai//om, Nama and Damara. Indeed, they are pretty much unique in the world, being found otherwise only in Papua New Guinea. They no longer, as far we can tell, occur to any great extent with Nama or Damara, and the actual names seem to be kept secret even among Hai//om (see Widlok 1999: 194–7).

Fourie (1928: 85) reports on the occurrence of bride capture, but adds that taking someone else's territory, rather than someone's wife, would be forbidden. His comment presumably refers to Hai//om, although it is not entirely clear here which group of Bushmen he describes. In any case, territory and territoriality are indeed of high importance for Hai//om. This is ironic given the dispute over who owns Etosha Pan (Dieckmann 2007). Ethnicity is always a complex phenomenon, and always constructed and relational (see Dieckmann 2007: 4–8). Almost nowhere is this more true than among Hai//om.

Etosha Pan

Perhaps the most salient feature of Hai//om social life is their proximity to Etosha Pan. Etosha is probably Namibia's greatest wonder, and indeed perhaps Africa's greatest wildlife reserve. But whose land does it lie in?

A recent source is Robert Hitchcock (2016), who has written on the continuing dispute between the government of the Republic of Namibia and the Hai//om over rights to Etosha. Etosha was in fact declared Namibian (at the time, German South West African) as early as 1907. Hithcock relates this fact in the context of challenges by incomers over land rights for the Ju/'hoansi. The dispute is very significant for the future of Namibia, where Etosha Pan has gained such notoriety because of its location as a major source of government revenue through tourism, as well as for its wildlife. In this context, it is worth noting that Namibia was the first country *in the world* to enshrine protection of the environment in its Constitution. Yet the Hai//om were forcibly removed from Etosha in 1954. Until that time, they were officially regarded as 'part of the conserved nature' of the reserve (Widlok 1999: 34).

In an intriguing paper, Thomas Widlok (2001) tries to account for the lack of comparativist interests in Namibian ethnography and even tries to take over ground previously occupied by the Kalahari Debate. Widlok attacks the positions of James Suzman (2000) who, Widlok argues, wants to turn anthropology into contemporary history, and Sian Sullivan (2001), who sees extreme reflexivity and deconstruction as a goal. Widlok's article is in essence a review article on Sullivan's paper and largely one that favours the representation of the Hai//om as an ethnic entity, against the revisionist understanding of Bushmen as merely an underclass. The latter is, of course, Wilmsen's (1989) view.

Of the many points Widlok makes, one that caught my eye is his remark on the lack of an anthropology department at the University of Namibia (UNAM). Instead, any anthropological interest has to be subsumed under other departments, and any comparative concerns at UNAM are distinctly sidelined. To some extent the same could be said of the University of Botswana, and the anxiety that Widlok suggests does imply that only South Africa among southern African nations has a claim to such comparative interests. The irony is that South Africa has this claim precisely because of its much longer history of involvement with Bushmen and the lack of prejudice against academics with comparativist interests. It is not without relevance that the Department of Social Anthropology at the University of Cape Town (UCT) has always been situated within the School of African Life and Languages (to give it its original name), founded by A. R. Radcliffe-Brown in the 1920s. Perhaps incidentally, that was the decade that saw the arrival of UCT's first black students. As far as I know, there are as yet no San in the university.

Is Herding Worthwhile?

The existence of the Hai//om does test the limit of the capacity of the land to support a herding lifestyle. In reference to the transition from the Mesolithic to the Neolithic in north-western Europe, I once speculated on differences between hunter-gatherers and herders (see Barnard 2007b). The differences depend on things like the accumulation of free time among hunter-gatherers versus the accumulation of goods among herders. Of course it is more complicated than this, but the gist is clear. Whether herding is truly worthwhile or not depends on any number of factors, and these are implied in Table 9.1.

In 1996 Widlok and I set about to compare the settlement patterns of Naro living on the Ghanzi farms and the 11,000 Hai//om living in various conditions in northern Namibia (Barnard and Widlok 1996) (Figure 9.2). Some live within the commercial farming area. This area is somewhat similar to the area where most Naro live. Some live in close association with Ovambo or with Damara, and others somewhat independently either in outlying areas or in centres of population. The latter pattern is becoming increasingly common.

Table 9.1 *Hunting and gathering versus herding livestock*

	Hunting and gathering	Herding livestock
Water	Fewer worries about water	Concern over water
Environment	Knowledge of the environment	Knowledge of herding skills
Food	Search for wild food	Search for grazing for livestock
Possessions	Lack of possessions	Chance to acquire possessions
Free time	Free time	Long working hours
Meat sharing	Sharing meat	Trading meat as well as sharing meat
Land and people	Need for individual space	Need of space for migration
Planning	Lack of planning	Long-term planning needed

Source: Based very loosely on Barnard 2007b: 16. On the impact of *cultivation*, see also Barnard 2007b: 17.

Figure 9.2 Northern Namibia

A brief outline of Widlok's text may be worthwhile. The first settlement was on communal land about 80 kilometres from the Angolan border. There, Hai//om assisted Ovambo in clearing fields and growing and harvesting millet and sorghum. This was from December or January until May or June. Ovambo, specifically Kwanyama, provided food and drink, while the Hai//om worked for them. The fireplace is for meeting visitors. It is called by various names in the Hai//om dialect, including *!hais* (men's fire) and *≠khoa-ais* (literally, elephant's place).

This refers to the medicine dance that is performed there. The layout is according to gender, in normal Hai//om fashion and probably borrowed from their agro-pastoralist neighbours. Food, notably mangetti, and beer are shared widely.

Then in July, we have the second pattern. The entire community moves to near their original waterhole. Each year there is a new campsite near that of the previous one, but the duration of settlement is for the remainder of the year. This is the season of hunting and gathering. Hunting is not difficult because foliage is thin, but the bulk of the diet consists of wild plants.

Another kind of settlement is found at the mangetti grove. At the height of the war between SWAPO and the South African Defence Force the population there was over 200, and that settlement has been occupied by Hai//om at least since the early twentieth century. A few men are employed in livestock management, but the bulk of the population is not. Some subsist by gathering food for the Ovambo, and they pay out with money that is used to buy alcohol. Three bands are recognized at the settlement, and the band or //gâus is the main point of identity. People there enjoy access to clean water, but residence is fluid.

Widlok's fourth example is of a commercial farm, where wage labour is the norm. Before the war farmers preferred Hai//om workers, whereas later they took on a preference for employing Ovambo or Kavango. There has also developed a new style of living, with the nuclear family taking on a greater significance. Private property is now tolerated and has to an extent replaced sharing. Some own donkey carts, have bank accounts and write their names or initials on possessions. Still, lending things is common, and universal kinship is practised. Clearly, these people are in a state of transition, but the //gâute (bands) remain important as foci of identity. Equally important is the !nus (territory), though this tends to mean the territory of the band cluster rather than the band.

So herding is worthwhile, though really only when both culturally and materially appropriate. It does take more effort to be a herder than to be a hunter-gatherer.

Mafisa and 'Inverse *Mafisa*'

In the 1990s, Widlok made an interesting discovery, which he called 'inverse *mafisa*'. *Mafisa* or 'loan cattle' is a common Tswana practice: poor people in Botswana (often Basarwa) herd the livestock of wealthy people (usually Tswana). In exchange for this service, the wealthy give the poor milk and sometimes the cattle or kids respectively of the cattle and goats they look after (Schapera 1984 [1953]: 28). They might also perform some labour for their masters, such as thatching. Obviously, the practice of *mafisa* serves to help equalize relative wealth.

However, 'inverse *mafisa*' (Widlok 1999: 113–19) is the opposite. It is a bit like keeping your money in the bank, and paying the bank interest to hold onto it for you! In other words, it makes no *economic* sense, although it does make *social* sense: it provides proof that the person has no apparent wealth. What happens is that poor San 'deposit' their livestock with wealthier Ovambo. The Ovambo then keep the livestock produced. This enables San not to be seen holding any animals, when in fact they have 'banked' them. There is also a vaguely similar practice in which San pay in mangetti nuts (as Herero call them) or mongongo nuts (as Tswana call them) for Ovambo to make fermented 'beer' (Widlok 1999: 100–6). The Hai//om do know how to make beer, but they prefer to have the free time rather than to spend time in the practice. This is a mark of what is of value to them: free time rather than the accumulation of money. They would probably have to give up any money in any case. Thus their values are maintained. The entire process of giving and of sharing is actually complicated, as Widllok (2017: 9–10, 65) later explained. Even *xaro* (*hxaro*) is complicated by its relation to the parties who are giving and receiving. Widlok likens *xaro* more to Trobriand *kula* exchanges than to the Northwest Coast *potlatch* or to the everyday sharing of food and goods among Ju/'hoansi. Indeed we know more about *xaro* than we do about such everyday sharing activities. Part of the point of *xaro* is that it encodes otherwise hidden rights to utilize resources.

I am not an economic anthropologist, but I have written a few papers on related issues, sometimes showing how opposite ways of thinking inform notions of sociality (for example, Barnard 2017). Of course Bushmen know that their values differ from our own, and sometimes the difference causes dilemmas: for example, when they have to choose between giving freely and accumulating (see again Figure 5.1). For them, this is not merely an ethical dilemma but a practical one too. The values of concern here refer to food and property, but is much the same in other spheres too: perceptions of land and the role of the state, the extent and nature of kinship (universal or judged by genealogical distance), perceptions of leadership and followership (for hunter-gatherers, followership is often valued more) and ethnic versus national identity (Barnard 1998b, 2001). It is not that they are better people than we are, but that their values drive them, just as ours do. That is why, as we saw in Chapter 5, hunter-gatherers can be said to think differently from the rest of us.

Clearly, Hai//om in a sense think differently from others. Yet *mafisa* and 'inverse *mafisa*' aside, what the Hai//om data suggest is that change is possible and sometimes appears in unexpected places. This is the lesson of Hai//om ethnography. These people are caught between different ideals, not quite Bushmen but surely not non-Bushmen either. Possibly there are lessons here for future generations of Bushmen or indeed for those who study their social lives (Figure 9.3).

Figure 9.3 Hai//om man with stick

The Mixed Economy

The Hai//om economy is 'mixed'. This works in several respects, and not least through things like 'inverse *mafisa*'. The complexity of sharing is shown in Widlok's (2017) book *Anthropology and the economy of sharing*. The social meaning of exchange, it seems, is ever present. Indeed, I hesitate to use words like 'exchange', 'gift' or 'reciprocity' in this context. Widlok warns against this.

Namibia gained its independence in 1990, and the ethnographic present Widlok (1999) refers to is the first six years after this. His base was at Mangetti West, a few kilometres east of Etosha. That site was inhabited by a few hundred Hai//om and by the Afrikaner family who ran the farm situated there. The Afrikaners, of course, live in European-style housing, while the

Hai//om live in huts made of grass or corrugated iron. Like the Ju/'hoansi, they have a staple food in the form of mongongo or mangetti nuts, which are more abundant there than in anywhere else on earth. Although the population stood at 300 at the time of the War of Liberation, that today is fewer, perhaps 200. Three groups are represented, and only those from the north call themselves, or even know the term, ≠Akhoe. For this reason, Widlok tends to call them Hai//om.

The old 'red line' of German colonial times continues to exist. It differentiated the traditional area of the Ovambo to the north and other groups to the south, although later it was simply a veterinary cordon. Still, this meant that Hai//om and others could not rear cattle for transfer across it. Early ethnographers like Louis Fourie (1928: 83) assumed that Hai//om were a mixture of Nama and !Xun or some unknown San group. Widlok (1999: 28–32) tries to debunk this idea on the grounds that Hai//om have no knowledge of it, although we do know that Hai//om do have Khoekhoe ancestry. The continuing dispute over land has to do with its commercial potential. The confusion over issues of settlement relates to the diversity of sites under review by different ethnographers over the last hundred years or so (Widlok 1999: 37–41). Every aspect of Hai//om life today is affected by the complexities of economic diversity: folklore, settlement patterns and getting along with Ovambo neighbours alike.

When I visited Widlok in the field one southern winter I was struck by the evidence of marked seasonality. This was at a time when Hai//om were generally maintaining their hunter-gatherer ways, but their temporarily abandoned horticultural sites told a different story. This was the dry season, and Hai//om were able to live traditionally. The abandoned sites were full of the debris of settlement: disused huts, grain, threshing floors and so on. Neither Hai//om nor their neighbours were present. They would return once the rains came again. However, subsistence flexibility, including hunting for profit, does occur when times dictate. Recall Silberbauer's (1981: 246) witnessing of good and poor tsama seasons. I remember similar ecological developments among the Naro in the 1970s and 1980s. Even social change is implicated, as Widlok (1999: 62) found out: life was different during the South African occupation of the 1970s and 1980s than later it became. Field research is only ever a snapshot in time. Occasionally, one can imagine a cycling as opposed to a shift. Meyer Fortes (1958) found this in West Africa some decades ago, when he *imagined* the changes that would take place if one could spend decades rather than years in one place: the life cycle of one family in the present resembles that of another in the past as it expands with births and contracts with deaths and with splits within families over a long period.

Widlok (1999: 62–106) documents the flexibility of subsistence regimes through environmental pressures and the role of outsiders (particularly Ovambo and commercial farmers) over time and through the seasons.

Rainfall is heaviest in December through February. Food-gathering is possible at almost any time of the year, and some Hai//om prefer to live by these means. Yet, both herding and agriculture are possible too. After the cutting of grass and poles in from November to January, Hai//om spend February to April in hoeing. Harvesting and threshing take place after that, with clearing the land beginning around August, then hoeing again. The mixed economy is normal for them, and they can utilize mangetti as they need it, or exchange mangetti for other things. Millet is commonly grown, and some prefer this as a subsistence base. Others prefer rice and maize, although growing rice in the Kalahari is rather more difficult. The trade in copper was once common, but since the early twentieth century trade in copper has been controlled by mining companies.

In a sense, Hai//om today are integrated into the Ovambo economy, but they maintain a very separate existence. Ovambo have headmen, chiefs and kings: Hai//om politics is flexible, and these categories are meaningless.

A Final Word on Settlement and on Ritual

Putting settlement and ritual together might seem an odd coupling. Yet there is a logic to it. Both are areas where one might expect tradition to be strongly maintained. As with band organization, cross-descent naming, the parallel/cross distinction and the patrilineal transmission of headmanship, tradition is maintained. However, certain aspects of settlement apparently common in the 1920s were no longer there in the 1990s. In Fourie's (1928) main article on 'The Bushmen of South West Africa' there is no Hai//om //gâus ground plan, but there is one in the preliminary version (Fourie 1926: 51). This is, of course, an idealized ground plan.

Key features have already been mentioned in passing: the men's fire and the dancing area. There is also a sacred tree or village tree, as there is among Damara. Indeed, the Hai//om band settlement bears a close resemblance to that of the Damara and also of the Herero (see Barnard 1992a: 205–7). Herero are different only for cultural reasons: because to be placed on the south side indicates inferiority, Herero tend to cluster towards the 'superior' north side. All these northern Namibian groups are in contact, and no doubt share similarities through cultural diffusion. Among Hai//om there were also gender divisions, and there were specific places for the headman, for widows and for visitors. In all these cases, the headman or chief occupied the easternmost hut, and the sacred or village tree was near the centre and livestock to the west. Widlok (1999: 135–78) discusses this at some length, and his conclusion is that adaptability and flexibility should not be underestimated. This does seem to be particularly true for Hai//om, and the similarities in the past would seem to be generally peculiar to northern Namibians, irrespective of language or any other cultural aspects. Other groups do keep other traditions though. For example, a Nama chief places his hut in the west rather than in the east. Such orientations may indeed reflect perceptions of hierarchy, as among Bantu-speakers (see Kuper 1982: 140–56).

The medicine dance is much the same as among other San groups (Widlok 1999: 213–58). Indeed, this does prove beyond doubt that Hai//om are indeed San. They are not simply Khoekhoe who have lost their language. Ovambo and members of other groups, in fact, seek out Hai//om as ritual specialists who can use their healing powers to good effect. Much the same is true of the female initiation ceremony. G/wi, Naro and Hai//om, and indeed Nama, all give priority to female rather than male initiation (Widlok 1999: 228–32). In other words, Khoe-speaking peoples regard female initiation as particularly important.

Plainly, Hai//om have their niche in an otherwise complex of ethnic relations in northern Namibia. As Widlok (1999: 265) puts it, 'In terms of language, economy, and ritual, no forager group in southern Africa has been completely isolated during the recent past. What needs emphasizing in the Hai//om case is that the foragers themselves have made efforts to decrease the distance, to link up with neighbouring groups by establishing common ground.'

Further Reading

The two leading texts are Widlok's (1999) *Living on mangetti* and Dieckmann's (2007) *Hai//om in the Etosha region*. These complement, rather than contradict, each other. Dieckmann makes the case that the rightful owners of the Etosha area are in fact the Hai//om. The case is presently under consideration in the Namibian courts. Fortunately, Namibia maintains a very fair judicial system, so there is a strong possibility that either the Hai//om will win or (much more likely) that a compromise can be found. Dieckmann's text presents a historical picture, whereas Widlok's is a straightforward and very interesting ethnography.

The comparison between Hai//om and Naro settlement patterns I wrote with Widlok (Barnard and Widlok 2006) illustrates the diversity found in each, especially for the Hai//om. I suspect that there may be lessons for the future in the Hai//om data, which illustrates well the possibilities of a mixed economy. This has been less successful, for example, among Ju/'hoansi. The difficulties for Ju/'hoansi though may be related to the small space on the land left for gardening. This and the lack of water, at Skoonheid in the Omaheke region, in particular, may make this less of a possibility there.

The G/wi, G//ana and Naro are all classic cases of 'Central Bushman' (to use Dorothea Bleek's phrase) ethnography. Other linguistically 'Central' groups include the so-called River Bushmen of the Okavango Delta. Their existence tests the limits of the idea of 'hunter-gatherers', as they are fishermen as well as hunter-gatherers. Their fishing lifestyle has had profound effects on their existence, as has the relatively recent impact of tourism in their ancestral lands.

A major ethnography on these groups was completed by 'Doc' Heinz (n.d.) in the late 1960s and early 1970s. I borrowed his typescripts and took notes on them in 1982. But very sadly, Heinz was murdered in the year 2000, and his manuscripts were lost. Only a very preliminary paper of his River Bushman material was ever published (Heinz 1969). Reading through the notes I took in 1982, I see that most of these were on kinship. Regrettably, I recorded little else. Yet happily, the main set of Heinz's River Bushman manuscripts has now been found, and these are in the hands of ethnographer Klaus Keuthmann. He has plans to publish them very shortly. They cover traditional cultural features of various River Bushman groups.

My student Michael Taylor did his PhD on River Bushmen, completed in 2000. He has now left academia and works for the World Food Program, but Taylor's own thesis sheds new light on the recent history of these groups. The Bushmen of the Okavango are a set of very similar ethnic groups who inhabit several parts of the Okavango swamps. They are dispersed and relatively isolated because of the terrain of that region. The Okavango is unique because it is a river delta that is entirely inland: it does not flow to any sea, but fills each year with water. The water comes from Angola in the north, the delta fills during the winter dry season and then the water evaporates. The seasonal cycle is the same as in the Kalahari (southern winter dry season, southern summer wet season), but because the filling and evaporation of the Okavango takes so long, the seasons are, in effect, reversed. Flooding occurs in the *dry* season. Indeed, the ecology of the Okavango delta is rather complicated (Biggs 1976).

Other work, apart from Heinz's, includes material on traditional life and on social development. The late linguist and ethnographer Oswin Köhler's (for example, 1966) work is also valuable. His major work (Köhler 1989) has recently been edited by Gertrud Boden and Anne-Maria Fehn and has now appeared in English (Köhler, with Boden and Fehn 2018). These are in the Kxoé or Khwe dialect, and are extensive and fully illustrated. Boden, incidentally, does not regard the Khwe as true 'River Bushmen', since they actually live in and around the Caprivi Strip to the immediate north of the Okavango (see also Boden 2018). In any case, Heinz's data and Köhler's on family and kinship do largely corroborate one another. Other material in the Köhler oeuvre concerns (among other things) religion and magic, healing, music, myth and legend. It is a spectacular source, albeit rather difficult to use, except for linguists who want to learn the language.

Community-Based Natural Resource Management

An important work is the thesis by Michael Taylor (2000). He contests the idea of 'development', or rather its indeterminate nature especially in light of the Botswana government's programme known as CBNRM (Community-Based Natural Resource Management). The river groups are not particularly different from each other, either in language, social structure or indeed in utilization of the environment, but we do now have sufficient records to make sense of these fascinating former hunter-gatherers on the fringes of the Kalahari.

Community-Based Natural Resource Management, or CBNRM, is a common phrase in Botswana and indeed in Namibia. The idea, and the phrase too, are common in other African countries as well. Michael Taylor (2000) jettisons the idea of 'hunter-gatherers' and views San ethnicity in the Okavango as a set of symbols. There is a loss of control over land and wildlife, key markers of San identity. Social development, Taylor argues, should be seen in this context and in light of the historical political and economic processes that have led to alienation. Taylor, by the way, is a (white) Botswana citizen and certainly not opposed to the goals of CBNRM. In the end he suggests that what needs to done is to refocus CBNRM to take better account of diversity, including the diverse goals of a variety of actors: the Basarwa (San) themselves as well as the government, conservationists and tourism industry. Another writer on CBNRM is the South African Julie Taylor (2012) who did similar work on the other side of the border in Namibia's Caprivi Strip. She also talks about the complexities of ethnicity, San identity and mapping among Khwe (her preferred spelling) and surrounding groups in that part of Namibia.

Michael Taylor began his field research in 1996. The timing was important, because at this time the Department for Animal Health and Production had just begun the unprecedented step of slaughtering all the 305,000 cattle in the district of Ngamiland. This was deemed necessary because of an outbreak of contagious bovine pleuropneumonia (CBPP), a lung disease that threatened the entire bovine population. Taylor (2000: 1) tells the story that when the Minister

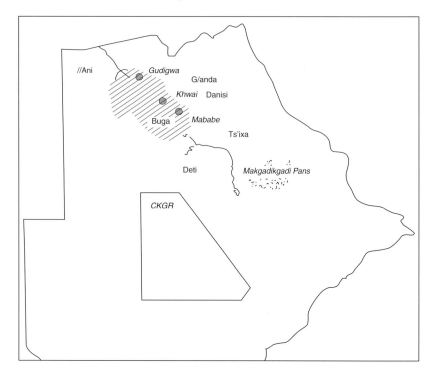

Figure 10.1 The Okavango swamps

of Agriculture arrived by helicopter: 'One elderly man I knew who had little else in material possessions other than the 400 cattle he had built up over the last five decades stood up and told the Minister that he might as well shoot his children; these cattle were his life's work. They spared his children, but shot his cattle.' Fortunately for the River Bushmen, *they* had virtually no cattle; their cattle had been wiped out because of the presence of tsetse flies in the area.

Taylor's thesis is based on fifteen months of field research. It covers his results from three villages, Gudigwa, Khwai and Mababe, all on the northern periphery of the delta. A map showing these villages is shown in Figure 10.1. Gudigwa is the farthest north. At the time of Taylor's fieldwork, it had a population of about 600. Khwai had a population of 360, and Mababe 290 (M. Taylor 2000: 3–11). Mababe is the oldest of the villages, and has been inhabited since at least the 1890s. However, in the past habitation was seasonal, whereas it is now regularly inhabited especially in the early rainy season. All the groups speak a closely related Khoe or Kxoe dialect: the term 'Khoe' refers to the subfamily, whereas 'Kxoe' (often spelled with an acute accent: Kxoé) tends to be used specifically for the dialects of the Okavango region. Basically, Khoe, Kxoe and Khwe are pronounced the same. Some ethnographers (such as Köhler) have preferred Kxoé, whereas others (such as Boden) have preferred Khwe. As Boden points out, there is both a dictionary and a grammar of Khwe (Kilian-Hatz 2003; 2008), and this was a reason for this choice.

As one of Taylor's (2000: 13) informants put it, it does not matter whether a person is called a Ts'ixa, a Danisani or a Shua: 'we are all of the same womb'. Central to their lives are, of course, their land, their livelihood and some degree of power over these. Bushmen, or at least these Bushmen, prefer to see their identity as in the present, rather than constructed on the basis of ancient claims. CBNRM might have been constructed as a conservation programme, but today it is perhaps best seen in the context of development. Indeed, ethnic identity has been affected by strange things, like the loss of clicks in various Khoisan languages. For example, in Ts'ixa, a dialect of eastern Shua: when the Ts'ixa moved to the western Mababe area they developed a close association with the Buga or Bugakhoe. This led directly to the re-introduction of clicks into the Ts'ixa dialect (Wilmsen and Vossen 1990: 23). On the other hand, Traill (1984: 16) writes:

[R]egarding the vexed question of 'names' of languages or groups, I can offer the following observations made by the informants I consulted at Shakawe, Khwaai and Mababe. The term *xuu khoe* is the generic term used by the Ts'ixa of Mababe to refer to all so-called 'Bushmen' (i.e. Masarwa or Basarwa in Tswana) and therefore to themselves as well. Whereas the Khwaai River groups called themselves *xuu khoe* or *buka khoe*, the Ts'ixa denied being *buka khoe* and emphasized their distinctiveness, somewhat facetiously I suspect, by referring to the Khwaai groups as *//gam dzira* (thorn birds).

Ts'ixa is an odd language. It has only about 200 speakers and is classified by some as standing in between the Eastern Khoe languages like Shua and the Western ones like Buga (Fehn 2017b: 122–3).

Khwai and Mababe are Bugakhoe settlements. In the nineteenth century, many people at Khwai were forced into servitude. Yet they remained loyal subjects of the Tawana chief. The Tawana hunted in the area in the late nineteenth century, but this became impossible when, in 1963, the Moremi Game Reserve was declared. That reserve occupies to this day a large part of the Okavango delta, and indeed the Tawana had a hand in its creation. The population not only has a complicated history but also has a complicated demography: there are a dozen ethnic groups listed in Schapera's (1952: 94) record of the 1946 census. These include Yei (13,261), Tawana (8,124), Herero (5,798) and Mbukushu (5,268), as well as 3,704 who consider themselves Basarwa. Some of the last were indeed subjects of Kgalagadi who, with

1,918 individuals, were the next most populous group. The population history of Ngamiland is well documented by the late Thomas Tlou (1985).

Interestingly, two papers (M. Taylor 2002a; Bolaane 2001, 2002) stress the idea that mapping is important to River Bushmen. Maitseo Bolaane notes that Basarwa drew maps in the dirt for her in order to indicate territorial possession. It would seem that Heinz's (1972) concern with this matter may not be exclusive to him, although I would still say that territoriality in other areas may not be quite as strong as he suggests. However, no two Bushman peoples could be more different than the !Xoõ and the Buga. The !Xoõ live in an extremely dry part of the Kalahari, whereas the Buga inhabit a vast swamp. The similarity is that both have to deal with pressures, whether these be of space (in the !Xoõ case) or of encroaching groups (for the Buga). Nor should we not be afraid that contact with outsiders, whether tourists or researchers, might have an effect: a point made by some of the latter in an assessment of the situation at Khwai (Damm, Lane and Bolaane 1998: 349–50; M. Taylor 2003).

Kinship and Social Life among River Bushmen

I mentioned earlier that in 1982 I was able to read and take notes on Heinz's (n.d.) River Bushman manuscripts. What they indicate is that the groups all had similar relationship terminology structures. These were, in fact, apparently quite similar to those of the G/wi and G//ana. As they are all Khoe speakers, this is quite understandable. The difficulty lay only in the fact that the River Bushmen seemed to be heavily influenced by surrounding groups.

All the River Bushmen distinguish parallel from cross-cousins, although the expected term for cross-cousins, n//odi- (with appropriate masculine and feminine suffixes), generally seems to be replaced with words such as djara or dzara. The rules of marriage are that only members of this category are possible as spouses, with a preference for marriage of a man with his matrilateral cross-cousins. Heinz later suggests that djara means 'playmate'. Heinz records among Buga the terms dashi for senior male cross-cousin, damashe for junior male cross-cousin and gwinke for female cross-cousin. The term for 'grandparent' is mamã, and for 'grandchild' //oli. The latter could indeed suggest a mis-recording of n//odi. His record is rather unsystematic, though, and I fear it cannot entirely be trusted. That said, Heinz's ethnography of !Xoõ is significantly better, although here too there are possible problems (see Barnard 2016c).

The terminology of the River //Anikhoe is similar to that of the Buga, and Heinz notes a close bond between grandparents and grandchildren, with avoidance between parents and children. He also records that relationship terms seem to have little to do with social behaviour. A boy is said to be 'afraid' of a sister. This is fairly standard among all San groups though. Yet there does seem to be some inconsistency otherwise, either in Heinz's account itself or in my rendering of it. He refers to the fact that /Xokhoe Buga or Bugakhoe consider themselves Mopani Bushmen rather than River Bushmen (they live in a mopani forest), and there are other details of location and ethnic group names that suggest either changes in individual preference or the transformation of the groups themselves and new identities. Small things are worth noting, such as the fact that some groups are said *not* to hunt with arrows. Presumably they hunt with snares instead.

Among other ethnographic details, levirate is said to be practised among some peoples, but denied among others. It is also the case that intermarriage with the Yei (Bayei) and Mbukushu will certainly have had its effects. Heinz reports that the River Bushmen have been in close contact with Yei and Mbukushu since around 1700. They owe allegiance to the Tawana chief, although as he is the Paramount Chief of all the Tawana (the north-eastern Tswana tribe) he is among their number. Some //Anikhoe have more than one wife, though no further detail is given. The girls' puberty ceremony is still in existence, but it is no longer significant. There do seem to be variants, however. The /Xokhoe Buga or 'Black Bushmen' live on the north bank of the river Kwaai, which lies immediately north of Moremi Game Reserve. Some groups cultivate land, and some of these practise shifting cultivation. The /Xokhoe are said to be patriarchal and patrilineal, with virilocal residence. The institutionalized headmanship is also transmitted patrilineally. There is no levirate or sororate among /Xokhoe, and food taboos are minimal. There is an abundance of game, but because of tsetse flies there is no animal husbandry.

Courtship is a little complicated among River Bushmen. A boy courts a girl by visiting her, preferably at night. When she agrees to marry him, the boy asks her father or 'uncle' (presumably the father's brother) to speak to the girl's father. He consults his daughter, and if she agrees then they can be married. To show that the couple or their parents are not short of possessions, the girl brings an ox. This is then slaughtered. The boy's parents prepare 'dowry' (bridewealth), and the boy sets out a mat for the couple. Eventually, the bride's parents leave her and go home. Two or three days later, the groom's sister takes an ox and accompanies the bride to her family. The bride travels from house to house within her own village as a sign of her freedom to visit. Bridewealth is paid at the birth of the first child: an ox or a goat, depending on wealth. It is not clear, however, to whom it is paid. There seems to be no other ceremonial activity. Normally, Heinz says, residence is virilocal, but occasionally it is uxorilocal. Most marriages are monogamous, though sometimes a man will take a second wife. There is no bridewealth for second marriages, though there is for first marriages.

In general, fathers are closer to their sons, and mothers to their daughters. Brothers and sisters maintain a 'fear' relationship. A joking relationship is said to occur only between a man and his father's *younger* sister. Heinz goes into some detail concerning rules of sitting: the wife sits to the left of her husband; sons sit to the right of their father; daughters sit to the left of their mother; and so on. There is also some discussion of demography and a bit on naming. There is gift exchange and meat sharing among brothers, the expected avoidance between in-laws and rules on when to tell and when not to tell sexual jokes. Among the /Andakhoe group bride service is practised, but does not seem to be common among other peoples. I hesitate to use the word 'peoples' here in any case, as the degree of clarity about these is not particularly obvious. Among most groups patrilineal descent would seem to be the norm. The Tzexa seem to have rules of naming, although not to the degree of the Naro or the Ju/'hoan systems.

Overall, in spite of a fair bit of detail on many small points, it is very difficult to make much of Heinz's River Bushman ethnography as a whole. To some extent these people would seem to be in the throes of change. They are also very mixed in descent and identities, and their dialects are very similar. It is, though, worth some reflection that we should not be too quick to reify our findings on other groups in a world that must be in constant change, both for River Bushmen and for San in general.

Beyond the Okavango

North-west of the Okavango is Angola, where at least until the 1920s lived a group called the Kwadi. We know very little about them, but they are known by several names: !Kwa/tsi, Cuepe, Ovakwepe, Coroca, Kuroca and so on. Thanks to recent work by Tom Güldemann and Rainer Vossen (2000: 119–20), based on data collected by Ernst Westphal (1971), we do know a bit about the Kwadi language. No one speaks it today, but from available accounts it is an SOV language (that is, subject-object-verb), like the Khoe languages. Westphal did fieldwork with a remnant population in 1965, and before that Father Carlos Estermann (1976 [1956]: 42) and António de Almeida (1965: 29) reported very small groups. It appears that, as with the N!aqriaxe, they were not teaching the language to their children, and with the devastation caused by tuberculosis and other diseases the Kwadi language is now quite extinct. Memories of it, however, probably survive among the descendants of this otherwise lost people. In addition to the Kwadi, whose land was to the western part of southern Angola, to the east lived !Xun, or !O !Kung as they are called. This group was known but not much studied by any ethnographers apart from a small handful in the Portuguese tradition (see Barnard 1992a: 42–3).

Needless to say, very little is known about these groups who live to the north. They must have been caught up in the war in Namibia, and apart from that greatly affected by food shortages and the political struggles of southern Angola. Angola became independent in 1975, and was transformed from Portuguese colonial rule to the one-party Marxist-Leninist system governed by the Popular Movement for the Liberation of Angola (MPLA). A new constitution in 1992 paved the way for elections. However, the civil war quickly began again. The leader of the opposition was killed in action in 2002, and constitutional government did not return until 2010. Obviously, this is but a very brief summary, but more detail is given, for example, in Martins Udenga's (2017) *Angola economy and political leadership*.

In *Hunters and herders* (Barnard 1992a: 131–3), I summarized what had been recorded on the Kwadi. I have visited River Bushman territory a couple of times, but unfortunately I never been to Kwadi country. I nearly did travel there in 1974, but alas never did. In *Hunters and herders*, I drew on a number of sources in English and in Portuguese. It seems that now no Kwadi-speakers remain, although they were once numerous. The Khoe-Kwadi language (as the language family is now known) they spoke resembled the dialects of eastern Botswana more than those now spoken in Angola. The Kwadi today seem to have given up a hunter-gatherer lifestyle almost entirely and subsist by cultivation and herding. They grow millet, yams and beans, as well as maize. They herd cattle, sheep and goats. Their rituals have elements of both those of their herding neighbours and of what was once, no doubt, their traditional way of life. The Kwadi wedding, for example, was reminiscent of that described by Dorothea Bleek (1928: 33–4) for the Naro. It was basically marriage by 'mock capture', involving both families. Male initiation, on the other hand, involves a collective circumcision ceremony. Female initiation is held at the time of a girl's first period and involves dancing, feasting and the requirement of food taboos, as well as being rubbed with fat.

The River Bushmen are unusual, even unique among San groups. They are still Bushmen, although it can be said that they are indeed making the transition to a lifestyle that is quite different. I well remember Michael Taylor's (pers. comm.) remark that when in the Okavango they share resources widely but when elsewhere (for example, attending school or university) they do not. Rather, they behave like any other people.

In the next chapter, we turn our attention briefly away from Bushmen to look at the other peoples of southern Africa. A basic understanding of them is essential in order to appreciate both southern Africa's hunter-gatherers in their own right and the relations between them and the groups that surround them.

Further Reading

Apart from Heinz's manuscripts, the main ethnography of the River Bushmen is a thesis on social development in the Okavango by Michael Taylor (2000). Another useful piece is Taylor's (2002b) 'The shaping of San livelihood strategies', which covers similar ground. There is a popular account of discovery by a journalist (Cowley 1969), but it is less useful for its ethnography. More important is Bolaane's (2013) DPhil thesis, published in 2013.

In addition, at least four papers in a special issue of *Pula* (volume 16, number 2 and issue number 27) deal in whole or in part with Bushmen of the Okavango. The word *pula*, incidentally, is Tswana (or Setswana) for 'rain' – with symbolic connotations of everything that is good. In his article there, Michael Taylor (2002a) presents a historical overview of territoriality.

Another very useful source is the work of the late Oswin Köhler. It is mainly in German, but summaries are given within Barnard (1992a; for references, see pages 318–19). Köhler's magnum opus (Köhler, with Boden and Fehn 2018) has recently been published in English. It contains 711 pages of text on the family and on customary law. It is written in Khwe, with grammatical notes and an English translation, essentially the fourth volume of Köhler's planned series of five volumes.

Finally, the Botswana Society (1976) organized a symposium on the delta that included thirty-two papers. These are summarized in Thompson (1976).

11   Sharing the Land with Others

Bushmen are not alone in the Kalahari. They are not even the majority people there. Rather, Bushman communities frequently share their land and its resources with Ovambo, Herero, Khoekhoe, Tswana, whites, 'Coloured people', Basters and many others. Even these groups are diverse in several ways, not only in traditional lifestyles (herder, rancher, white-collar worker and so on), but also in terms of social class and education. The purpose of this penultimate chapter is to sketch in some of the ethnographic background. It should also serve to highlight some differences between the foragers and others, as well as to show some of the ways in which foragers and others can maintain a mutual relationship in spite of their ethnic differences. The relationship is not always benign, however, due to 'occlusion' on the part of colonial regimes. Ann Laura Stoler (2016) makes no mention of Bushmen, but her book *Duress* is revealing of conditions that have affected Bushmen throughout their history.

The Kalahari happens to be one of the least populous regions of the earth. Yet the environments are fragile, water is limited and activities like livestock rearing require lots more land than other existences. In hard times, pastoralists suffer most. Foraging may be difficult, but Kalahari foragers do know how to make the most of what they have. Lee (1979: 464–5), for example, reports that Ju/'hoansi know some 220 species of plant. They also know where to find them and how to prepare them as well as their seasonal availability, and nearly all of these plants are edible.

My earliest intention as a field researcher had been to study ethnicity, and in this chapter I return to that topic at a theoretical level. Part of my goal here is to explore what it means to adhere to any of these labels: Bushman, San, Kua or whatever. 'Bushmen' are generally presumed to be *hunter-gatherers*, but what does that label mean in a post-hunting-and-gathering world? What does it mean in a world where generations have grown up alongside herders, and many themselves now herd their own livestock? What does it mean in a world where other changes in subsistence (such as in the 'River Bushman' case) make classification difficult? So how do such changes in lifestyle affect the ideology of being a 'forager' or 'hunter-gatherer', or indeed what does it mean to be a '*traditional* hunter-gatherer'? Most people called Bushmen or San in some sense already inhabit the margins of tradition. And some others, such as Tswana, are quite capable to live to an extent by hunting and gathering.

Arrival of the Khoekhoe and Bantu-Speakers

Almost everywhere, the first inhabitants of southern Africa are but a tiny minority. Namibia is Africa's least populous country by population density, with only 3 people per square kilometre on a landmass of (according to Wikipedia) 823,290 square kilometres. San in Namibia number only about 27,000 or 34,000, depending on which source one trusts. Nearly half the population speak an Ovambo dialect as their first language, and Afrikaans is the lingua franca. They must share their lands, dry and wet, with groups who are far more numerous. Table 11.1 shows very approximate numbers of people of different ethnic groups in southern Africa today. But, of course, this is all dependent on what we mean by 'southern Africa', and, for example, we find Tswana in Namibia (as well as in Botswana and South Africa) and so on.

In anthropology, if not beyond it, the numerical strength of ethnic groups tends to matter far less than their diversity. That is one reason why Bushmen are regarded as so 'important'; they are numerically insignificant, whereas, say, Han Chinese are vastly more numerous. It is, of course, almost impossible to suggest truly reliable figures for any of these groups. This is not least because of definitions of 'ethnic groups', and also because of the significant fact that so many Bushmen or San are multilingual as well as of mixed ancestry. Who is a real Naro, and who is half Naro and half Ju/'hoan?

The Khoekhoe (formerly called 'Hottentots') came first, arriving in southern Africa perhaps around 2,000 years ago. There are also Damara, a Khoekhe-speaking group of northern Namibia of 'black' origin. In many respects they are like any other Khoekhoe, but there are, as we saw in Chapter 9, some cultural differences. After the Khoekhoe came the Bantu-speaking peoples. These included first Nguni-speakers, arriving in present-day South Africa around the year 1500 and later settling in the northern parts of the country and eventually in the Cape. Nguni languages, like Khoekhoe and Bushman ones, are characterized by containing clicks. These languages include Zulu, Xhosa and Swati (Swazi), among others. They have three clicks (excluding the 'click releases'): / (written *c*), // (written *x*) and ! (written *q*). These were acquired initially from San languages. The other major division of the Bantu family within southern Africa is the Sotho branch, consisting of Sesotho and Tswana (Setswana). All these people are agro-pastoralists; herding livestock is the ideal, but growing crops is an acceptable alternative for them.

Many treatises on the languages have been published, although the standard one remains Clement Doke's (1954) *The southern Bantu languages*. Apart

Table 11.1 *Approximate populations of non-Bushman groups in southern Africa*

Northern Namibian groups	
Ovambo	1,830,000
Herero (including Himba)	350,000
Far northern groups	200,000
Khoekhoe-speakers	
Khoekhoe	100,000
Damara	200,000
Mixed origin in Namibia	170,000
Sotho-speakers	
Southern Sotho	6,000,000
Northern Sotho or Pedi	5,200,000
Tswana (in Botswana and RSA)	6,000,000
Nguni-speakers	
Xhosa	8,000,000
Zulu	12,000,000
Swati (Swazi) and others	1,300,000
Lemba, Venda and Tsonga	4,000,000
Afrikaners and mixed origin in RSA	7,000,000

Source: Adapted from Wikipedia
Note: These figures are very rough and intended only to give a vague idea of relative populations.

from Nguni and Sotho, southern Bantu languages also include Tsonga (Thonga), spoken in Mozambique and in the far north of South Africa, and Venda, also spoken in the far north of South Africa. The Bantu family of languages is very widespread, and has its origin in central Africa. It seems that Bantu-speakers interbred with Khoisan over a long period of time, with male Bantu-speaker and female Khoisan unions being most common (see Bajić *et al.* 2018). The linguistic prehistory of these groups is, of course, more complicated than that, but these are the basics. A definitive chapter on the classification of cultural groups is contained in W. D. Hammond-Tooke's *Bantu-speaking peoples* (Van Warmelo 1974). Beyond that, it is worth mentioning that there are some northern groups who never came into South Africa at all, and one of the Bantu-speaking peoples, the Lemba, probably have a Semitic origin. According to their own folklore, this small group, centred in Zimbabwe, is Jewish in origin.

The most numerous ethnic group in the lands Bushmen inhabit are the Tswana, made famous through Isaac Schapera's (for example, 1984 [1953]) work. Most Tswana, over 4,000,000 of them, live within the Republic of South Africa. Only about 1,600,000 live in Botswana. Yet again, the numbers are difficult to estimate. Like the Khoekhoe, the Tswana are traditionally a cattle-keeping people, and they have long lived in large villages, divided into wards. Many Tswana also live 'on the lands', and some occupy cattle posts. All these modes of residence are traditional, and demographically the ages of village residents, cattle-post residents and those on the lands vary depending on activity. For example, women engaged in agriculture live often on the lands, and elderly men and young boys commonly prefer to live at cattle posts (see Gulbrandsen 1996: 311–53). Although the villages are 'large', relative to other African villages, we should also remember those who are not present. The Tswana are also divided into tribes, each with a chief. In colonial times, these chiefs were sometimes described as kings. Most of the Tswana tribes, of which there are about fifty, live in South Africa, with just seven in Botswana.

The Tswana population of Botswana is about 80 per cent of the total, so who are the others? Many Bantu-speakers in Botswana are Kgalagadi, a group closely related to the Tswana. The word 'Kalahari' comes from this designation. Many others are Herero, a group that escaped from Namibia in the genocide of the War of 1904–08. Their escape took them mainly to Botswana, but since Namibian independence in 1990 a fair number have moved back into Namibia. The ethnocide attempted was supposed to kill all Herero, athough today around a quarter of a million survive. This number is rather more than the total number of San. The War of 1904, by the way, did last longer than expected, although it was over by 1908. Also it was the last of several wars between Germans and Herero, and some of these also involved other ethnic groups, particularly Nama and Damara. Damara, it is said, tended to support Germany (see Olusoga and Erichsen 2010; Sarkin 2010). Altough Bushmen were not particularly affected by that war, they were by many other attempts at ethnocide in both South Africa and Namibia. With their simple technology and their vulnerability in other ways, they were easy targets and have long been. Reports of subjecting Bushmen to hard labour and even of shooting them 'for sport' were not uncommon in the nineteenth century, and even early in the twentieth century (Gordon 1992: 77–85).

If the Tswana are about 80 per cent, other groups are smaller: Kalanga around 11 per cent and Kgalagadi around 7 per cent. Only perhaps 3 per cent are San. Herero has a number of dialects. Oluthimba or Otjizemba, for example, is spoken in the north and in Angola. All these other languages are Bantu ones, Herero being 'central Bantu' and the others 'southern Bantu'. Nearly everyone in Botswana, San included, has Setswana as a second language. Before the Tswana came the Kgalagadi (see Kuper 1970). Kazunobu Ikeya (1999) has written on historical dimensions of contact with them in the Ghanzi district of Botswana. They arrived in what is now Botswana in the before the nineteenth century and in what became the CKGR by late in the nineteenth century. The CKGR in the 1930s had a Kgalagadi headman. The population of the CKGR was mainly G/wi in the east and G//ana in the west, but also with two smaller groups: Tsila and Hai/nu. The presence of the former was confirmed by Valiente-Noailles, and the latter, who only arrived in the 1980s, by Ikeya. It does seem that there was a shift in identity of Kgalagadi *becoming* San over recent years (Ikeya 1999: 28–9). Of course we are talking about mixed populations here, so the shift is not very surprising. It does, however, suggest that identifying as San and therefore as members of a lower-status group is not necessarily regarded as problematic. Ikeya is not explicit about whether these are G/wi or G//ana, but the implication is that this matters little. G//ana are often said to claim Kgalagadi ancestry, though the individuals Ikeya mentions do include some G/wi.

Relations between Bushmen and Kgalagadi in general were embedded in the *mafisa* system, whereby Bushmen looked after cattle for the Kgalagadi. Much the same has been true of relations between Bushmen and Tswana (London Missionary Society 1935; Barnard 1992a: 119–21). The idea is that Bushmen become clients of wealthier patrons and get to keep the milk and the offspring of their cattle. This traditional system was supplemented by a similar one involving goats, from around 1980. Around the same time, Bushmen began to assist in gathering and growing tsama melons. Later they also assisted Kgalagadi in hunting, and so relations between the two groups grew closer and clientship became more embedded. To some extent they also intermarried, and there is a folk belief that G//ana (though not G/wi) tend to be part Kgalagadi as well as part Bushmen. In a sense this matters little, and perhaps what we have here is a system of ethnicity that is taking on new dimensions as people adapt to individual circumstances.

The Tswana, like the Kgalagadi, are part of the Sotho-speaking population of southern Africa. The majority live within South Africa, but a significant number inhabit the present-day Republic of Botswana (see Schapera 1984 [1953]). The Kgalagadi number just 40,000. Kalanga (a mainly Zimbabwean group) number about 11 per cent of the population of Botswana, and ethnic Tswana just below 80 per cent. By comparison, San are just 3 per cent. Yet as the shifting identities reflect larger concerns beyond those of particular families, the numbers and percentages here should not be taken to mean that the 'realities' are always 'real'.

In addition to Southern Bantu groups such as those mentioned above, southern Africa also boasts several Central Bantu ones. These include Herero and Ovambo, among others. The Herero have a distinctive style of dress: women wear a large volume of petticoats and a headdress with 'ears' to resemble those of cattle. Girls do not dress in this way, but married women do. Herero also possess a rare, double descent system (also known as duolineal descent). Each Herero belongs to two decent groups: an *oruzo*, or patrilineal group, and an *eanda*, or matrilineal group. The existence of such a system was famously noted by A. R. Radcliffe Brown (1924) and has been more definitively described by Gordon Gibson (1956). It is especially important for inheritance: essentially, a man inherits ordinary cattle through his *eanda* and sacred cattle and ancestral spirits through his *oruzo*. The cattle coming through the *eanda* are inherited from the man's mother's brothers. There have been attempts to circumvent the system in recent times, but it does seem to be holding, at least in modern Namibia. Finally, the Himba, who speak a dialect of Herero, have a distinct style of dress yet again. They wear few clothes and cover themselves in red ochre.

For the South African and neighbouring groups, further details are contained in N. J. van Warmelo's (1974) chapter on ethnic classification and in Basil Sansom's (1974) on traditional economic systems and, for the Namibian groups, in J. S. Malan's (1995) *Peoples of Namibia*. See also Gibson, Larson and McGurk (1981). An additional rather short text is *Owambo* (Anon. [a] 1971). This gives cattle population figures of 379,000 in 1962 and 567,000 in 1970, with goats numbering 420,000 and 338,000 respectively (Anon. [a] 1971: 13). The increase in cattle numbers between these years could be due to a number of factors, including the vaccination campaigns and the creation of quarantine facilities. The decrease in the goat population is unexplained.

Arrival of the Whites

The first encounter between Bushmen and whites was between Portuguese explorers and Strandlopers. This was in 1497. Whites began to settle in 1652, after arriving in Cape Town in that year. Here at last we have a measure of 'reality', though we should recall that the second governor of the Cape, Simon van der Stel, married a Khoekhoe woman, and so too did many others. The third governor was his son, Willem Adriaan Van der Stel. South Africa, one might say, was virtually founded by 'Coloureds', and so the saga continued through the arrival of later 'Coloured' groups, the formation of the Baster community and so on (see Marais 1939: 1–31). My point here is that this does not matter much: the population of southern Africa was 'mixed race' almost from the beginning. Apartheid and all that followed was of relatively short duration, and people of mixed ancestry along with the idea of being 'Coloured' both long predate apartheid. Its effect, even so, has been very significant: racial tension was very important before 1948 and remains so today. The problem for Bushmen is that they have always held a low social status, which, sadly, they retain. During the decades of apartheid, Bushmen were not discriminated against to the degree that blacks were.

The population of southern Africa as a whole has always been diverse, just as it has always been mixed. The construction of cultural identities has little to do with biology and a lot to do with the politics of belonging. We see this, for example, with Griqua identity (see A. G. Morris 1998; De Jongh 2012). Their self-identity as a First People is contingent on acceptance of that label by others.

Margo and Martin Russell (1979) produced an excellent, though perhaps little known, monograph on the Kalahari Afrikaners. Since Afrikaners settled among the Naro, I knew some of them fairly well in the 1970s. Things had changed a bit by then, as the Russells (1979: 1–9) describe life before, when until 1964 only whites occupied the veranda and bar at the Kalahari Arms. This was the watering hole of both British officials and Afrikaner farmers. Bushmen and Kgalagadi tended to prefer the off-licence. I am not certain, but I may have helped integrate that hotel when I introduced a few Naro there around 1975. By that time, the bar was well populated by black civil servants, and they were both tolerant and friendly with the Naro they met. Yet the Naro were still outsiders, presumably because they had no money. 'Race' mattered, and there was no way that Bushmen, blacks, Coloureds, Anglophones and Afrikaners could have mixed on equal terms. 'No way', that is, except in an idealized, imaginary society.

Education was integrated in 1964, two years before Botswana's independence, and Afrikaner teachers and pupils promptly abandoned the Tswana-medium schools. Then and in later times, Afrikaners preferred Afrikaans language learning even if this meant attending schools abroad, mainly in Namibia. This is in spite of the fact that nearly all of them understood and spoke perfect Tswana. The shops in Ghanzi were always integrated: anyone's money was as good as anyone else's. The Russells (1979: 8) heard many a strange story about the Afrikaners before they departed England for the Kalahari: 'Their cattle are so wild that they have to hunt them with guns', and so on. Their monograph paints a fascinating picture of them, but it is an idealized picture and perhaps less a true one. Certainly, there was no notion that the first Afrikaners were settlers. As the Russells (1979: 15) put it,

Terms like 'settlement', 'European' and 'farmer' easily obscure the fact that the people so described were neither settled, European nor farmers, but trekkers, a fact which alone explains much of the failed expectations n both sides, and the marked hostility which characterised colonial attitudes to trekkers in the western Kalahari. Ghanzi in 1898 was a wilderness, and it would be difficult to conceive how a settlement of European farmers there could ever have been successful.

The first white settler in Ghanzi was a man called Hendrik van Zyl. He was a dealer in ivory and is reputed to have had a hundred Bushman concubines (Russell and Russell 1979: 10–11). He hunted in the Ghanzi area between 1862 and 1872 and settled there around 1877 (Tabler 1973: 113–15). Permanent settlement in Ghanzi, however, did not begin until 1898, after reconnaissance efforts and attempts by Afrikaners to explore possibilities farther north, including Angola. This began as a result of efforts by Cecil Rhodes to prevent German expansion from German South-West Africa (later known just as South West Africa, modern Namibia) into the western Kalahari. Germany had already colonized that country in 1884, and German rule lasted until the First World War. Specifically, it lasted until Jan Smuts's army captured Windhoek in 1915. Formal administration was eventually as a League of Nations Class C mandate.

Decades of fragile economic relations followed, and generations of multilingual children grew up. Typically they spoke both Afrikaans and Naro, as well as Tswana, Kgalagadi, English and (sometimes) Herero. Afrikaner influence on the Naro was mixed, with separate camps being maintained but with concubinage fairly common. Today Naro often attend church, although it is difficult to say with certainty that their religious beliefs are truly Christian or a mix of Christian and Naro ones. I suspect the latter, and indeed much the same has been said of the religious world-view of the Ghanzi Afrikaners (see Russell and Russell 1979: 79–117). In the 1930s, there were plans to put a railway through the area, but this never materialized. Cattle production has had mixed fortunes, and dependency is the norm. That is, the Naro of Ghanzi ridge remain dependent on the good will of the Afrikaners, with whom they share both their land and their languages.

Bushmen have for a very long time been on the wrong side of history. Nowhere is this more obvious than through the ethnography of Robert Gordon (for example, 1997, 1999), who was born in the colony that later became Namibia. In his most poignant book Gordon (1992) describes Bushmen as an underclass. He also describes numerous attempts variously to 'civilize', enslave and murder Bushmen. The issue of class today seems to dominate Bushman studies. This is particularly true for the ≠Khomani of South Africa. They live a generally miserable existence in the Northern Cape, though often in intense contact, not only with Afrikaners but also with a variety of other ethnic groups as well as a proliferation of NGOs. The right to land, even very poor land, is very important for them, but so too are housing, food and water, education, health care, sanitation, employment and so on. Cultural tourism is growing in importance, and I suspect that this may partly be an answer for them (Grant 2011: 133–44). It has also been proven as a possibility farther west, at !Khwa ttu. The settlement, museum and educational programme there are in their infancy, but they do hold hope for the future.

But can that ever be the future for all Bushmen? I doubt it. They will have to learn to accommodate with other inhabitants of the subcontinent, and vice versa.

Further Reading

There is a good deal of literature on the Tswana. Most important is Schapera's (1984 [1953]) short monograph *The Tswana*. However, it does not contain much useful material on Bushmen except in relation to their employment as servants of the Tswana. The classic source on the Bantu-speaking peoples is Schapera's (1937) edited volume on the subject, updated and largely rewritten by W. D. Hammond-Tooke (1974) and his colleagues. Each has snippets on Bushmen here and there, but a knowledge of Bantu-speakers in their own right is necessary for comprehending southern Africa as a whole. Also important is the relevant work of Adam Kuper (1970, 1982, 1987). He first worked with the Kgalagadi and later did comparative studies on other groups.

The book by Margo and Martin Russell (1979) is another interesting place to start. It covers both the history of Afrikaner settlement from the 1890s to life in recent times, including relations between Bushman and Afrikaners on the Ghanzi ranches. To some extent the relationship between Bushmen and Afrikaners is symbiotic, and indeed much the same can be said of relations between Bushmen and Tswana. Finally, J. S. Malan's *Peoples of Namibia* offers an overview of ethnic groups in that country, although in places it is a little old-fashioned in its coverage.

12   Conclusions

Concluding a work of this kind is usually easy. Yet I shall give here what might well be regarded as a fairly unorthodox conclusion, simply because there are a few loose ends for me to tie up. My intension here is less to summarize and more to see what we can explain through our studies of the San. What are the key issues? For example, is there any such thing today as a hunter-gatherer? Can the positivist notion of ethnic groups as discreet entities ever be justified, especially in light of self-definition, multilingualism, long-term social change and intermarriage? Is a deep history implied in Bushman studies, for example in the retention of religious ideas from one end of southern Africa to the other? We know that the various groups are linked linguistically as a *Sprachbund* (a set of languages related through convergence, rather than through common descent). Might this have implications for the study of ethnicity? Language history? And can we conclude anything about deep history based on the fact that the rock art of southern Africa is so old? Indeed, are relations between southern Africa and other parts of the continent implicated too?

The definition of a 'hunter-gatherer' depends on context. Broadly, virtually all San are hunter-gatherers because of the way they view things like exchange and preparation for the future (Barnard 2017). The literal definition is there in the background, but is not an essential component. As for ethnic groups, they exist to some extent, but they are not discreet entities at all. Through history they are made and remade. Multilingualism is important here, not just for the understanding of ethnicity but for explaining much in deep history as well. We should remember that language evolved in southern Africa, and it is still evolving. The timespan of a language family is but a blink of an eye in comparison (Barnard 2016b). Language is fundamental to San studies both through history and today. Religion in its broadest sense is equally fundamental to Bushman thought, but it is flexible (see Barnard 1988b).

Part of this is explained through the prevalence of rock art through thousands of years of San prehistory. And yes, rock art is found on every continent, but in southern Africa it exhibits an almost unique uniformity. It is something that has been around not just for centuries, but for millennia. Indeed, it helps to confirm the quest of Father Schmidt (1939) and his team of early twentieth-century priests in their search for an 'original' monotheistic religion. They may have been wrong that monotheism was earlier than any other belief system, but this idea did indeed have a place in the foundation of Bushman studies (see Schmidt 1929). That is why Schmidt sent his priests to hunter-gatherer communities in Africa, Asia and South America: to locate, in a way, its source among what we presumed to be the most primitive of peoples. Deep history, the search for the earliest language, the origins of religion and so on all take us to the same place: southern Africa.

Language and Ethnicity

My earliest intention as a field researcher had been to study ethnicity. This was all the rage in the early 1970s, perhaps partly because of Fredrik Barth's (1969) important edited volume *Ethnic groups and boundaries*. Yet from an individual point of view, Bushman ethnicity is far more stable than in Pakistan, where Barth did some of his most important work. This is probably to do with the more collective ethos of Bushman society, or even of hunter-gatherer society in general.

Yet, considering the enormous time scale inherent in Bushman society, as we think of it (as almost everlasting) this is perhaps not surprising. Individuals do not change ethnicity on a whim, nor for strategic reasons, but in fact because of intermarriage among neighbouring groups. Remembering the Naro case, we can easily see that when very small groups interact, even language is up for grabs. This does not mean that Ju/'hoansi *become* Naro; rather, it means that both ethnic groups and ethnic boundaries are fluid entities. In this sense, it is meaningful to think in terms of multilingual clusters of peoples, maintaining stability as they choose. There truly is stability, since kinship systems, above all other aspects of culture, require it. It is not that individuals impose structures on such things, but rather as with language, linguistic structures impose themselves on peoples.

Is there any such thing today as a hunter-gatherer? Indeed, has there ever been? The notion of the hunter-gatherer has a history in European social thought, from a time (in the seventeenth century) when this was dominated by political considerations to a time (in the eighteenth century) when economic considerations came to the fore (see Finlayson and Warren 2017b: 2–4). Can the positivist notion of ethnic groups as discreet entities ever be justified, especially in light of self-definition, multilingualism, long-term social change and intermarriage? Religious ideas are fluid for Bushmen, though there is a consistency across ethnic boundaries. Is a deep history implied in Bushman studies, for example in the retention of religious ideas from one end of southern Africa to the other? We know that the various groups are linked linguistically as a *Sprachbund*. Might this have implications for the study of ethnicity? Or for the study of language history – especially in light of the fact that nearly all Bushmen, even today, are multilingual? And can we conclude anything about deep history based on the fact that the rock art of southern Africa is so old? Indeed, are relations between southern Africa and other parts of the continent implicated too? I think they are, and this comes out through my general theoretical perspective, which is known as regional structural comparison. To some extent it is in practice inherent in most anthropological research, and therefore hardly worth mentioning, let alone building a theory around. However, it does help see explicitly as a method. We might also, as I have suggested above, think in terms of a *Kulturbund* or group of peoples that have come together, rather as in a *Sprachbund* indicating a convergence of linguistic features.

Edmund Leach (pers. comm.) used to say that the basic method of anthropological field research was functionalist; it is only after that that other perspectives (like structuralism) come into play. On the other hand, as E. E. Evans-Pritchard (1965) was supposed to have put it: 'There is only one method in social anthropology, the comparative method – and that is impossible.' In fact, I doubt if he ever quite said that in those exact words, although the notion has stuck. There may be a grain of truth in both, but broadly I side more with Leach. It is what we do after field research that counts.

Regional Structural Comparison

Methodologically, my early work was exactly following the lead of my supervisor, Adam Kuper. This was not because of blind adulation on my part, but because of a chance discovery that we both made when we were 14,000 kilometres apart.

Kuper left his post at University College London in 1976, and I replaced him there as a temporary lecturer until my move to Edinburgh two years later. Ironically, he and I came to our theoretical viewpoint at the same time: he was on sabbatical in Sweden in the academic year 1974–1975 and working on similarities among Bantu-speaking groups in southern Africa. I was doing fieldwork in Botswana and thought up the same approach in talking with Bushmen. That is, Bushmen knew their own kinship systems and how they related to other systems of the subcontinent – just as often reported among Australian Aborigines. Kuper named our theoretical perspective 'regional structural comparison'. This was exemplified in his inaugural lecture at Leiden (Kuper 1979) and in his books *Wives for cattle* (1982) and *South Africa and the anthropologist* (1987) and in my book *Hunters and herders of southern Africa* (Barnard 1992a) – as well as in many articles both before and since.

The name of the approach (regional structural comparison) never caught on, but the idea is to look for structures on a regional basis and not either across all humanity, as in French structuralism, or just in one society, as in British structuralism. Rather, our approach was rather like that of the Dutch structuralism of the 1920s and 1930s (for example, Josslin de Jong 1977 [1935]): regional rather than global or local. Occasionally others have developed similar approaches, for example A. R. Radcliffe-Brown (1913), Fred Eggan (1954), David Damas (1975), John Davis (1977) and, in the Kalahari, Elizabeth Cashdan (1983). Yet very rarely (except here in Eggan's case) is the theory behind the approach made clear. In a recent discussion I had with a climate scientist, it emerged that similar approaches occur there too: a big change in local circumstances can have a significant effect on a much larger scale.

Ironically, Kuper took a chair in the Netherlands in 1976, sometime after Dutch anthropology had essentially abandoned the regional approach of long before. Dutch anthropology was at that time mainly preoccupied with development issues, as to some extent it still is. I believed in regional structural comparison because the approach worked, especially in explaining similarities in kinship structures. This was my main interest, as indeed it still is. Bushmen do not have just one kinship system, but a series of related systems. Each is a permutation of the one next door. Much the same is true of other things too: settlement patterns (another early interest of mine), religious ideology and so on. One can understand each as a system of systems, whose full explanation is only revealed through an exploration of the relationship between one system and the next. Looking at one system on its own does not allow one to see the wood for the trees. Looking at them all together, or rather one in relation to another, does. Although the present book is not framed in quite those terms, these terms do still hold true. By analogy, think of languages: it is easier to pick up Italian if one already has a bit of French; it is easier to learn Dutch if one already speaks some German, and so on.

Broadly, I still hold to the idea of regional structural comparison, although my work in recent years has focused instead mainly on human evolution. The idea here is to add a social anthropological perspective to evolutionary studies, which had always been dominated by biological thinking. Both these approaches reveal wider truths, but the first (regional structural comparison) is ethnographic and comparative and the latter (evolutionary studies) is plainly evolutionary.

Much of my own work has focused on kinship or relationship terminologies. These are, of course, important in regulating social organization, but beyond that such terminology structures offer profound insight into language change, especially in multilingual contexts. I was not fully aware of this in my early work. Terminology structures are self-regulating, as they tend to move towards regulation through the rule of uniform reciprocals. Recursion in them is a mirror of recursion in other linguistic areas, and sheds considerable light on cognition and even on the evolution of grammar in general (D. Jones 2010). It also helps explain things like why a system of father's sister's daughter marriage, once envisaged or initially practised, tends to break down so easily (see Lévi-Strauss 1969: 438–55). It is demographically 'ungrammatical'.

Is There a Unity in Anthropology?

I would say no, but this, of course, depends on what we mean by 'anthropology'. Recently, Glynn Custred (2016) has argued that anthropology retains a unity through its history. In a sense it does, with cultural anthropology, biological anthropology, anthropological linguistics and prehistoric archaeology traditionally making up the subject, at least as it is seen in North America. Of course the historical development of the subject suggests this, and this had been the intention of Franz Boas at the end of the nineteenth century. However, ideas change. Bushmen today are hardly the same as they were perceived then, and issues such as social change, social development and so on hardly existed as issues a century ago. Genetics, as the term is understood today, did not exist at all.

It is meaningful to think of what, for example, Dorothea Bleek or for that matter Wilhelm Bleek might have thought of the changing images of Bushmen throughout history. Mathias Guenther (1980) comments on this, at least implicitly, in his article, 'From "brutal savages" to "harmless people"'. There is, I suppose, no 'real Bushman'. In my early field research, outsiders often tried to lead me to 'him', but 'he' did not really exist. Essentially, Guenther is specialist in the anthropology of religion. The idea of the earliest theories of religion (by which I mean religion in the Middle Stone Age) has cropped up here and there throughout this book, but only in passing. We have left behind what is actually more interesting. This is the problem of human spirituality in general, a problem that surfaced in the very beginning of the book when I quoted a philosophical piece by Peter Nilssen and Craig Foster. They suggest that the earliest human societies had their roots in art, music, myth and symbolism and more specifically in animistic religion. If there were a global religion prior to 10,000 years ago, it was Animism. Or, as they put it: 'At our core, we are all Animists, carrying remnants of a profoundly imprinted mindset and way of life based on a reverent and functional relationship with nature' (Nilssen and Foster 2017: 5). The implication is that humanity should try to reconnect with this ancient and nature-friendly spiritual tradition.

Although I would not go quite that far myself, I think the effort deserves the utmost respect. And rather than quarrelling about who is or is not indigenous to whatever piece of land, we should think about our common origin as a species all those millennia ago, whether our ancestors were in the Kalahari, at Pinnacle Point or wherever. At the risk of causing offence to those who truly are, I would say that in a sense we are all Bushmen. That is, we are all descendants of hunter-gatherers, and the non-hunter-gatherer lifestyle that we enjoy is really very, very recent (see, for example, Barnard 2011).

We must always remember how very far we have come as intellectuals, since the nineteenth century. Take, for example, just one early twentieth-century account: that of the medical doctor, Justice of the Peace and expert on leprosy S. P. Impey. He cites a considerable number of authorities, including Dorothea Bleek. However, he disagrees with Bleek on a number of points: Impey (1926: 1–2) did not believe that Bushmen painted the pictures attributed to them, or even that they were the original inhabitants of southern Africa. Instead, he thought that Bushmen are recent arrivals. Further, he considered both black Africans and 'Grimaldi man' (an Italian form of Cro-Magnon) originated in central Asia, and that the Strandlopers (or 'beach rangers' of the southern African west coast) were the ancestors of Bushmen (Impey 1926: 58–82). He is right though that we humans are all members of a mixed species. No one today would agree, though, on his surmises on origins of Bushmen or any other specific peoples he mentions. Still, we are moving forward, if not quite forward enough for some. The idea of 'indigeneity' is today hotly analysed and hotly disputed, for example in the work of the legal anthropologist Ronald Niezen (2003, 2010: 105–36). And of course, also among indigenous groups themselves. This is played out too in understandings of *precedent* (in Common Law) and *principle* (in Roman-Dutch law). The former is common in many legal systems, and the latter particularly in those of southern Africa.

In the late twentieth century, many things changed. We have the arrival of the Marshall family (for example, Marshall 1976, 1999) and their tremendous insights, all with true anthropological field research. This fed rapidly into the wider cultural understanding of Bushmen or San. Agnes Jackson (1956), for example, only a few years after fieldwork by the Marshalls, wrote a splendid short monograph on Bushmen. It is apparently for young people, but it avoids the speculations of earlier writers like Impey. Both Lorna Marshall's material and that of Elizabeth Marshall Thomas had yet to appear in print at that time, so Jackson had had no access to these. Rather, the 1950s marked a cultural shift both in our understanding of San and in social anthropology. Bushmen were no longer to be portrayed as primitive. With the *Man the hunter* volume (Lee and DeVore 1968b), other events of 1968 and Richard Lee's research a few years later, another paradigm shift occurred. No longer were they to be thought of as merely impoverished. Their 'original affluence', whether real or imagined, had come to be recognized. Anthropology had come of age. As for the Kalahari Debate, Tanaka and Sugawara (1996: 4) explained it like this:

Although the epistemological reflection on the radical condition of the discipline is worthy of respect, we believe that anthropological theory can only be renewed only by continuing good fieldwork, rather than by nullifying all products brought about by previous fieldwork. And good fieldwork is possible only if the fieldworker respects the people he/she studies.

Obviously this a roundabout way of saying it, but the work of Wilmsen and the rest of us is only possible because we are standing on the shoulders of the Bleeks, Lee and the Marshalls, and not really because we have something truly new to add.

Too Many, or Not Enough References?

The number of references is a common problem in academia: too many, or too few? I completed the text of *Hunters and herders of southern Africa* (Barnard 1992a) in 1991 and promptly put a manuscript copy of it in the departmental library. One of the students complained that the book was over-referenced. Perhaps it was, but the cause of the student's concern was actually that it *appeared to* have too many citations, simply because 'the book' was a double-spaced manuscript. A year later, I produced the rather shorter *The Kalahari debate* (Barnard 1992b), to a large extent with the same bibliography, 582 items and 88 pages, though with the subtitle *a bibliographical essay*. It was single-spaced and has never had that complaint. Indeed, it still gets rather more hits on a certain website than I would ever have expected for a booklet that old. Even the 'preliminary list' of publications on non-Bantu click languages, compiled by Ernst Westphal's secretary (Levy 1968), contains references to several hundred works, including, for example, 16 by Dorothea Bleek and 15 by Wilhelm Bleek. If such a list were to be compiled today, it would have to contain *a great many thousands* more. The two-volume Khoe and San bibliography compiled by Shelagh Willet and her colleagues (Willet *et al.* 2002; Willet 2003) contains 1,470 items. The present work contains rather fewer. The moral of this story is that there is *no correct number of references*, and no correct number of books and articles in a bibliography.

However, I am conscious of meeting the needs of readers. These are quite diverse, and especially so in the case of the San. The literature on these groups is vast, both on their diversity and in respect of their similarities.

Bushmen: Some Similarities and Differences

Whether we truly are all Bushmen or not, let me sum up what we have learned in this book. I shall divide this into two categories, similarities (things shared among all Bushmen) and differences (things that are different among different Bushman groups).

Similarities

- Wet and dry seasons
- Detailed knowledge of the environment
- Small group size
- Egalitarian social structure
- Emphasis on giving
- Universal kinship
- Absolute distinction between joking and avoidance
- Knowledge of the spirit world
- Belief in one male god
- Belief in minor deities
- Minor deities include Mantis, etc.
- Common folklore, with similar tales
- Belief in male moon and (usually) female sun
- Moon is 'good', sun often is not
- Medicine dance, mainly male trance performers
- Medicine dance, female clappers and singers
- Male initiation common
- Female initiation very common
- Flexibility in almost everything

Differences

- Diverse environments with no shared subsistence base
- Very diverse patterns of aggregation and dispersal
- These depend on specific environmental circumstances
- Extremely diverse kinship systems
- Extremely diverse languages: no common features

Of course, most of these indicate the same things, and the similarities are more numerous than the differences. Some similarities are generally common to hunter-gatherers, and so, less significant than the others: they know their environments and make good use of them, for example. A small number, though, are extremely significant, especially among the differences. The idea of diverse patterns of aggregation and dispersal is clearly dependent on knowing the availability of resources: water is the most crucial here. If one has no water at all in the dry season, then dry season aggregation is simply not possible (see again Barnard 1979a; Cashdan 1983). This affects especially the G/wi and G//ana. Diversity in kinship systems may not seem significant, but in such small-scale societies it is (Barnard 2009). As for diverse language, this is exactly what one should expect when these peoples have been in the same area for millennia.

Bushmen are a diverse set of peoples. They are expert in what they know. The fact that they choose free time over the accumulation of property is their own choice. Their kinship systems are complicated, but they are adaptive. Extreme flexibility allows them to adapt to their surroundings. Only time will tell how much longer their precise lifestyles can continue.

Will the Bushmen Survive?

This, of course, is a difficult question. They have survived for tens of thousands of years, so why not? But let me answer in a different way, by quoting from an obscure manuscript written by Dorothea Bleek. The exact date is not easy to determine: it is given in a catalogue as between 1911 and 1915, but the material included appears in a notebook dated 1918. It is a record of the //ŋ !ke of Griqualand West, on the fringe of the Kalahari near Upington. According to D. F. Bleek (2000: 16),

The //ŋ !ke danced as other Bushmen did, the men circling round while the women clapped and sang. In some dances young women joined in one at a time. They stated that they only played the bow, not the drum. Among members of the tribe near Upington a Ramki was found, but that was an adopted instrument.

Of religious ceremonies and beliefs little was to be learnt from the tribe. Certain stars were said to bring certain foods, which points to their sharing the worship of the heavenly bodies of the /xam .... Of course the older people knew much of their old lore, but would not disclose it. The present generation probably knows nothing and is being absorbed by their neighbours, marrying Bechuana, Griqua, Basters or any coloured people.

What this indicates to me is simply that change is the norm. The Naro probably once lost their language, but they still exist. The //ŋ !ke are becoming absorbed through intermarriage, but they too still exist. Old people cannot be relied on to forever keep to the old ways. Chris Low (2014), a specialist in traditional medicine, locates /Xam beliefs and practices specifically in a wider Khoisan setting, while noting differences. He concentrates on four themes in /Xam belief: the eland, buchu (a medicinal herb) and the idioms of 'behaving nicely' and 'standing'. The eland is a pervasive symbol in Khoisan belief, and buchu has been widely used in Khoisan medicine for centuries. The latter two are more subtle. Both occur frequently in Lucy Lloyd's manuscripts and refer to maintaining sociality while doing things correctly and to standing one's ground. What unites them all is a consistent vocabulary for expressing them across language and even language family boundaries. They are thus part of a wide Khoisan *Sprachbund* that is not only linguistic but also societal, a *Kulturbund*. Even the 'vanished voice' of the N//ŋ of the Drakensberg can, in a sense, still be heard through its rock art record as well as in its folklore (Wessels 2014). The complexity of issues surrounding the San, especially in reference to dealings with nation states, has been well documented (Hohmann 2003). The San know where they stand, and fortunately southern Africa has some of the most enlightened of governments and, although poor in comparison to the West, still relatively well-off states in comparison to others in Africa.

In short, we should not fear change. If we are always on the lookout for pure hunter-gatherers we will not find them. The point is that everyone changes. Just as the Karretjie People were once the /Xam (De Jongh 2012), others can adapt too. It follows that there is 'no true Bushman'. His or her existence is always dependent of context. Thomas (2016: 159–71) comments on this dilemma with reference to whether Bushmen can understand the concept (or the need for) money. Of course they can, but they do not need it when living 'traditionally'. Bushman or San tradition depends on different assumptions, such as giving freely, the lack of hierarchy and universal kinship. To some extent, these values occur in all societies, of course, but we cannot assume that they occur equally or by exactly the same rules. They do not, and the unity and difference between societies or social formations may be very subtle indeed. That said, I am never surprised by the primitivist imagery in writings on the San. For example, the closing cover blurb of one short book by the resident beekeeper of London's Natural History Museum (Dixon 2015) reads: 'This remarkable novella is a vivid evocation of a lost age, the world of the hunter gatherers of southern Africa.' Of course this could have been written by a skilled copywriter, but that is not relevant. Whoever wrote the words, the sentiment is the same.

So what future should we see for the San? And what do they need most? In a way these are closely related questions. Let me start with the second. What San need is, of course, the alleviation of poverty. What could be more obvious? Yet as James Suzman's (2017) book implies, they can be affluent without abundance. Marshall Sahlins (1974: 1–39) said much the same thing. But bearing in mind the rhetorical complexity of this let me make a simple list:
• alleviation of poverty,
• improvement of infrastructure (particularly the provision of water),
• rights to land and
• housing (but does this imply permanent settlement?).

The list could go on. My vote though would emphasize more the things that others deny them. At the Twelfth International Conference on Hunting and Gathering Societies in 2018 (CHAGS12), linguist Anne-Maria Fehn (pers. comm.) made an interesting suggestion. She urged educators to be more aware of the stigma attached to speaking a minority language. She suggested that children be encouraged to be tolerant of them as well as being aware of this as a potential problem. The suggestion found favour with several of the Tswana present. Yet I would go even further: San already speak many languages. It is not that unusual for one to be able to speak three, four or half a dozen. So why not encourage the children not just to be tolerant, but to speak each other's languages? Obviously, it is appropriate for all citizens of Botswana to be able to speak Setswana: that is why Tony Traill's (2018) latest !Xoõ dictionary is trilingual. If everyone in Botswana could speak a Bushman language, this magnificent country would be even more magnificent. Much the same is true of Namibia (where English is the only official language) and of South Africa (which has eleven official languages).

In a real sense, Bushmen are part of nature. That is, they are better exemplars of natural humanity than the rest of us. Yet Bushmen are fully cultural and, indeed, completely cultured. What makes them different from us at all is that they have different values. Some of these are listed above: they give freely, they lack social hierarchy, and they possess practices of universal kinship. I would not suggest that tolerance is everything, but awareness and appreciation of Bushman values might make all the difference. An important reader on hunter-gatherers (Gowdy 1998: 219–325) closes with four largely pessimistic chapters on the future. John Yellen (1998 [1990]) presents a disturbing view of contact with capitalist economies. Tim Flannery (1998 [1995]) adds an assessment of environmental consumption in Australia, after some 60,000 years of relative stability. Ilisa Barbash (2016: 164), quoting from an obituary of ≠Toma in *Anthropology News*, notes that he 'was born to and grew up in an autonomous and self-sufficient life of hunter-gathering [*sic*]. His death represents the end of that era.' ≠Toma was the Marshalls' chief informant. He died in 1988 at the age of 75. On the other hand, John Zerzan (1998 [1994]) argues the case for the superiority of hunter-gatherer lifestyles over 'modern' ones. Paul Shepard (1998 [1992]) makes a similar case for Palaeolithic primitivism in the 'post-historic' times of our Neanderthal ancestors. But read another way, perhaps these various suggestions are not so pessimistic at all.

San have been known to Europeans since around the year 1660. Yes, they will survive for a long time to come, but the *way* in which they survive will not necessarily be as expected.

References

Almeida, António de. 1965. *Bushmen and other non-Bantu peoples of Angola.* Johannesburg: Witwatersrand University Press

Ambrose, Stanley H. 1998. 'Late Pleistocene human population bottlenecks, volcanic winter, and differentiation of modern humans', *Journal of Human Evolution* 34(6): 633–51

Andersson, Charles John. 1856. *Lake Ngami; or explorations and discoveries during four years' wanderings in the wilds of south western Africa.* London: Hurst and Blackett

1861. *The Okavango river: a narrative of travel, exploration, and adventure.* London: Hurst and Blackett

Anon. [a]. 1971. *Owambo.* Pretoria: Department of Foreign Affairs

Anon. [b]. 2002. 'NGOs involved in San development and advocacy', in Lee, Hitchcock and Biesele, p. 59

Anon. [c]. 2002. 'Films on the San (Bushmen)', in Lee, Hitchcock and Biesele, p. 57

Arthreya, Sheena and Xinzhi Wu. 2017. 'A multivariate assessment of the Dali hominin cranium from China: morphological affinities and implications for Pleistocene evolution in East Asia', *American Journal of Physical Anthropology* 164: 679–701

Asch, Michael and Colin Sampson, Dieter Heinen, Justin Kenrick and Jerome Lewis, Sidsel Saugestad, Terry Turner and Adam Kuper. 2004. 'Discussion: on the return of the native', *Current Anthropology* 45: 261–7

Atkinson, Quentin D. 2011. 'Phonemic diversity supports a serial founder effect model of language expansion from Africa', *Science* 332: 246–9

Bailey, Geoff and Penny Spikins (eds.). 2008. *Mesolithic Europe.* Cambridge University Press

Bajić Vladimir, Chiara Barbieri, Alexander Hübner, Tom Güldemann, Christfried Naumann, Linda Gerlach, Falko Berthold, Hirosi Nakagawa, Sununguko W. Mpoloka, Lutz Roewer Josephine Purps, Mark Stoneking and Brigitte Pakendorf. 2018. 'Genetic structure and sex-biased gene flow in the history of southern African populations', *American Journal of Physical Anthropology* 167(1): 1–16

Bank, Andrew (ed.). 1998. *The proceedings of the Khoisan identities and cultural heritage conference.* Cape Town: Institute for Historical Research, UWC/ InfoSOURCE CC

2006. *Bushmen in a Victorian world: the remarkable story of the Bleek-Lloyd collection.* Cape Town: Double Storey

Barbash, Ilisa. 2016. *Where the roads all end: photography and anthropology in the Kalahari.* Cambridge, MA: Peabody Museum Press

Barham, Lawrence and Peter Mitchell. 2008. *The first Africans: African archae-ology from the earliest toolmakers to most recent foragers*. Cambridge University Press

Barnard, Alan. 1976. Nharo Bushman kinship and the transformation of Khoi kin categories. PhD thesis, University of London

1978. 'Universal systems of kin categorization', *African Studies*, 37: 69–81

1979a. 'Kalahari Bushman settlement patterns', in Philip Burnham and Roy F. Ellen (eds.), *Social and ecological systems* (ASA Monographs 18). London: Academic Press, pp. 131–44

1979b. 'Nharo Bushman medicine and medicine men', *Africa* 49: 68–80

1980. 'Sex roles among the Nharo Bushmen of Botswana', *Africa* 50: 115–24

1982. 'The kin terminology system of the Nharo Bushmen', *Cahiers d'études africaines*, 18: 607–29

1986. 'Rethinking Bushman settlement patterns and territoriality', *Sprache und Geschichte in Afrika* 7(1): 41–60

1988a. 'Kinship, language and production: a conjectural history of Khoisan social structure', *Africa* 58: 29–50

1988b. 'Structure and fluidity in Khoisan religious ideas', *Journal of Religion in Africa* 18: 216–36

1989. 'The lost world of Laurens van der Post?', *Current Anthropology* 30: 104–14

1992a. *Hunters and herders of southern Africa: a comparative ethnography of the Khoisan peoples*. Cambridge University Press

1992b. *The Kalahari debate: a bibliographical essay* (Occasional Papers No. 35). Edinburgh: Centre of African Studies, University of Edinburgh

1992c. 'Social and special boundary maintenance among southern African hunter-gatherers', in Michael J. Casimir and Aparna Rao (eds.), *Mobility and territori-ality: social and special boundaries among foragers, fishers, pastoralists and peripatetics*. New York: Berg, pp. 137–51

1996. 'Regional comparison in Khoisan ethnography: theory, method and practice', *Zeitschrift für Ethnologie* 121: 203–20

1998a. 'Être Bushman aujourd'hui', in Olivier and Valentin, pp. 65–85

1998b. 'Hunter-gatherers and bureaucrats: reconciling opposing worldviews', in Sidsel Saugestad (ed.), *Indigenous peoples in modern nation-states* (Occasional Papers, Series A, No. 90). Tromsø: Faculty of Social Science, University of Tromsø, pp. 63–76

2000. *History and theory in anthropology*. Cambridge University Press

2001. *Los pueblos cazadores recolectores: tres conferencias dictadas en Argentina/ The hunter-gatherer peoples: three lectures presented in Argentina* (translated by Florencia Rodriguez). Buenos Aires: Fundación Navarro Viola

2003. '!Ke e: /xarra //ke – Multiple origins and multiple meanings of the motto', *African Studies* 62: 243–50

2004. 'Hunting-and-gathering society: an eighteenth-century Scottish invention', in Alan Barnard (ed.), *Hunter-gatherers in history, archaeology and anthropology*. Oxford: Berg Publishers, pp. 31–43

2006. 'Kalahari revisionism, Vienna and the "indigenous peoples" debate', *Social Anthropology* 14: 1–16

2007a. *Anthropology and the Bushman*. Oxford: Berg

2007b. 'From Mesolithic to Neolithic modes of thought'. *Proceedings of the British Academy* 144: 5–19

2009. 'Social origins: sharing, exchange, kinship', in Botha and Knight, pp. 219–35

2011. *Social anthropology and human origins*. Cambridge University Press

2012. *Genesis of symbolic thought*. Cambridge University Press

2014. 'The Ju/'hoan-Naro contact area', in Barnard and Boden, pp. 209–22

2016a. 'Nothing wrong with reasoned speculation', *Antiquity* 90 (352): 1084–5

2016b. *Language in prehistory*. Cambridge University Press

2016c. 'Some puzzles in !Xóõ kinship terminology', in Vossen and Haacke, pp. 21–32

2017. 'Egalitarian and non-egalitarian sociality', in Jon Henrik Ziegler Remme and Kenneth Sillander (eds.), *Human nature and social life: essays in honour of Professor Signe Howell*. Cambridge University Press, pp. 83–96

Barnard, Alan (ed.). 2004. *Hunter-gatherers in history, archaeology and anthropology*. Oxford: Berg Publishers

Barnard, Alan and Gertud Boden (eds.). 2014. *Southern African Khoisan kinship systems* (Quellen zur Khoisan-Forschung/Research in Khoisan Studies 30). Cologne: Rüdiger Köppe

Barnard, Alan and Justin Kenrick (eds.). 2001. *Africa's indigenous peoples: 'first peoples' or 'marginalized minorities'?* Edinburgh: Centre of African Studies

Barnard, Alan and Thomas Widlok. 1996. 'Nharo and Hai//om settlement patterns in comparative perspective', in Kent, pp. 87–107

Barras, Colin. 2017. 'Losing the plot: everything we thought we knew about who we are and where we came from needs a major rethink', *New Scientist* 3140: 28–33

Barth, Fredrik (ed.). 1969. *Ethnic groups and boundaries: the social organization of culture difference*. Oslo: Universitetsforlaget

Beach, David. 1998. 'Cognitive archaeology and imaginative history at Great Zimbabwe', *Current Anthropology* 39: 47–72

Behar, Doron M., Richard Villems, Himla Soodyall, Jason Blue-Smith, Luisa Pereira, Ene Metspalu, Rosaria Scozzari, Heeran Makkan, Shay Tzur, David Comas, Jaume Bertranpetit, Lluis Quintana-Murci, Chris Tyler-Smith, R. Spencer Wells, Saharon Rosset and the Genographic Consortium. 2008. 'The dawn of human matrilineal diversity', *American Journal of Human Genetics* 82: 1–11

Bennun, Neil. 2005 [2004]. *The broken string: the last words of an extinct people*. London: Penguin Books

Bétaille, André. 1998. 'The idea of indigenous people', *Current Anthropology* 39: 187–91

Bicchieri, M. G. (ed.). 1972. *Hunters and gatherers today: a socioeconomic study of eleven such cultures in the twentieth century*. New York: Holt, Rinehart and Winston

Biesele, Megan. 1978. 'Sapiens and scarce resources: communication systems of the !Kung and other foragers', *Social Science Information* 17: 921–47

1986. 'How hunter-gatherers' stories "make sense": semantics and adaptation', *Cultural Anthropology* 1: 157–70

1993. *Women like meat: the folklore and foraging ideology Kalahari Ju/'hoan*. Johannesburg: Witwatersrand University Press

2016. 'Language development and community development in a San community', in Vossen and Haacke, pp. 49–70

Biesele, Megan and Robert K. Hitchcock. 2011. *The Ju/'hoan San of Nyae Nyae and Namibian independence: development, democracy, and indigenous voices in southern Africa*. New York: Berghahn Books

Biggs, R. C. 1976. 'The effects of the seasonal flood regime on the ecology of Chief's Island and the adjacent floodplain system', in Botswana Society, pp. 113–20

Bleek, D. F. 1924. 'Bushman terms of relationship', *Bantu Studies* 2: 57–70

1928. *The Naron: a Bushman tribe of the central Kalahari*. Cambridge University Press

1929. *Comparative vocabularies of Bushman languages*. Cambridge University Press

1928/29. 'Bushman grammar: a grammatical sketch of the language of the /xam-ka-!k'e', *Zeitschrift für Eingeborenen-Sprachen* 19: 81–98

1929/30. 'Bushman grammar: a grammatical sketch of the language of the /xam-ka-!k'e (continuation)', *Zeitschrift für Eingeborenen-Sprachen* 20: 161–74

1956. *A Bushman dictionary*. New Haven: American Oriental Society (American Oriental Series 41)

2000. 'The //ŋ!ke or Bushmen of Griqualand West', *Khoisan Forum* (working paper no. 15), pp. 14–16

(ed.). 1931 to 1936. 'Customs and beliefs of the /Xam Bushmen (from material collected by Dr W. H. I. Bleek and Miss L. C. Lloyd between 1870 and 1880)', *Bantu Studies* 5: 167–79; 6: 47–63; 6: 233–49; 6: 323–42; 7: 297–312; 7: 375–92; 9: 1–47; 10: 131–62

Bleek, W. H. I. 1858. *The library of his excellency sir George Grey, KCB: philology Vol. I. South Africa*. London: Trübner and Co.

1869. *On the origin of language* (translated by Thomas Davidson). New York: L. W. Schmidt

1874. 'Remarks on Orpen's "Mythology of the Maluti Bushmen"', *Cape Monthly Magazine* (n.s.) 9: 10–13

Bleek, W. H. I. and L. C. Lloyd. 1911. *Specimens of Bushman folklore*. London: George Allen & Company

Blurton Jones, Nicolas and Melvin J. Konner. 1976. '!Kung knowledge of animal behavior (or: The proper study of mankind is animals)', in Lee and DeVore, pp. 325–48

Boden, Gertrud. 2014a. 'Tuu kinship classifications – a diachronic perspective', in Barnard and Boden, pp. 161–84

2014b. 'Language contact and flexible kin categories', in Barnard and Boden, pp. 241–62

2017. 'Variation and change in Taa kinship terminologies', in Vossen and Haacke, pp. 213–43

2018. 'The Khwe collection in the academic legacy of Oswin Köhler: formation and potential future', in Puckett and Ikeya, pp. 129–46

Boden, Gertrud (compiler and editor). 2007. *!Qamtee /aa ≠xanya: the book of traditions. Histories, texts and illustrations from the !Xoon and 'N/ohan peoples of Namibia*. Basil: Basler Afrika Bibliographien

Bolaane, Maitseo M. M. 2001. 'Fear of the marginalized minorities: the Khwai community determining their boundary in the Okavango, Botswana, through a Deed of Trust', in Barnard and Kenrick, pp. 145–71

2002. 'Bugakhwe San community of Khwai: mapping its own territory', *Pula: Botswana Journal of African Studies* 16: 86–97

2013. *Chiefs, hunters, and San in the creation of the Moremi Game Reserve, Okavango delta: multiracial interactions and initiatives, 1956–1979* (Senri Ethnological Studies 83). Osaka: Senri Ethnological Studies

Botha, Rudolf and Chris Knight (eds.). 2009. *The cradle of language* (Studies in the Evolution of Language 12). Oxford University Press

Botswana Society. 1976. *Proceedings of the symposium on the Okavango delta and its future utilisation.* Gaborone: Botswana Society

Brenzinger, Matthias. 2007. 'Language endangerment in southern and eastern Africa', in Matthias Brenzinger (ed.), *Language diversity endangered.* Berlin: Mouton de Gruyter, pp. 179–204

Brody, Hugh. 2001. *The other side of Eden: hunter-gatherers, farmers and the shaping of the world.* London: Faber and Faber

Brooks, Alison S. 1984. 'San land use patterns, past and present: implications for southern African prehistory', in M. Hall, G. Avery, D. M. Avery, M. L. Wilson and A. J. B. Humphreys (eds.), *Frontiers: southern African archaeology today* (BAR International Series 207). Oxford: British Archaeological Reports, pp. 40–52

Cameron, David W. and Colin P. Groves. 2004. *Bones, stones and molecules: 'Out of Africa' and human origins.* Burlington, MA: Elsevier Academic Press

Carsten, Janet. 2004. *After kinship.* Cambridge University Press

Carsten, Janet (ed.). 2000. *Cultures of relatedness: new approaches to the study of kinship.* Cambridge University Press

Cashdan, Elizabeth A. 1983. 'Territoriality among human foragers: ecological models and an application to four Bushman groups', *Current Anthropology* 24: 47–66

1984. 'G//ana territorial organization', *Human Ecology* 12: 443–63

1986. 'Competition between foragers and food-producers on the Botletli River, Botswana', *Africa* 56: 299–318

1987. 'Trade and its origins on the Botletli river, Botswana', *Journal of Anthropological Research* 43: 121–38

Cassidy, Lin, Ken Good, Isaac Mazonde and Roberta Robberts. 2001. *An assessment of the status of the San in Botswana* (Regional Assessment of the Status of the San in Southern Africa, Report 3). Windhoek: Legal Assistance Centre

Chennells, Roger. 2014. 'Some reflections', in Deacon and Skotnes, pp. 417–22

Childers, Gary W. 1976. *Report on the survey/investigation of the Ghanzi farm Basarwa situation.* Gaborone: Government Printer

Clement, A. J. 1967. *The Kalahari and its lost city.* Johannesburg: Longmans

Clottes, Jean and David Lewis-Williams. 1998. *The shamans of prehistory: trance and magic in the painted caves.* New York: Harry Abrams

Collier, Jane F. and Michelle Z. Rosaldo. 1981. 'Politics and gender in simple societies', in Sherry B. Ortner and Harriet Whitehead (eds.), *Sexual meanings: the cultural construction of gender and sexuality.* Cambridge University Press, pp. 275–329

Collins, Chris and Jeffrey S. Gruber. 2014. *A grammar of ǂHòã.* (Quellen zur Khoisan-Forschung / Research in Khoisan Studies 32). Cologne: Rüdiger Köppe

Corry, Stephen. 2003. 'Bushmen – the final solution and blaming the messenger', *Before Farming* 3(2): 1–10

Cowley, Clive. 1969. *Fabled tribe: a journey to discover the river Bushmen of the Okavango swamps*. London: The Travel Book Club

Critical Arts. 1985. *Critical arts: a journal of cultural studies*, vol. 9, no. 2. Durban: University of Natal

Custred, Glynn. 2016. *A history of anthropology as a holistic science*. Lanham, MD: Lexington Books

Da Gama, Vasco. 1947 [1497]. 'The route to India, 1497-8' (translated by E. G. Ravenstein), in Charles David Ley (ed.), *Portuguese voyages, 1498–1663: tales from the great age of discovery*. London: J.M. Dent & Sons, pp. 3–38

Damas, David. 1975. 'Three kinship systems from the central Arctic', *Arctic Anthropology* 12(1): 10–30

Damm, Charlotte, Paul Lane and Maitseo Bolaane. 1998. 'Bridging the River Khwai: archaeology, tourism and cultural identity in eastern Ngamiland, Botswana', in Bank, pp. 344–50

Davis, John. 1977. *People of the Mediterranean: an essay in comparative social anthropology*. London: Routledge and Kegan Paul

Deacon, Janette. 1996. 'Archaeology of the flat and grass Bushmen', in Deacon and Dowson, pp. 245–70

Deacon, Janette and Thomas A. Dowson (eds.). 1996. *Voices from the Past: /Xam Bushmen and the Bleek and Lloyd collection*. Johannesburg: Witwatersrand University Press

Deacon, Janette and Pippa Skotnes (eds.). 2014. *The courage of //kabbo: celebrating the 100th anniversary of the publication of Specimens of Bushman folklore*. Cape Town: UCT Press

De Jongh, Michael. 2012. *Roots and routes: Karretjie people of the great Karoo, the marginalisation of a South African first people*. Pretoria: UNISA Press

De Jongh, Michael and Riana Steyn. 1994. 'Itinerancy as a way of life: the nomadic sheep-shearers of the South African Karoo', *Development Southern Africa* 11: 217–28

De Prada-Samper, José Manuel. 2017. '"I have //gubbo": //Kabbo's maps and place-lists and the /Xam concept of !xoe', *South African Archaeological Bulletin* 72(206): 116–24

d'Errico, Francesco, Lucinda Backwell, Paola Villa, Ilaria Degano, Jeannette J. Lucejko, Marion K. Bamford, Thomas F. G. Higham, Maria Perla Colombini and Peter B. Beaumonti. 2012. 'Early evidence of san material culture represented by organic artifacts from Border Cave, South Africa', *PNAS* 109(33): 13214–9

d'Errico, Francesco, Christopher Henshilwood, Marian Vanhaeren, and Karen Van Niekirk. 2005. 'Nassarius kraussianus shell beads from Blombos Cave: evidence for symbolic behaviour in the middle stone age', *Journal of Human Evolution* 48: 3–24

Dickens, Patrick. 1994. *English-Ju/'hoan, Ju/'hoan-English dictionary* (Quellen zur Khoisan-Forschung / Research in Khoisan Studies 8). Cologne: Rüdiger Köppe Verlag

Dieckmann, Ute. 2007. *Hai//om in the Etosha region: a history of colonial settlement, ethnicity and nature conservation*. Basil: Basler Afrika Bibliographien

2009. *Born in Etosha: homage to the cultural heritage of the Hai//om*. Windhoek: Xoms /Omis Project

Dixon, Luke. 2015. *A time there was: a story of rock art, bees and Bushmen*. Hebdon Bridge: Northern Bee Books

Doke, C. M. 1954. *The southern Bantu languages: handbook of African languages*. London: International African Institute

Dornan, S. S. 1917. 'The Tati Bushmen (Masarwas) and their language', *Journal of the Royal Anthropological Institute* 47: 37–112

1925. *Pygmies and Bushmen of the Kalahari*. London: Seeley, Service and Co.

Douglas, Kate. 2018. 'Out of Asia: it's time to rethink the map of human evolution', *New Scientist*, no. 3185 (7 July 2018): 28–31

Dowson, Thomas A. 1992. *Rock engravings of southern Africa*. Johannesburg: Witwatersrand University Press

Dowson, Thomas A. and David Lewis-Williams (eds.) 1994. *Contested images: diversity in southern African rock art research*. Johannesburg: Witwatersrand University Press

Dunbar, R. I. M. 2003. 'The social brain: mind, language and society in evolutionary perspective', *Annual Review of Anthropology* 32: 163–81

Dyll-Myklebust, Lauren. 2015. 'Development narratives: the value of multiple voices and ontologies in Kalahari research', in Tomaselli and Wessels, pp. 57–74

Eggan, Fred. 1954. 'Social anthropology and the method of controlled comparison', *American Anthropologist* 56: 743–60

Eibel-Eibesfeldt, I. 1975. 'Aggression in the !Ko Bushmen', in Thomas R. Williams (ed.), *Psychological anthropology*. The Hague: Mouton, pp. 317–33

Estermann, Carlos. 1976 [1956]. *The ethnography of southwestern Angola*, Vol. I: The non-Bantu peoples: the Ambo ethnic group (edited by Gordon D. Gibson). New York: Africana Publishing Company

Evans-Pritchard, E. E. 1965. 'The comparative method in social anthropology', in *The position of women in primitive societies and other essays*. London: Faber and Faber, pp. 13–36

Farini, G. A. 1896. *Through the Kalahari desert: a narrative of a journey with gun camera, and note-book to Lake N'gami and back*. London: Sampson, Low, Marston, Searle & Rivington

Fehn, Anne-Maria. 2017b. 'Marking direct objects in Ts'ixa (Kalahari Khoe)', in Fehn 2017a, pp. 121–56

Fehn, Anne-Maria (ed.). 2017a. *Khoisan languages and linguistics: proceedings of the 4th international symposium* (Quellen zur Khoisan-Forschung / Research in Khoisan Studies 36. Cologne: Rüdiger Köppe Verlag

Felton, Silke and Heike Becker. 2001. *A gender perspective on the status of the San in southern Africa* (Regional Assessment of the Status of the San in Southern Africa, Report 5). Windhoek: Legal Assistance Centre

Finlayson, Bill and Graeme Warren (eds.). 2017a. *The diversity of hunter-gatherer pasts*. Oxford: Oxbow Books

2017b. 'The diversity of hunter-gatherer pasts: an introduction', in Finlayson and Warren 2017a, pp. 1–13

Flannery, Tim. 1998 [1995]. 'So varied in detail, so similar in outline', in Gowdy, pp. 237–54

Fortes, Meyer. 1958. 'Introduction', in Jack Goody (ed.), *The developmental cycle in domestic groups*. Cambridge University Press, pp. 1–14

Fourie, Louis. 1926. 'Preliminary notes on certain customs of the *Hei//om* Bushmen', *Journal of the S. W. A. Scientific Society* 1: 49–63

    1928. 'The Bushmen of south west Africa', in C. H. L. Hahn, H. Vedder and L. Fourie, *The native tribes of south west Africa*. Cape Town: Cape Times, pp. 79–105

Fritsch, Gustav. 1872. *Die Eingeborenen Südafrikas: ethnographisch und anatomisch Beschreiben*. Breslau: Ferdinand Hirt

    1880. 'Die afrikanischen Buschmänner als Urrasse', *Zeitschrift für Ethnologie*,12: 289–300

    1906. 'Die Buschmänner der Kalahari von S. Passarge', *Zeitschrift für Ethnologie* 38: 71–9, 411–15

Gall, Sandy. 2001. *The Bushmen of southern Africa: slaughter of the innocent*. London: Chatto & Windus

Garfield, Zachary H., Melissa J. Garfield and Barry S. Hewlett. 2016. 'A cross-cultural analysis of hunter-gatherer social learning', in Hideaki Terashima and Barry S. Hewlett (eds.), *Social learning and innovation in contemporary hunter-gatherers* (Replacement of Neanderthals by Modern Humans Series). Tokyo: Springer, pp. 19–34

Gerlach, Linda and Falko Berthold. 2014. 'N!aqriaxe (≠'Amkoe) spatial terms from a genealogical and areal perspective', in Güldemann and Fehn, pp. 209–32

Gibson, Gordon. 1956. 'Double descent and its correlates among the Herero of Ngamiland', *American Anthropologist* 58: 109–39

Gibson, Gordon D., Thomas J. Larson and Cecilia R. McGurk. 1981. *The Kavango peoples* (Studien zur Kulturkunde 56). Wiesbaden: Franz Steiner

Good, Kenneth. 2003. *Bushmen and diamonds: (un)civil society in Botswana* (Discussion Paper 23). Uppsala: Nordiska Afrikainstitutet

    2008. *Diamonds, dispossession and democracy in Botswana*. Oxford: James Currey

Goodwin, A. J. H. and Van Riet Lowe, C. 1929. 'The Stone Age cultures of South Africa', *Annals of the South African Museum* 27(7): 1–289

Gordon, Robert J. 1992. *The Bushman myth: the making of a Namibian underclass*. Boulder, CO: Westview Press

    1997. *Picturing Bushman: the Denver African expedition of 1925*. Athens, OH: Ohio University Press

    1999. '"Bain's Bushmen": scenes at the Empire Exhibition, 1936', in Lindfors, pp. 266–89

Gorelik, Boris. 2017. *Rooibos: an ethnographic perspective*. Pniel, WC: Rooibos Council

Gowdy, John M. (ed.). 1998. *Limited wants, unlimited means: a reader on hunter-gatherer economics and the environment*. Washington, DC: Island Press

Grant, Julie. 2011. Rural development in practice? The experience of the ≠Khomani Bushmen in the Northern Cape, South Africa. PhD thesis, University of Edinburgh

Greenberg, Joseph H. 1955. *Studies in African linguistic classification*. New Haven: Compass Publishing Company

Griffiths, Tom. 1985. *Indigenous peoples and the World Bank: experiences with participation*. Moreton-in-Marsh: Forest Peoples Programme

Gruber, Jeffrey S. 1973. '≠Hòã kinship terms', *Linguistic Inquiry* 4: 427–49

Grün, Rainer and Peter Beaumont. 2001. 'Border Cave revisited: a revised ESR chronology', *Journal of Human Evolution* 40(6): 467–82

Grün, R., P. B. Beaumont and C. B. Stringer. 1990. 'ESR dating evidence for early modern humans at Border Cave in South Africa', *Nature* 344(6266): 537–9

Gulbrandsen, Ørnulf. 1996. *Poverty in the midst of plenty: socio-economic marginalization, ecological deterioration and political stability in a Tswana society.* Bergen: Norse Publications

Güldemann, Tom. 2014. '"Khoisan" linguistic classification today', in Güldemann and Fehn, pp. 1–41

Güldemann, Tom and Anne-Maria Fehn (eds.). 2014. *Beyond Khoisan: historical relations in the Kalahari Basin.* Amsterdam: John Benjamins Publishing Company

Güldemann, Tom and Rainer Vossen. 2000. 'Khoisan', in Bernd Heine and Derek Nurse (eds.), *African languages: an introduction.* Cambridge University Press, pp. 99–122

Guenther, Mathias Georg. 1973. Farm Bushmen and mission Bushmen: socio-cultural change in a setting of conflict and pluralism of the San of the Ghanzi District, Republic of Botswana. PhD dissertation, University of Toronto

1979a. *The farm Bushmen of the Ghanzi District, Botswana.* Stuttgart: Hochschul Verlag

1979b. 'Bushman religion and the (non)sense of anthropological theory of religion', *Sociologus* 29(2): 102–32

1980. 'From "brutal savages" to "harmless people": notes on the changing Western image of the Bushmen', *Paideuma* 26: 123–40

1981. 'Bushman and hunter-gatherer territoriality', *Zeitschrift für Ethnologie* 106(1/2): 109–20

1986. *The Nharo Bushmen of Botswana: tradition and change* (Quellen zur Khoisan-Forschung 3). Hamburg: Helmut Buske Verlag

1989. *Bushman folktales: oral traditions of the Nharo of Botswana and the /Xam of the Cape.* Stuttgart: Franz Steiner Verlag

1992. '"Not a Bushman thing': witchcraft among the Bushmen and hunter-gatherers', *Anthropos* 87: 83–107

1996. 'Attempting to contextualise /Xam oral tradition', in Deacon and Dowson, pp. 77–99

1999. *Tricksters and trancers: Bushman religion and society.* Bloomington, IN: Indiana University Press

2006. '*N//àe* (talking): the oral and rhetorical base of San culture', *Journal of Folklore Research* 43: 241–61

2014a. 'Dreams and stories', in Deacon and Skotnes, pp. 195–209

2014b. 'War and peace among Kalahari San', *Journal of Aggression, Conflict and Peace Research* 6(4): 229–39

2017. '. . . the eyes are no longer wild: you have taken the kudu into your mind': the supererogatory aspect of San hunting', *South African Archaeological Bulletin* 72 (205): 3–16

Guenther, Mathias, Justin Kenrick, Adam Kuper, Evie Plaice, Trond Thuen, Patrick Wolfe, Werner Zips and Alan Barnard. 2006. 'The concept of indigeneity', *Social Anthropology* 14: 17–32

Hahn, Theophilus. 1881. *Tsuni-//goam: the supreme being of the Khoi-khoi.* London: Trübner and Co.

Hammond-Tooke, W. D. (ed.). 1974. *The Bantu-speaking peoples of Southern Africa.* London: Routledge & Kegan Paul

Heine, Bernd and Henry Honken. 2010. 'The Kx'a family: a new Khoisan genealogy', *Journal of Asian and African Studies* 79: 5–36

Heinz, H. J. 1969. 'Search for Bushman tribes of the Okavango', *The Geographical Magazine*, July 1969: 742–50

   1972. 'Territoriality among the Bushmen in general and the !ko in particular', *Anthropos* 67: 405–16

   1978. 'The male initiation of the !ko Bushmen and its acculturative changes'. Unpublished paper delivered at the (First) International Conference on Hunting and Gathering Societies, Paris

   1994 [1966]. *The social organization of the !Kõ Bushmen* (edited by Klaus Keuthmann) (Quellen zur Khoisan-Forschung / Research in Khoisan Studies 10). Cologne: Rüdiger Köppe Verlag

   n.d. [*c.* 1970–3]. 'The people of the Okavango delta'. Unpublished series of six manuscripts comprising: I The /xokwe Bugakwe; II The end of a people (the swamp //anakwe); III The river //anekwe; IV The /anadekwe Bugakwe; V The Tzexa; VI Tales and fables of the //anekwe, Yei, and Bugakwe

Heinz, Hans-Joachim and Marshall Lee. 1978. *Namkwa: life among the Bushmen.* London: Jonathan Cape

Henn, Brenna M., Christopher R. Gignoux, Matthew Jobin, Julie M. Granka, J. M. Macpherson, Jeffrey M. Kidd, Laura Rodríguez-Botigué, Sohini Ramachandran, Lawrence Hon, Abra Brisbin, Alice A. Lin, Peter A. Underhill, David Comas, Kenneth K. Kidd, Paul J. Norman, Peter Parham, Carlos D. Bustamante, Joanna L. Mountain and Marcus W. Feldman. 2011. 'Hunter-gatherer genomic diversity suggests a southern African origin for modern humans', *PNAS* 108(13): 5154–62

Henshilwood, Christopher. 2009. 'The origins of symbolism, spirituality, and shamans: exploring Middle Stone Age material culture in South Africa', in Colin Renfrew and Iain Morley (eds.), *Becoming human: innovation in prehistoric material and spiritual culture.* Cambridge University Press, pp. 29–49

Henshilwood, Christopher S., Francesco d'Errico and Ian Watts. 2009. 'Engraved ochres from the Middle Stone Age levels at Blombos Cave, South Africa', *Journal of Human Evolution* 57: 27–47

Henshilwood, Christopher S. and Francesco d'Errico (eds.). 2011. *Homo symbolicus: the dawn of language, imagination and spirituality.* Amsterdam: John Benjamins Publishing Company

Hewitt, Roger L. 1986. *Structure, meaning and ritual in the narratives of the Southern San* (Quellen zur Khoisan-Forschung 2). Hamburg: Helmut Buske Verlag

High Court of Botswana. 2005. *Judgement.* Lobatse: Misca. No. 52 of 2002 in the Matter between Roy Sesana, Keiwa Setlhobogwa and others, and the Attorney General

Hitchcock, Robert K. 1978. *Kalahari cattle posts: a regional study of hunter-gatherers, pastoralists, and agriculturalists in the western sandveld region, Central District, Botswana* (two volumes). Gaborone: Ministry of Local Government and Lands

   1987. 'Socioeconomic change among the Basarwa in Botswana: an ethnohistorical analysis', *Ethnohistory* 34: 220–55

2016. 'Hunter-gatherers, herders, agropastoralists and farm workers: Hai//om and Ju/'hoansi San and their neighbors in Namibia in the 20th and 21st centuries', in Ikeya and Hitchcock, pp. 269–90

Hitchcock, Robert K. and Megan Biesele. 2014. 'Bitter roots: the ends of a Kalahari myth', *Canadian Journal of African Studies / La Revue canadienne des études africaines* 48(2): 373–6

Hobbes, Thomas. 1991 [1651]. *Leviathan* (revised student edition). Cambridge University Press

Hohmann, Thekla (ed.). 2003. *San and the state: contesting land, development, identity and representation.* Cologne: Rüdiger Köppe Verlag

Hollmann, Jeremy C. (ed.). 2004. *Customs and beliefs of the /Xam Bushmen.* Johannesburg: Wits University Press

How, Marion Walsham (with illustrations by James Walton). 1970 [1958]. *The Mountain Bushmen of Basutoland* (second edition). Pretoria: J. L. van Schaik

Hublin, Jean-Jacques, Abdelouahed Ben-Ncer, Shara E. Bailey, Sarah E. Freidline, Simon Neubauer, Matthew M. Skinner, Inga Bergmann, Adeline Le Cabec, Stefano Benazzi, Katerina Harvati and Philipp Gunz. 2017. 'New fossils from Jebel Irhoud, Morocco and the pan-African origin of *Homo sapiens*', *Nature* 546: 289–92

Ikeya, Kazunobu. 1999. 'The historical dynamics of the socioeconomic relationships between the nomadic San and the rural Kgalagadi', *Botswana Notes and Records* 31: 19–32

2000. 'Environment and resource management among the San in Botswana', *Nomadic Peoples* (n.s.) 4(1): 67–82

2016. 'Interaction of the San, NGOs, companies, and the state', in Ikeya and Hitchcock, pp. 255–6

2017. 'Introduction: studies of sedentarization', in Kazunobu Ikeya (ed.), *Sedentarization among nomadic peoples in Asia and Africa.* (Senri Ethnological Studies 95). Osaka: National Museum of Ethnology

2018. 'Settlement patterns and sedentarization among the San in the Central Kalahari (1930–1966)', in Puckett and Ikeya, pp. 177–96

Ikeya, Kazunobu and Robert K. Hitchcock (eds.). 2016. *Hunter-gatherers and their neighbors in Asia, Africa, and South America* (Senri Ethnological Studies 94). Osaka: National Museum of Ethnology

Impey, S. P. 1926. *Origin of the Bushmen and the rock paintings of South Africa.* Cape Town: Juta & Co.

International African Institute. 1933. 'Summary of proceedings of the twelfth meeting of the Executive Council', *Africa* 6: 472–82

International Labour Organization C. 169. 1989. *Convention concerning Indigenous and Tribal peoples in independent countries.* Geneva: ILO

Izumi, Hiroaki. 2006. *Towards the Neo-Kyoto School: history and development of the primatological approach of the Kyoto School in Japanese primatology and ecological anthropology* (Occasional Papers No. 101). Edinburgh: Centre of African Studies, University of Edinburgh

Jackson, Agnes. 1956. *The Bushmen of South Africa.* Oxford University Press

Jobling, Mark, Edward Hollox, Matthew Hurles, Toomas Kivisild and Chris Tyler-Smith. 2014. *Human evolutionary genetics* (second edition). New York: Garland Science

Jolly, Peter. 2002. 'Therianthropes in San rock art', *South African Archaeological Bulletin* 57(176): 85–103

Jones, Doug. 2010. 'Human kinship, from conceptual structure to grammar', *Behavioral and Brain Sciences* 33: 367–416

Jones, Sir William. 1824. *Discourses delivered before the Asiatic Society: and miscellaneous papers, on the religion, poetry, literature, etc., of the nations of India.* London: C. S. Arnold

Josselin de Jong, J. P. B. de. 1977 [1935]. 'The Malay Archipelago as a field of ethnological study', in P. E. de Josselin de Jong (ed.), *Structural anthropology in the Netherlands.* The Hague: Marinus Nijhoff, pp. 166–82

Katz, Richard. 1982. *Boiling energy: community healing among the Kalahari Kung.* Cambridge, MA: Harvard University Press

Katz, Richard, Megan Biesele and Verna St Denis. 1997. *Healing makes our hearts happy: spirituality and cultural transformation among the Kalahari Ju/'hoansi.* Rochester, VT: Inner Traditions

Keeney, Bradford. 2002. *The Bushman way of tracking God.* New York: Atria Books
  2015. *The way of the Bushman: spiritual teachings and practices of the Kalahari Ju/'hoansi.* Rochester, VT: Bear & Company

Keeney, Bradford and Hillary Keeney. 2013. 'Reentry into the first creation: a contextual frame for the Ju/'hoan Bushman performance of puberty rites, storytelling, and healing dance', *Journal of Anthropological Research* 69: 65–86

Kegl, Judy. 2012. 'Language emergence in a language-ready brain: acquisition', in Gary Morgan and Bernice Woll (eds.), *Directions in sign language acquisition.* Amsterdam: John Benjamins, pp. 207–54

Kelly, Robert L. 2013. *The lifeways of hunter-gatherers: the foraging spectrum.* Cambridge University Press

Kent, Susan (ed.). 1996. *Cultural diversity among twentieth-century foragers: an African perspective.* Cambridge University Press
  2002. *Ethnicity, hunter-gatherers, and the 'other': association or assimilation in Africa.* Washington: Smithsonian Institution Press

Kieama, Kuela. 2010. *Tears for my land: a social history of the Kua of the Central Kalahari Game Reserve, Tc'amnqoo.* Gaborone: Mmegi Publishing House

Kilian-Hatz, Christa. 2003. *Khwe dictionary with a supplement on Khwe place names in the West Caprivi by Matthias Brenzinger* (Namibian African Studies 7). Cologne: Rüdiger Köppe Verlag
  2008. *A grammar of modern Khwe (Central Khoisan)* (Quellen zur Khoisan-Forschung / Research in Khoisan Studies 23). Cologne: Rüdiger Köppe Verlag

Knight, Alec, Peter A. Underhill, Holly M. Mortensen, Lev A. Zhivotovsky, Alice A. Lin, Brenna M. Henn, Dorothy Lewis, Merritt Ruhlen and Joanna L. Mountain. 2003. 'African Y chromosome and mtDNA divergence provides insight into the history of click languages', *Current Biology* 13(6): 464–73

Knight, Chris. 2010. 'The origins of symbolic culture', in Ulrich J. Frey, Charlotte Störmer and Kai P. Willführ (eds.), *Homo novus – a human without illusions.* Berlin: Springer-Verlag, pp. 193–211

Köhler, Oswin. 1962. 'Studien zum Genussystem und Verbalbau der zentralen Khoisan-Sprachen', *Anthropos* 57: 529–46

1966. 'Tradition und Wandel bei den Kxoé-Buschmännern von Mutsiku', *Sociologus* 16(2): 122–40

1989. *Die Welt der Kxoé Buschleute im südlichen Afrika. Eine Selbstdarstellung in ihrer eingenen Sprache*, Vol. 1. Berlin: Dietrich Reimer

Köhler, Oswin, with Gertrud Boden and Anne-Maria Fehn (editors). 2018. *The world of the Khwe Bushmen in southern Africa: a self-portrait in their own language – Die Welt der Kxoé-Buschleute im südlichen Afrika: Eine Selbstdarstellung in ihrer eigenen Sprache*. Berlin: Dietrich Reimer

Kordsmeyer, Tobias, Pádraig MacCarron and R. I. M. Dunbar. 2017. 'Sizes of permanent campsite communities reflect constraints on natural human communities', *Current Anthropology* 58: 289–94

Kuper, Adam. 1970. *Kalahari village politics: an African democracy*. Cambridge University Press

1979. 'Regional comparison in African anthropology', *African Affairs* 78: 103–13

1982. *Wives for cattle: bridewealth and marriage in southern Africa*. London: Routledge and Kegan Paul

1987. *South Africa and the anthropologist*. London: Routledge and Kegal Paul

2003. 'The return of the native', *Current Anthropology* 44: 389–402

2005. *The reinvention of primitive society: transformations of a myth*. London: Routledge

Kuper, Adam and Jonathan Marks. 2011. 'Anthropologists unite!', *Nature* 470: 166–8

Kusimba, Siebel Barut. 2003. *African foragers: environment, technology, interactions*. Walnut Creek: AltaMira Press

Leacock, Eleanor and Richard Lee (eds.). 1982. *Politics and history in band societies*. Cambridge University Press

Lee, Richard B. 1969. '!Kung Bushman subsistence: an input-output analysis', in Andrew P. Vayda (ed.), *Environment and cultural behavior*. New York: Natural History Press, pp. 47–79

1972. 'The !Kung Bushmen of Botswana', in Bicchieri, pp. 327–68

1979. *The !Kung San: men, women, and work in a foraging society*. Cambridge University Press

1984. *The Dobe !Kung*. New York: Holt, Rinehart and Winston

1990. 'Primitive communism and the origin of social inequality', in Steadman Upham (ed.), *The evolution of political systems: sociopolitics in small-scale sedentary societies*. Cambridge University Press, pp. 225–46

1993. *The Dobe Ju/'hoansi* (second edition). Fort Worth: Harcourt Brace College Publishers

1998. 'Gumi kwara: I kwara e ba n//a basi o win si !kwana: oral histories from Nyae Nyae-Dobe and the Khoisan renaissance', in Bank, pp. 67–73

2003. *The Dobe Ju/'hoansi* (third edition). Stamford, CT: Thomson Learning

2013. *The Dobe Ju/'hoansi* (fourth, International edition). London: Wadsworth, Cengage Learning

2014. 'Hunter-gatherers on the best-seller list: Steven Pinker and the "Bellicose School's" treatment of forager violence', *Journal of Aggression, Conflict and Peace Research* 6(4): 216–28

2018. 'Persistence of foraging among Tsumkwe Ju/'hoansi in the 21st century', in Puckett and Ikeya, pp. 161–76

Lee, Richard B. and Irven DeVore. 1968a. 'Problems in the study of hunters and gatherers', in Richard B. Lee and Irven DeVore (eds.), *Man the hunter*. Chicago: Aldine, pp. 3–12

Lee, Richard B. and Irven DeVore (eds.). 1968b. *Man the hunter*. Chicago: Aldine

Lee, Richard B. and Irven DeVore (eds.). 1976. *Kalahari hunter-gatherers: studies of the !Kung San and their neighbors*. Cambridge, MA: Harvard University Press

Lee, Richard B. and Mathias Guenther. 1991. 'Oxen or Onions: the search for trade (and truth) in the Kalahari', *Current Anthropology* 32: 592–601

1993. 'Problems in Kalahari historical ethnography and the tolerance of error' *History in Africa* 20: 185–235

Lee, Richard B., Robert Hitchcock and Megan Biesele (guest eds.). 2002a. 'The Kalahari San: self-determination in the desert', *Cultural Survival Quarterly* 26 (1) (spring issue)

Lee, Hitchcock and Biesele. 2002b. 'Introduction: foragers to First Peoples, the Kalahari San today', in Lee, Hitchcock and Biesele 2002a, pp. 9–12

Lévi-Strauss, Claude. 1968. 'The concept of primitiveness', in Lee and DeVore 1968b, pp. 349–52

1969. *The elementary structures of kinship* (revised edition, translated by James Harle Bell, John Richard von Sturmer and Rodney Needham). Boston: Beacon Press

Levy, Leah. 1968. *A preliminary list of publications referring to non-Bantu click languages* (Communications from the School of African Studies, n.s. 33). Cape Town: Department of African Languages, School of African Studies

Lewis, Jerome. 2009. 'As well as words: Congo Pygmy hunting, mimicry, and play', in Botha and Knight, pp. 236–56

Lewis-Williams, J. D. 1980. 'Ethnography and iconography: aspects of Southern San thought and art', *Man* (n.s.) 15: 467–82

1981. *Believing and seeing: symbolic meanings in Southern San rock paintings*. London: Academic Press

1983. *The rock art of southern Africa*. Cambridge University Press

1990. *Discovering southern African rock art*. Cape Town: David Philip

1996. '"A visit to the lion's house', the structure, metaphors and socio-political significance of a nineteenth-century Bushman myth', in Deacon and Dowson, pp. 122–41

2002a. *The mind in the cave: consciousness and the origins of art*. London: Thames & Hudson

2002b. *A cosmos in stone: interpreting religion and society through rock art*. Walnut Creek: AltaMira Press

2010. *Conceiving God: the cognitive origin and evolution of religion*. London: Thames & Hudson

2015. *Myth and meaning: San-Bushman folklore in global context*. Walnut Creek: Left Coast Press

2018. 'Three nineteenth-century Southern African San myths: a study in meaning', *Africa* 88: 138–59

Lewis-Williams, J. D. (ed.). 2000. *Stories that float from afar: ancestral folklore of the San of southern Africa*. Cape Town: David Philip

Lewis-Williams, David and Sam Challis. 2011. *Deciphering ancient minds: the mystery of San Bushman rock art*. London: Thames & Hudson

Lewis-Williams, David and Thomas Dowson. 1989. *Images of power: understanding Bushman rock art*. Johannesburg: Southern Book Publishers

Lewis-Williams, David and David Pearce. 2005. *Inside the Neolithic mind: consciousness, cosmos the realm of the gods*. London: Thames & Hudson

Lew-Levy, Sheina, Noa Lavi, Rachel Reckin, Jurgi Cristóbal-Azkarate and Kate Ellis-Davies. 2018. 'How do hunter-gatherer children learn social and gender norms? A meta-ethnographic review', *Cross-Cultural Research* 52: 213–55

Lindfors, Bernth (ed.). 1999. *Africans on stage: studies in ethnological show business*. Bloomington: Indiana University Press / Cape Tow: David Philip

Lombard, Marlize, Lyn Wadley, Janette Deacon, Sarah Wurz, Isabelle Parsons, Molboheng Mohapi, Joane Swart and Peter Mitchell. 2012. 'South African and Lesotho Stone Age sequence updated (I)', *South African Archaeological Bulletin* 67 (195): 123–44

London Missionary Society. 1935. *The Masarwa (Bushmen): report of an inquiry by the South African District Committee of the London Missionary Society*. Alice: Lovedale Press

López, Saioa, Lucy van Dorp and Garrett Hellenthal. 2015. 'Human dispersal out of Africa: a lasting debate', *Evolutionary Bioinformatics* 11(S2): 57–68

Low, Chris. 2014. 'Locating /Xam beliefs and practices in a contemporary KhoeSan context', in Deacon and Skotnes, pp. 349–61

McBrearty, Sally and Alison A. Brooks. 2000. 'The revolution that wasn't: a new interpretation of the origin of modern human behaviour', *Journal of Human Evolution* 39: 453–563

McGranaghan, Mark. 2015. '"Different people" coming together: representations of alterity in /Xam Bushman (San) narrative', in Tomaselli and Wessels, pp. 206–25

McGregor, William B. 2014. 'Shua kinship terminology', in Barnard and Boden, pp. 39–62

McWhorter, John H. 2011. *Linguistic simplicity and complexity: why do languages undress?* Boston: De Gruyter Mouton

Maddock, Kenneth. 1973. *The Australian Aborigines: a portrait of their society*. London: Allen Lane the Penguin Press

Malan, J. S. 1995. *Peoples of Namibia*. Wingate Park: Rhino Publishers

Mandela, Nelson. 1997. 'Message from President Nelson Mandela to the International Conference on Khoisan Identities and Cultural Heritage', in Bank 1998, p. vi

Marais, J. S. 1939. *The Cape Coloured People, 1652–1937*. London: Longmans, Green & Co.

Marean, Curtis W. 2010. 'Pinnacle Point Cave 13B (Western Cape Province, South Africa) in context: the Cape Floral kingdom, shellfish, and modern human origins', *Journal of Human Evolution* 59 (3–4): 425–43

Marshall, John. 1957. *The hunters*. Watertown, MA: Documentary Educational Resources

2012 [1993]. 'Filming and learning', in Jay Ruby (ed.), *The cinema of John Marshall*. London: Routledge, pp. 1–134

Marshall, John and Claire Ritchie. 1984. *Where are the Ju/wasi of Nyae Nyae? Changes in a Bushman society: 1958–1981* (CAS Communications 9). Cape Town: Centre for African Studies, University of Cape Town

Marshall, Lorna J. 1976. *The !Kung of Nyae Nyae*. Cambridge, MA: Harvard University Press

   1999. *Nyae Nyae !Kung beliefs and rites*. Cambridge, MA: Peabody Museum of Archaeology and Ethnology

Mason, John. 2006. 'Apollo 11 Cave in southwest Namibia: some observations on the site and its rock art', *South African Archaeological Bulletin* 61(183): 76–89

Mbeki, Thabo. 2000. *Address by President Thabo Mbeki at the unveiling of the Coat of Arms, Kwagafontein, 27 April 2000*. Pretoria: Office of the Presidency

Mguni, Siyakha. 2015. *Termites of the gods: San cosmology in southern African rock art*. Johannesburg: Wits University Press

Miller, G. H., O. B. Beaumont, H. J. Deacon, A. S. Brooks, P. E. Hare, and A. J. T. Jull. 1999. 'Earliest modern humans in South Africa dated by isoleucine epimerization in ostrich eggshell', *Quaternary Science Reviews* 18: 1537–8

Mitchell, Peter. 2002. *The archaeology of southern Africa*. Cambridge University Press

Mithen, Steven. 1996. *The prehistory of the mind: a search for the origins if art, religion and science*. London: Thames & Hudson

Mogwe, Alice. 1992. *Who was (t)here first: an assessment of the human rights situation of Basarwa in selected communities in the Ghanzi district, Botswana* (Occasional Paper 10). Gaborone: Botswana Christian Council

Mohr, Susanne and Anne-Maria Fehn. 2013. 'Phonology of hunting signs is two Kalahari Khoe-speaking groups (Ts'ixa and //Ani)', *LSA Annual Meeting Extended Abstracts* S.I. vol. 4, 29: 1–4. DOI:10.3765/exabs.v0i0.616

Moran, Shane. 2009. *Representing Bushmen: South Africa and the origin of language*. Rochester: University of Rochester Press

Morris, Alan G. 1998. 'The Griqua and the Khoikhoi: biology, ethnicity and the construction of identity', in Bank, pp. 367–73

Morris, Brian. 1994. *Anthropology of the self: the individual in cultural perspective*. London: Pluto Press

Mphinyane, Sethunya Tshepho. 2002. 'Power and powerlessness: when support becomes overbearing – the case of outsider activism on the resettlement issue of the Basarwa of the central Kalahari game reserve', *Pula: Botswana Journal of African Studies* 16: 75–85

Myburgh, Paul John. 1985. *People of the great sand face*. Norwich: Anglia Television for Channel Four

   2013. *The Bushman winter has come: the true story of the last band of /Gwikwe Bushmen on the great sand face*. Cape Town: Penguin Books

Niezen, Ronald. 2003. *The origins of indigenism: human rights and the politics of identity*. Berkeley: University of California Press

   2010. *Public justice and the anthropology of law*. Cambridge University Press

Nilssen, Peter and Craig Foster. 2017. 'The key to our future is in our past: philosophical thoughts on saving us from ourselves', *The Digging Stick* 34(1): 1–6

Olivier, Emmanuelle. 1998. 'La musique ju/'hoan: de la creation à la consumation', in Olivier and Valentin, pp. 171–8

   2001. 'Categorizing the Ju/'hoan musical heritage', *African Study Monographs*, Supplement 27: 11–27

Olivier, Emmanuelle and Manuel Vallentin (eds.). 1998. *Les Bushmen dans l'histoire*. Paris: CNRS Éditions

Olusoga, David and Casper W. Erichsen. 2010. *The Kaiser's holocaust: Germany's forgotten genocide and the colonial roots of Nazism*. London: Faber and Faber

Ono, Hitomi. 2014. 'Extra-marital relationships and spouse exchange among G//ana peoples', in Barnard and Boden, pp. 85–98

Oppenheimer, Stephen. 2004. *The real Eve: modern man's journey out of Africa*. New York: Carroll & Graf

2009. 'The great arc of dispersal of modern humans: Africa to Australia', *Quaternary International* 201: 2–13

Orpen, Joseph M. 1874. 'A glimpse into the mythology of the Maluti Bushmen', *Cape Monthly Magazine* (n.s.) 9: 1–9

Pakendorf, Brigitte. 2014. 'Molecular anthropological perspectives on the Kalahari Basin Area', in Tom Güldemann and Anne-Maria Fehn (eds.), *Beyond Khoisan: historical relations in the Kalahari Basin*. Amsterdam: John Benjamins Publishing Company, pp. 45–68

Parsons, Neil. 1999. '"Clicko": Franz Taaibosch, South African Bushman entertainer in England, France, Cuba, and the United States, 1908–1940', in Lindfors, pp. 203–27

2009. *Clicko, the wild dancing Bushman*. Chicago: University of Chicago Press

Passarge, Siegfried. 1905. 'Das Okavangosumpfland und seine Bewohner', *Zeitschrift für Ethnologie* 37: 649–716

1907. *Die Buschmänner der Kalahari*. Berlin: Dietrich Reimer

Penn, Nigel. 1996. '"Fated to perish": the destruction of the Cape San', in Skotnes, pp. 81–91

Pickrell, Joseph K., Nick Patterson, Chiara Barbieri, Falko Berthold, Linda Gerlach, Tom Güldemann, Blesswell Kure, Sununguko Wata Mpoloka, Hirosi Nakagawa, Christfried Naumann, Mark Lipson, Po-Ru Loh, Joseph Lachance, Joanna Mountain, Carlos D. Bustamante, Bonnie Berger, Sarah A. Tishkoff, Brenna M. Henn, Mark Stoneking, David Reich and Brigitte Pakendorf. 2012. 'The genetic prehistory of southern Africa', *Nature Communications* 3, Article number: 1143 doi:10.1038/ncomms2140

Power, Camilla and Ian Watts. 1997. 'The woman with the zebra's penis: gender, mutability and performance', *Journal of the Royal Anthropological Institute* (n.s.) 3: 537–60

Potgieger, E. F. 1955. *The disappearing Bushmen of Lake Chrissie: a preliminary survey*. Pretoria: J. L. van Schaik

Puckett, R. Fleming and Kazunobu Ikeya (eds.). 2018. *Research and activism among the Kalahari San today: ideas, challenges, and debates* (Senri Ethnological Studies 99). Osaka: National Museum of Ethnology

[Radcliffe-]Brown, A. R. 1913. 'Three tribes of Western Australia', *Journal of the Royal Anthropological Institute* 43: 143–70

1924. 'The mother's brother in South Africa', *South African Journal of Science* 21: 542–55

1952. *Structure and function in primitive society*. New York: Cohen & West

Ritterband, Salomé. 2018. *Tracking indigenous heritage: Ju/'hoansi San learning, interpreting, and staging tradition for a sustainable future in cultural tourism in the Tsumkwe District of Namibia*. Zurich: LIT Verlag

Rivière, Peter. 1969. *Marriage among the Trio: a principle of social organization.* Oxford: Clarendon Press

Robins, Steven, Elias Madzudzo and Matthias Brenzinger. 2001. *An assessment of the status of the San in South Africa, Angola, Zambia and Zimbabwe* (Regional Assessment of the Status of the San in Southern Africa, Report 2). Windhoek: Legal Assistance Centre

Rosenberg, Harriet G. 1990. 'Complaint discourse, aging, and caregiving among the !Kung San of Botswana', in Jay Sokolovsky (ed.), *The cultural context of aging: worldwide perspectives.* New York: Bergin & Garvey, pp. 19–41

Ruby, Jay (ed.). 2012 [1993]. *The cinema of John Marshall.* London: Routledge

Russell, Margo and Martin Russell. 1979. *Afrikaners of the Kalahari: white minority in a black state.* Cambridge University Press

Sahlins, Marshall. 1968. 'La première société d'abondance', *Les Temps modernes*, 268: 641–80
    1974. *Stone age economics.* London: Tavsitock Publications

Sands, Bonnie. 1998. *Eastern and southern African Khoisan: evaluating claims for distant linguistic relationships* (Quellen zur Khoisan-Forschung / Research in Khoisan Studies 14). Cologne: Rüdiger Köppe Verlag

Sansom, Basil. 1974. 'Traditional economic systems', in Hammond-Tooke, pp. 135–76

Sapignoli, Maria. 2015. 'Dispossession in the age of humanity: human rights, citizenship, and indigeneity in the Central Kalahari', *Anthropological Forum* 25: 285–305
    2018. *Hunting justice: displacement, law, and activism in the Kalahari.* Cambridge University Press

Sapir, Edward. 1921. *Language: an introduction to the study of speech.* New York: Harcourt Brace & Co.

Sarkin, Jeremy. 2010. *Germany's genocide of the Herero: his general, his settlers, his soldiers.* Cape Town: UCT Press

Saugestad, Sidsel. 2001a. *The inconvenient indigenous: remote area development in Botswana, donor assistance, and the first people of the Kalahari.* Uppsala: Nordiska Afrikainstitutet
    2001b. 'Contested images: "First Peoples" or "marginalized minorities" in Africa?', in Barnard and Kenrick, pp. 299–322
    2011. 'Impact of international mechanisms on indigenous rights in Botswana', *International Journal of Human Rights* 15: 37–61

Scerri, Eleanor. 2018. 'The origin of our species', *New Scientist*, no. 3175 (28 April 2018): 34–7

Schapera, Isaac. 1927. 'Bows and arrows of the Bushmen', *Man* 27: 113–17 (article no. 72)
    1930. *The Khoisan peoples of South Africa: Bushmen and Hottentots.* London: George Routledge & Sons
    1952. *The ethnic composition of Tswana tribes* (LSE Monographs on Social Anthropology 11). London: London School of Economics
    1984 [1953]. *The Tswana.* London: KPI in Association with the International African Institute

Schapera, Isaac (ed.). 1937. *The Bantu-speaking tribes of South Africa.* London: George Routledge & Sons

Schmidt, P. W. 1929. 'Zur Erforschung der alten Buschmann-Religion', *Africa* 2: 291–301

1939. *Primitive revelation* (translated by Joseph J. Baierl). St Louis: B. Herder Book Co.

Schmidt, Sigrid. 2013a. *A catalogue of Khoisan folktales of southern Africa*, 2nd, revised edition (Quellen zur Khoisan-Forschung / Research in Khoisan Studies 28.1, Part 1: Introduction, types, indices, sources). Cologne: Rüdiger Köppe Verlag

2013b. *A catalogue of Khoisan folktales of southern Africa*, 2nd, revised edition (Quellen zur Khoisan-Forschung / Research in Khoisan Studies 28.2, Part 2: The tales and analyses). Cologne: Rüdiger Köppe Verlag

Schneider, David M. 1984. *A critique of the study of kinship*. Ann Arbor: University of Michigan Press

Shepard, Paul. 1998 [1992]. 'A post-historic primitivism', in Gowdy, pp. 281–325

Shostak, Marjorie. 1976. 'A !Kung woman's memories of childhood', in Lee and DeVore, pp. 246–78

1981. *Nisa: the life and words of a !Kung woman*. Cambridge, MA: Harvard University Press

2000. *Return to Nisa*. Cambridge, MA: Harvard University Press

Shrubsall, F. 1898. 'The crania of African bush races', *Journal of the Anthropological Institute* 27: 263–90

Silberbauer, George B. 1963. 'Marriage and the girl's puberty ceremony of the G/wi Bushmen', *Africa* 33: 12–24

1965. *Report to the government of Bechuanaland on the Bushman survey*. Gaberones [Gaborone]: Bechuanaland Government

1972. 'The G/wi Bushmen', in Bicchieri, pp. 271–326

1981. *Hunter and habitat in the central Kalahari desert*. Cambridge University Press

1982a. 'Review of *The San, hunter-gatherers of the Kalahari* (Jiro Tanaka)', *Man* (n.s.) 17: 803

1982b. 'Political process in G/wi bands', in Leacock and Lee, pp. 23–35

1996. 'Neither are your ways my ways', in Kent, pp. 21–64

Sion, Vivianne, Fabrizio Mafessoni, Benjamin Vernot, Cesare de Filipo, Steffi Grote, Bence Viola, Mateja Hajdinjak, Stéjane Peyrégregne, Sarah Nagel, Samantha Brown, Katerina Douka, Tom Higham, Maxim B. Kozlikin, Michael V. Shunkov, Anatoly P. Derevianko, Janet Kelso, Matthias Meyer, Kay Prüfer, and Svante Pääbo. 2018. 'The genome of the offspring of a Neanderthal mother and a Denisovan father', *Nature* 561: 113–16

Skotnes, Pippa. 2007. *Claim to the country: the archive of Lucy Lloyd and Wilhelm Bleek*. Johannesburg: Jacana

Skotnes, Pippa (ed.). 1996. *Miscast: negotiating the presence of the Bushmen*. Cape Town: University of Cape Town

Smith, Andrew B. 1985. 'Concepts of Khoi and San in South African history', *African Languages Association of Southern Africa, Khoisan Special Interest Group, Newsletter* 3: 10–12

Solway, Jacqueline S. and Richard B. Lee. 1990. 'Foragers, genuine or spurious? Situating the Kalahari San in history', *Current Anthropology* 31: 109–46

Spikens, Penny, Gail Hitchins and Andy Needham. 2017. 'Strangers in a strange land? Intimate sociality and emergent creativity in Middle Pleistocene Europe', in Finlayson and Warren, pp. 132–47

Spoor, Otto H. 1962. *Wilhelm Heinrich Immanuel Bleek: a bio-bibliographical sketch*. Cape Town: University of Cape Town Libraries

Steyn, H. P. 1971. 'Aspects of the economic life of some nomadic Nharo Bushman groups', *Annals of the South African Museum* 56: 275–322

Stoler, Ann Laura. 2016. *Duress: imperial durabilities in our times*. Durham, NC: Duke University Press

Stopa, Roman. 1972. *Structure of Bushman and its traces in Indo-European*. London: Curzon Press

Stow, George W. 1905. *The native races of South Africa: a history of the intrusion of the Hottentots and Bantu into the hunting grounds of the Bushmen, the aborigines of the country*. London: Swan Sonnenschein

Stringer, Chris. 2011. *The origin of our species*. London: Allen Lane

Strong, Adrian. 2015. *Filming real people: John Marshall, Ju/'hoansi, and the Bushman myth*. Aarhus: Intervention Press

Sugawara, Kazuyoshi. 2004. 'The modern history of Japanese studies on the San hunter-gatherers', in Barnard (ed.), pp. 115–28

Sullivan, Sian. 2001. 'Difference, identity, and access to official discourses. Hai//om, "Bushmen", and a recent Namibian ethnography', *Anthropos* 96: 179–92

Sullivan, Sian, compiler, with Mike Hannis, Angela Impey, Chris Low and Rick Rohde. 2017. *Future pasts: landscape, memory and music in west Namibia*. Bath, England: Future Pasts (Bath Spa University)

Suzman, James. 2000. *'Things from the bush': a contemporary history of the Omaheke Bushmen* (Namibia Studies Series 5). Basel: P. Schlettwein

2001a. *An introduction to the regional assessment of the status of the San in southern Africa* (Regional Assessment of the Status of the San in Southern Africa, Report 1). Windhoek: Legal Assistance Centre

2001b. *An assessment of the status of the San in Namibia* (Regional Assessment of the Status of the San in Southern Africa, Report 4). Windhoek: Legal Assistance Centre

2002. 'Kalahari conundrums: relocation, resistance and international support in the Central Kalahari Botswana', *Before Farming* 2002(3): 1–10

2017. *Affluence without abundance: the disappearing world of the Bushmen*. New York: Bloomsbury

Sylvain, Renée. 1999. 'We work to have life': Ju/hoan women, work and survival in the Omaheke region, Namibia. PhD dissertation, University of Toronto

Tabler, Edward C. 1973. *Pioneers of South West Africa and Ngamiland, 1738–1880*. Cape Town: A. A. Balkema

Takada, Akira. 2015. *Narratives of San ethnicity: the cultural and ecological foundations of lifeworld among the !Xun of north-central Namibia*. Kyoto: Kyoto University Press/Melbourne: Trans Pacific Press

Takada, Akira (ed.). 2016. 'Natural history of communication among the Central Kalahari San', *African Study Monographs*, Supplementary Issue No. 52.

Tanaka, Jiro. 1976. 'Subsistence ecology of Central Kalahari San', in Lee and DeVore, pp. 98–119

1978. *A San vocabulary of the central Kalahari: G//ana and G/wi dialects*. Tokyo: Institute for the Study of Languages and Cultures of Asia and Africa

1980. *The San, hunter-gatherers of the Kalahari: a study in ecological anthropology.* Tokyo: University of Tokyo Press

2014. *The Bushmen: a half-century chronicle of transformations in hunter-gatherer life and ecology* (translated by Minako Sato). Kyoto: Kyoto University Press / Melbourne: Trans Pacific Press

2016. 'Social integration of the San society from the viewpoint of sexual relationships', in Takada, 27–40

Tanaka, Jiro and Kazuyoshi Sugawara. 1996. 'Introduction', *African Study Monographs,* Supplement 22: 3–9

Tanaka, Jiro and Kazuyoshi Sugawara (eds.). 2010. *An encyclopedia of /Gui and //Gana culture and society.* Kyoto: Laboratory of Cultural Anthropology

Taylor, Julie J. 2012. *Naming the land: San ethnicity and community conservation in Namibia's West Caprivi.* Basil: Basler Afrika Bibliographien

Taylor, Michael John. 2000. Life, land and power: contesting development in northern Botswana. PhD thesis, University of Edinburgh

2002a. '"Mapping the land" in Gudigwa: Bugakhwe land, history and territoriality', *Pula: Botswana Journal of African Studies* 16: 98–109

2002b. 'The Shaping of San livelihood strategies: government policy and popular values', *Development and Change* 33: 467–88

2003. '"Wilderness", "development", and San ethnicity in contemporary Botswana', in Hohmann, pp. 255–79

Thackeray, J. Francis. 2018. 'A painting of a gemsbok in the "White Lady" panel in the Brandberg, Namibia', *The Digging Stick* 35(1): 11

Thomas, Elizabeth Marshall. 1959. *The harmless people.* London: Secker and Warburg

1994. 'Management of violence among the Ju/wasi of Nyae Nyae: the old way and a new way', in S.P. Reyna and R.E. Downs (eds.), *Studying war: anthropological perspectives.* Langhorne, PA: Gordon and Breach, pp. 69–84

2006. *The old way: a story of the first people.* New York: Farrar, Strauss, Giroux

Thomas, Roie. 2016. *Bushmen in the tourist imaginary.* Newcastle upon Tyne: Cambridge Scholars Publishing

Thompson, Keith. 1976. 'The Okavango delta and its future utilisation: an attempt at a synthesis of the proceedings', in Botswana Society, pp. 3–12

Tlou, Thomas. 1985. *A history of Ngamiland, 1750–1906: the formation of an African state.* Gaborone: Macmillan

Tobias, Phillip V. 1978. 'The San: an evolutionary perspective', in Phillip V. Tobias (ed.), *The Bushmen: San hunters and herders of southern Africa.* Cape Town: Human & Rousseau, pp. 16–32

Tomaselli, Keyan G. 1995. 'Introduction', *Critical Arts* 9(2): i–xxi

1999 (ed.). 'Encounters in the Kalahari', special issue of *Visual Anthropology* 12 (2–3): 131–364

2017. 'Filming real people', *Visual Anthropology* 30(2): 170–3

Tomaselli, Keyan G. and Michael Wessels (eds.). 2015. *San representation: politics, practice and possibilities.* London: Routledge

Traill, A. 1973. ' "N4 or S7": another Bushman language', *African Studies* 32: 25–32

1974. *The compleat guide to the Koon* (ASI Communication No. 1). Johannesburg: African Studies Institute

1984. 'Correspondence', *African Languages Association of Southern Africa, Khoisan Special Interest Group, Newsletter* 2: 16–18

1994. *A !Xóõ dictionary* (Quellen zur Khoisan-Forschung / Research in Khoisan Studies 9). Cologne: Rüdiger Köppe Verlag

1996. '!Khwa-Ka Hhoutiten Hhoutiten 'The rush of the storm': the linguistic death of the /Xam', in Skotnes, pp. 161–83

2018. *A trilingual !Xóõ dictionary* (edited by Hirosi Nakagawa and Andy Chebanne) (Quellen zur Khoisan-Forschung / Research in Khoisan Studies 37). Cologne: Rüdiger Köppe Verlag

Trubetzkoy, Nikolai S. 1923. 'Vavilonskaja bašnja i smešenie jazykov' [The Tower of Babel and the confusion of languages], *Evrazijskij vremennik* 3: 107–24

Udenga, Martins. 2017. *Angola economy and political leadership: history of Angolan Civil War in detail.* CreateSpace

Useb, Joram. 2002. 'Land crisis: a San perspective', in Lee, Hitchcock and Biesele 2002a, p. 32

Uys, Jamie. 1980. *The gods must be crazy.* Johannesburg: Ster-Kinekor

Valiente-Noailles, Carlos. 1988. *El circulo y el fuego: sociedad y derecho de los kúa.* Buenos Aires: Ediar

1993. *The Kua: life and soul of the Central Kalahari Bushmen.* Rotterdam: A. A. Balkema

1994. Les sexes chez les Kúa (Bochiman) du centre, du sud et de l'est de la Réserve Centrale du Kalahari, au Botswana: relations, differences et complémentairités dans les roles et les symbols (two volumes), doctoral thesis, École des Hautes Études en Sciences Sociales, Paris

Van der Post, L. 1958. *The lost world of the Kalahari.* London: The Hogarth Press

1961. *The heart of the hunter.* London: The Hogarth Press

Van Vuuren, Helize. 2016. *A necklace of springbok ears: /Xam orality and South African literature.* Stellenbosch: Sun Press

Van Warmelo, N. J. 1974. 'The classification of cultural groups', in Hammond-Tooke, pp. 56–84

Vierich, Helga. 1982. The Kũa of the southern Kalahari: a study of the socio-ecology of dependency. PhD dissertation, University of Toronto

2015. 'Rational and emotional intelligence through group selection in a wild primate: reflections on culture, evolution, and human nature'. Unpublished paper delivered at the Eleventh International Conference on Hunting and Gathering Societies, Vienna

2018a. 'When the sacred circle is broken'. Unpublished manuscript

2018b. 'Economies as trophic flows'. Unpublished manuscript

Vierich, Helga I. D. and Robert K. Hitchcock. 1996. 'Kũa: farmer/foragers of the eastern Kalahari, Botswana', in Kent, pp. 108–24

Vinding, Diana and Cæcilie Mikkelsen (eds.). 2016. *The indigenous world 2016.* Copenhagen: IWGIA

Vinnicombe, Patricia. 1976. *People of the eland: rock paintings of the Drakensberg Bushmen as a reflection of their life and thought.* Pietermaritzburg: University of Natal Press

Visser, Hessel. 2001. *Naro dictionary: Naro-English, English-Naro* (fourth edition). Gantsi: Naro Language Project / SIL International Swann

Visser, Hessel and Cobi Visser. 1998. 'Analysis of Naro names', in Bank, pp. 225–31

Vogelsang, Ralf, Jürgen Richter, Zenobia Jacobs, Barbara Eichhorn, Veerle Linseele and Richard G. Roberts. 2010. 'New excavations of Middle Stone Age deposits at Apollo 11 rockshelter, Namibia: stratigraphy, archaeology, chronology and past environments', *Journal of African Archaeology* 8(2): 185–218

Von Wielligh, Gideon Retief. 2017. *Bushman stories, volumes 1–4* (translated by Philip John, edited by Chris Low and Neil Rusch). Cape Town: !Khwa ttu & Mantis Books

Vossen, Rainer. 1991. 'What do we do with irregular correspondences? The case of the Khoe languages', *History in Africa* 18: 359–79

Vossen, Rainer and Wilfrid H. G. Haacke (eds.). 2016. *Lone Tree – scholarship in the service of the Koon: essays in memory of Antony T. Traill*. Cologne: Rüdiger Köppe Verlag

Waddell, Gene. 2018a. *Bushmen: were we like them? Volume 4*. CreateSpace
2018b. *Bushmen: were we like them? Volume 5*. CreateSpace

Wallace, Marion with John Kinahan. 2011. *A history of Namibia*. London: Hurst & Co.

Wang, Ning. 1999. 'Rethinking authenticity in tourism experience', *Annals of Tourism Research* 26: 349–70

Watts, Ian. 2017. 'Rain Serpents in northern Australia and southern Africa: a common ancestry?', in Camilla Power, Morna Finnegan and Hilary Callan (eds.), *Human origins: contributions from social anthropology*. New York: Berghahn Books, pp. 248–71

Watts, Ian, Michael Chazan and Jayne Wilkins. 2016. 'Early evidence for brilliant ritualized display: specularite use in the Northern Cape (South Africa) between ~500 and ~300 Ka', *Current Anthropology* 57: 287-

Weintroub, Jill. 2014. 'Colonial adventurer, loyal follower or problematic afterthought? Revisiting the life and scholarship of Dorothea Bleek', in Deacon and Skotnes, pp. 151–68

Wells, Spencer. 2007. *Deep ancestry: inside the genographic project*. Washington, DC: National Geographic

Wessels, Michael. 2010. *Bushman letters: interpreting /Xam narrative*. Johannesburg: Wits University Press
2014. 'Bushman literature of the Drakensberg: the re-emergence of a "vanished voice"', in Deacon and Skotnes, pp. 265–74

Westphal, E. O. J. 1971. 'The click languages of southern and eastern Africa', in Thomas A. Sebeok (ed.), *Current trends in linguistics*, Vol. 7, Linguistics in Sub-Saharan Africa. The Hague: Mouton, pp. 376–420

Widlok, Thomas. 1994. The social relationships of changing Hai//om hunter-gatherers in northern Namibia, 1990–1994. PhD thesis, University of London
1999. *Living on mangetti: 'Bushman' autonomy and Namibian independence*. Oxford University Press
2001. 'Living on ethnography and comparison: what difference do Hai//om "Bushmen" make to anthropology (and vice versa)?', *Anthropos* 96: 359–78
2016. 'Hunter-gatherer situations', *Hunter-Gatherer Research* 2(2): 127–43
2017. *Anthropology and the economy of sharing*. London: Routledge

Wiessner, Pauline Wilson [Polly]. 1977. Hxaro: a regional system of reciprocity for reducing risk among the !Kung San (vol. 1). PhD dissertation, University of Michigan, Ann Arbor

1982. 'Risk, reciprocity, and social influence on !Kung San economics', in Leacock and Lee, pp. 61–84

2014. 'Embers of society: firelight talk among the Ju/'hoansi Bushmen', *PNAS* 111 (39): 14027–35

Willcox, A. R. 1984a. *Rock art of Africa*. Beckenham: Croom Helm

1984b. *The Drakensberg Bushmen and their art, with a guide to rock painting sites.* Winterton, Natal: Drakensberg Publications

Willet, Shelagh. 2003. *The Khoe and San: an annotated bibliography* (volume 2). Gaborone: University of Botswana

Willet, Shelagh, Stella Monageng, Sidsel Saugestad and Janet Hermans. 2002. *The Khoe and San: an annotated bibliography* (volume 1). Gaborone: University of Botswana

Wilmsen, Edwin N. 1989. *Land filled with flies: a political economy of the Kalahari.* Chicago: University of Chicago Press

2003. 'Further lessons in Kalahari ethnography and history', *History in Africa* 30: 327–420

Wilmsen, Edwin N. and James R. Denbow. 1990. 'Paradigmatic history of San-speaking peoples and current attempts at revision', *Current Anthropology* 31: 489–24

Wilmsen, Edwin N. and Rainer Vossen. 1990. 'Labour, language and power in the construction of ethnicity in Botswana', *Critique of Anthropology* 10(1): 7–37

Wilson, M. L. 1986. 'Notes on the nomenclature of the Khoisan', *Annals of the South African Museum* 97(8): 251–66

Wilson, Monica. 1969. 'The hunters and herders', in Wilson and Thompson, vol. 1, pp. 40–74

Wilson, Monica and Leonard Thompson (eds.). 1969. *The Oxford history of South Africa* (2 vols.). Oxford University Press

Winkelman, Michael. 2010. *Shamanism: a biopsychosocial paradigm of consciousness and healing* (second edition). Santa Barbara: Praeger

Winter, J. C. 1979. 'Language shift among the Aasáx, a hunter-gatherer tribe in Tanzania: an historical and sociolinguistic case-study', *Sprache und Geschichte in Afrika* 1: 175–204

Woodburn, James. 1980. 'Hunters and gatherers today and reconstruction of the past', in Ernest Gellner (ed.), *Soviet and western anthropology*. London: Duckworth, pp. 95–117

1982. 'Egalitarian societies', *Man* (n.s.) 17: 431–51

Wurz, Sarah. 2002. 'Variability in the Middle Stone Age lithic sequence, 115,000–60,000 years ago at Klasies River, South Africa', *Journal of Archaeological Science* 29: 1001–15

Wynn, Thomas and Frederick L. Coolidge. 2012. *How to think like a Neanderthal.* Oxford University Press

Yellen, John E. 1977. *Archaeological approaches to the present: models for reconstructing the past*. New York: Academic Press

1998 [1990]. 'The transformation of the Kalahari !Kung', in Gowdy, pp. 223–35

Zerzan, John. 1998 [1994]. 'Future primitive', in Gowdy, pp. 255–80

Index